Lecture Notes in Computer Science 8264

Commenced Publication in 1973
Founding and Former Series Editors:
Gerhard Goos, Juris Hartmanis, and Jan van Leeuwen

Sebastiaan A. Meijer   Riitta Smeds (Eds.)

Frontiers in Gaming Simulation

44th International Simulation and Gaming Association Conference,
ISAGA 2013 and 17th IFIP WG 5.7 Workshop on
Experimental Interactive Learning in Industrial Management
Stockholm, Sweden, June 24-28, 2013, Revised Selected Papers

 Springer

Volume Editors

Sebastiaan A. Meijer
Royal Institute of Technology (KTH)
School of Architecture and the Built Environment
Division for Traffic and Logistics
Gaming and Participatory Simulation Labs
100 44 Stockholm, Sweden
E-mail: smeijer@kth.se

Riitta Smeds
Aalto University
School of Science
Department of Industrial Engineering and Management
Enterprise Simulation Laboratory SimLab
P.O. Box 15500
00076 Aalto, Finland
E-mail: riitta.smeds@aalto.fi

ISSN 0302-9743   e-ISSN 1611-3349
ISBN 978-3-319-04953-3   e-ISBN 978-3-319-04954-0
DOI 10.1007/978-3-319-04954-0
Springer Cham Heidelberg New York Dordrecht London

Library of Congress Control Number: 2014930987

CR Subject Classification (1998): H.5, H.4, C.2, I.2, I.6.8, H.3, D.2, K.6.5

LNCS Sublibrary: SL 3 – Information Systems and Application,
incl. Internet/Web and HCI

Typesetting: Camera-ready by author, data conversion by Scientific Publishing Services, Chennai, India

Printed on acid-free paper

Springer is part of Springer Science+Business Media (www.springer.com)

Preface

When talking about games, the last decades have shown a rapidly increasing societal and academic interest in their use for purposes other than entertainment. The book that you hold in your hands gives an overview of the frontiers in gaming simulation as of 2013. The volume consists of contributions selected as the best papers from the jointly held 44th International Simulation and Gaming Association conference 2013 and the 17th IFIP WG 5.7 Workshop on Experimental Interactive Learning in Industrial Management held in Stockholm, Sweden. The conference and workshop were organized and hosted by KTH Royal Institute of Technology, the oldest and largest technical university of Sweden, in collaboration with the EU Network of Excellence GaLA and the International Simulation and Gaming Association.

The two activities attracted a lively discussion among the attendees on the value of gaming and simulation in an increasingly complex society. Centered around an intriguing set of papers and five keynote speeches, new perspectives on gaming for design, research, and education were shared that can push the envelope of the maturing field of gaming. Societal trends like urbanization, the need for sustainability in people, profit, and planet dimensions, and the increasing demands for smart city solutions in transport, energy, and health bring excellent future prospects for the gaming simulation domain with its capabilities to address multi-actor systems in a holistic fashion.

The school around "serious gaming" developed quickly into a community of the assessment of learning effectiveness and the specific learning objectives that can be made by using games. The first section in this book, titled "Frontiers in Gaming Simulation for Education", brings you a selection of papers that witness the trends toward a merger of gaming and realistic interactive simulations. Augmented reality, simulation sandboxes, virtual worlds, and realistic logistics simulators are on the frontier of this branch of gaming. The search for effectiveness brings up a range of questions on how realistic, flexible, and predictable the gaming simulations need to be.

Where in the education application of gaming the predominant paradigm is what can be learned by the player, the section "Frontiers in Gaming Simulation for Design and Experimentation" presents a set of papers in which real-world solutions are designed or tested by using the gaming simulation environment as a version of reality. Measuring behaviour, the project management aspects of using games, and how to design the right environments are questions at the forefront of scientific exploration.

The theme of the conference was related to transportation, industrial processes, and logistics. With a high success rate on receiving theme-related papers, the section "Frontiers in Gaming Simulation for Transportation and Logistics" brings together an excellent range of papers in this area that is of crucial importance for the future of our society. Transportation modeling, choice experiments, logistics improvements, and even an overview article show where the traditional transportation research methods are enriched by the use of games. This section also includes the best paper award winner of the conference: Hajime Mizuyama, Shuhei Torigai, and Michiko Anse with their paper, titled "A Prediction Market Game to Route Selection Under Uncertainty," received the highest rankings from the peer-review process.

Last but not least, the section "Professionalism and Business in Gaming Simulation" presents two intriguing papers on rarely discussed aspects of the gaming simulation sector: the professionalism of facilitators that is parallel to the on going movement on professionalization in the consultancy business, and the commercialisation aspect to be able to make a living out of running and exploiting gaming simulations. In the era in which Facebook and Zynga are making a lot of their money from online game revenues, the serious gaming business is facing challenges.

We hope that this book provides you with inspiration for designing, using, or evaluating games up to the current state of the art. The frontiers of gaming simulation will always be moving forward. Taking stock now through this book shall prove a valuable exercise for setting the research agenda!

The editors wish to thank all the authors for their work on improving the papers after the conference. Looking forward to meeting you in future ISAGA and IFIP SIG conferences! A tremendous thank-you goes out to the people who helped realize this conference and this book: Jayanth, Aram, Max, Lennart, Julia and Jop, you did more than your job's worth!

December 2013   Sebastiaan A. Meijer
                                                                 Riitta Smeds

Organization

Conference Chairs

Sebastiaan A. Meijer   KTH Royal Institute of Technology, Sweden
Riitta Smeds   Aalto University, Finland

Organizing Committee

Aram Azhari   KTH Royal Institute of Technology, Sweden
Jayanth Raghothama   KTH Royal Institute of Technology, Sweden
Jop van den Hoogen   Delft University of Technology,
     The Netherlands
Julia Lo   Delft University of Technology,
     The Netherlands
Lennart Leo   KTH Royal Institute of Technology, Sweden
Maksims Kornevs   KTH Royal Institute of Technology, Sweden
Sebastiaan A. Meijer   KTH Royal Institute of Technology, Sweden

Joint Scientific Committee

Riitta Smeds   Aalto University, Finland
Sebastiaan A. Meijer   KTH Royal Institute of Technology, Sweden
Anders Frank   Förvarshögskolan, Sweden
Thomas Duus Henriksen   Aalborg Universitet, Denmark
Marco Taisch   Politecnico di Milano, Italy
Alessandro da Gloria   University of Genova, Italy
Johann Riedel   University of Nottingham, UK
Olivier Irrmann   Aalto University, Finland
Jannicke Baalsrud Hauge   BIBA, University of Bremen, Germany
Gabriele Hoeborn   University of Wuppertal, Germany
Maria-Eugenia Iacob   University of Twente, The Netherlands
Christiaan Katsma   University of Twente, The Netherlands
Toshiko Kikkawa   Keio University, Japan
Martijn Koops   Hogeschool Utrecht, The Netherlands
Rens Kortmann   Delft University of Technology,
     The Netherlands
Heide Lukosch   Delft University of Technology,
     The Netherlands

Willy Kriz   University of Vorarlberg, Austria
Elyssebeth Leigh   FutureSearch, USA
Vincent Peters   Samenspraak Advies, The Netherlands
Sebastian Schwägele   DHBW Stuttgart, Germany
Elizabeth Jane Tipton   Eastern Washington University, USA
Luiz Antonio Titton   Universidade de Sao Paulo, Brazil
Eric Treske   Intrestik, Germany
Shigchisa Tsuchiya   Chiba Institute of Technology, Japan

Table of Contents

Part I: Frontiers in Gaming Simulation for Education

Part II: Frontiers in Gaming Simulation for Design and Experimentation

Part III: Frontiers in Gaming Simulation for Transportation and Logistics

Part IV: Professionalism and Business in Gaming Simulation

Part I
Frontiers in Gaming Simulation for Education

Part I
Frontiers in Gaming Simulation
for Education

Playing Science: Role-Playing Games as a Way to Enter Scientific Activity

Alexey Fedoseev and Daria Vdovenko

Center of Interactive Educational Technologies,
Lomonosov Moscow State University

Abstract. The problem of introducing science, scientific method and scientific way of thinking to schoolchildren and students is very familiar today. Simulations and games can extend regular education in this field. In this paper we describe how the framework of Vygotsky's activity theory and the thought-activity pedagogics can be used as a theoretical basis for reconstructing scientific activity inside a game. We describe the experience of creating and conducting several educational role-playing games for presenting the essence of biological science to students. These games recreated the main aspects of scientific activity: experimental and theoretical work, scientific conflict and scientific management. The educational outcome proves the effectiveness of the method.

1   Introduction

Nowadays people often consider science to be about solving mathematical equations, studying graphs within a computer, pouring coloured liquids from one test tube into another – i.e., often taking into account only external or visual attributes of research activity, whereas the difference between scientific and common views of the world together with the goal and methods of science are left beyond mass culture framework. Most people do not understand scientific knowledge, and often try to think in this way as little as possible. Television and advertising force upon us all kinds of "clever" terms and "research" results, but who ever thinks about what they really mean?

It is clear that popularization of science is an important task which seems necessary for modern society. But how can we achieve such a difficult mission? There are many examples of engaging schoolchildren and students in scientific activity: student research projects, youth scientific contests, even popular science events. Students temporarily become "scientists" and have an experience of feasible research guided by competent advisers. However, these approaches have obvious disadvantages: modern scientific equipment is quite expensive (and the price of a mistake is very high), some experiments cannot be even reproduced in a learning environment and require field expeditions or guided tours to a laboratory. But the most distressing problem of these learning methods is the predetermination of the students' role: usually students do not have an ability to choose object/method/theory for the research, they just do the assistant's work. This means that the most interesting scientific issues (choosing the proper research object, hypothesizing, participating in a scientific conflict, comparing contradictory theories, etc.) remain inaccessible for the students [9].

S.A. Meijer and R. Smeds (Eds.): ISAGA 2013, LNCS 8264, pp. 3–12, 2014.

A very different approach is provided by the field of simulation and games. We can try to reproduce scientific activity in vitro and highlight the scientific way of thinking and common issues of philosophy rather than merely imparting particular knowledge. In this way students are able to become full participants of research activity [7], and therefore will not just understand the scientific method but feel the sense of scientific work [21].

But how can these simulations be constructed, and is it really an effective method? We will answer these questions using the results of our researches and experiments based on a number of educational role-playing games created for schoolchildren and university students in 2009-2012. To implement scientific activity inside the educational process we use the activity theory framework [28] introduced and developed mostly by soviet philosophers and psychologists.

2   Activity Theory and Modern Educational Technologies

This small introduction to the modern activity theory is required because there is not so many publications on the achievements of activity theory available in English [18, 19, 28]. Looks like many western authors equate Vygotsky's results with the Leontiev's activity theory school [6, 14, 20]. There is still lack of good translations of original Vygotsky's works [27]. At the same time, there are many other followers of Vygotsky's available in Russian [5, 3, 10, 24], but only several works has been translated to English.

In this paper we will use the terminology typical for activity theory and Vygotsky's cultural-historical school in psychology. The most complex term here is "activity". One should keep in mind that in this philosophic approach activity is not a peculiarity of a person, but a social system of knowledge, rules, values, cultural patterns. This means that a person does not make an activity, quite the contrary, the activity embraces the person [4].

Activity theory is deeply associated with the problems of development and education. The theory developed by Vygotsky was ahead of his time but now it is becoming widely known about [4]. It is also clear that modern education is being transformed from knowledge-based to activity-based (e.g. competences, cultures or ethics). The reasons and conclusions for such a shift across society may be considered. But the results are obvious: in the modern world of Internet, Wikipedia and globalization we cannot limit ourselves to studying a knowledge, we need also to study how one can find, check and use that knowledge. The conclusions of the activity theory are quite similar to the constructivist approach to learning [17].

The great basis for activity-related aspects of education was built by the Soviet and Russian philosophers and psychologists. Here we will use not only original Vygotsky's results, but the ideas of thought-activity pedagogics [10] – the modern implication of Vygotsky's activity theory for the practical education. Traditional educational technologies (like lectures or tests) are not effective for teaching an activity [2]. Traditionally the learning process was considered as an one-way transfer of culture and knowledge from teacher to student. But studying an activity implies specially organized communication not only between teacher and students but also between   students   and   professionals,   students   themselves,   including   such psychological processes as thought, understanding, projecting, modelling, reflection and others [24]. This new educational content requires new methods.

Simulations and games (both computer-based and live) are considered as effective methods of teaching competences and "soft skills" by many authors [1, 29]. The educational potential of live-action role-playing games was confirmed recently [11, 12]. At the same time there is solid theoretical framework for building educational/research communication-based games within activity theory [25]. Here we will use the results of synthesis of educational live-action role-playing games and activity theory framework [8].

We will describe how the method of educational role-playing games within activity theory has been applied to the particular activity – scientific activity. Let us continue with considering scientific activity from the activity theory viewpoint.

3   Scientific Activity

So, what is science, and what are specific features of scientific activity? Let us consider the definition from Wikipedia[1]: 'Science is a systematic enterprise that builds and organizes knowledge in the form of testable explanations and predictions about the universe'.

We will try to understand what this definition means, and how science became divided from other types of human activities[23]. Initially, human activities were aimed at getting a certain final product, and their knowledge about the surrounding world had the following form: "In order to get product A, it is necessary to take object B and to perform actions c, d and e towards it" (see fig. 1a). We face this type of knowledge most often, let us call it "practical knowledge". Here is a trivial example: "in order to recuperate, it is necessary to make a restorative drink: mix chamomile flowers with ginger root, grind the mixture and infuse it in boiling water".

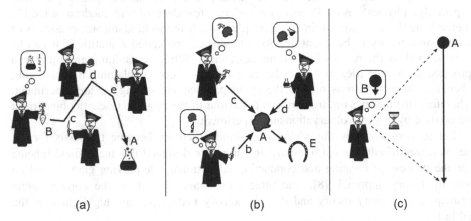

(a)   (b)   (c)

Fig. 1. Human knowledge: practical, technical and scientific

---

[1] http://en.wikipedia.org/wiki/Science [06.02.2013]

When a person is occupied with getting a certain product for a long time, from the variety of practical skills he has mastered he derives and accumulates a special type of knowledge, which describes the object of labour itself and everything that may happen to it. Typically, this knowledge assumes the following form: "*If object A is subjected to actions b, c and d, as a result we will get object E*" (see fig. 1b). This knowledge is not scientific yet, let us call it "technical knowledge". Experience accumulated in materials processing can provide us with examples of such knowledge ("diamond can be processed only with another diamond" or "after melting ice, we will get water").

In order for science to appear, people need a paradigm shift. From a practical person point of view, objects always change during some actions, and the changes are directly related to the products of these actions. Whereas scientific cognition requires understanding of the fact that such changes are natural processes, taking place independently from any actions of this practical person and complying with their own internal mechanisms and laws. This taken into account, the above statements assume the following form: "*Under conditions a and b object C will be subjected to changes d, e and f*" or, more abstractedly, "*Changes happening to object A comply with law B*" (see fig. 1c). This way there appears gravity affecting a stone or a shell, or the law of evolution defining the development of all living organisms.

It is of importance that here we speak not just about specific actions performed by people (all three cases may feature the same action, for instance, mixing solutions in a test tube), but of the knowledge and the way of thinking they are using.

The work of a scientist implies revealing the true relations in this most complicated reality featuring a great variety of different dependencies. It is important to note, that science always requires an object of research which is, in crucial respect, detached from the scientist and exists according to its own laws, beyond the scientist's will. In general, such and object is represented by the nature around [13].

Speaking of scientific method, we usually think of natural philosophy and, especially, physics[2]. Karl Popper, one of the founders of the modern scientific method, used the notion of *falsifiability* [22] which is the fundamental condition of admitting a theory to be scientific. So, a theory can be called scientific if it can be contradicted by the result of a test, an experiment. While researching an object or a process, a scientist tries to derive the most reliable theory explaining its behaviour, checking the conclusions of this theory in practice via setting up an experiment. Therefore, the theories on structure and behaviour of the in-game research object must be verified by in-game observation and experiment.

Let us consider how this vision of scientific activity became the basis for the development of educational role-playing game. We designed this methodical schema for the process of creating and conducting educational role-playing game based on activity theory approach [8]. The three main stages based on the corresponding principles of activity theory and thought-activity pedagogics are highlighted in the table 1.

---

[2]   By the example of physics one can see very well that science in based, first of all, on observation, derivation of theory and on experiment.

Table 1. The main stages of the educational role-playing game development process

The stages of development	The activity theory principles	The example
Designing the game: first of all, fixing the content of the game, analysing the players' knowledge and abilities. For sure, usually we are limited by time and resources, and, therefore we have to create the model of the considered activity (this can be a complex simulation model or just a set of rules).	The educational content of the game should be separated from the educational method and the matter used [10]. The activity (as a part of a culture) can be considered as the educational content of the game/lesson. In this case one should design the number of situations in which the activity will be implemented (and thus internalized) by the participants. The created model will represent the required elements of the activity.	Let us use the scientific activity as the content of the educational game. Let the target audience be schoolchildren, so we have to limit ourself to the core element of the scientific activity – arranging experiments and correcting theories – wrapping this to the model of research. We also have to use the comprehensible but actual matter, e.g. the botany or mechanics (but not the quantum physics).
Conducting the game: preparing and involving players (depends on size and complexity of the game, it could be a text, a presentation, a workshop, or even a mini-game), controlling the model of the activity during the game (one should also control the game dynamics and use all the game stuff available: in-game conflicts, encounters, non-player characters, events, etc.).	Role-playing games are familiar for people in the modern society from youth [5]. But the particular game could require a lot of preparations: reading the rules, understanding the roles, immersing into the situations presented. The participants should manage with the proper terms and notions to understand the educational content [3]. At the same time, the organizers of the game should maintain the model of the activity operable and consistent.	The preparation may consist of: reminding the required for the game school matter, discussing with the teacher what the words 'experiment' and 'theory' mean, choosing the roles in the laboratory. During the game the model for experiments (including the object of the research and the social relations inside the group of characters) should be maintained.

Table 1. (*continued*)

| Discussing the experience: helping players to consider self experience (right after the game ends one should discuss the process and the results with the participants and try to figure out all the meaningful experience), carrying out the players' reflection process to reconstruct the underlying activity – the organizers use specific questions to direct participants' reflection. | The players' experience of processing the activity can be internalized [26]. This can be done if the participant of the activity reflects the performed actions and the self way of thinking [24]. The reflection process should be prepared and organized properly – the teacher should allow participants to reconstruct the means of own thinking and activity independently, through the communication rather than throw out the fixed knowledge on the students [10]. | After the finish of the game, the children should have time to rest and debrief the results – what experiments were successful, and what were failed. But after that the teacher should not only organize communication between the game participants to help them highlight the characteristics of the methods they used, but bind these with the actual research methods presented in the culture. |

4   The Game "Pandora"

We will use the particular example of role-playing game designed in the way described above and targeted to the reproducing scientific activity. The game called "Pandora"[3] was created and conducted in 2009. The game duration was one day plus night. Number of participants – 50 players. The two quite similar role-playing games were conducted in 2010 and 2012.

The research process was the major content of the game. From the very beginning, we as the organizers of the game, involved scientific experts into the development process[4]. The revolutionary idea of this game implied reconstruction of a full-scale model for living ecosystem of the planet – this ecosystem was the research object.

---

[3]   The aesthetics and the story of the game was based on the science fiction book "Disquiet" by Strugatsky brothers. The book states an essential philosophic problem: how far a man can go studying nature, before he faces an insoluble moral conflict, for instance, "whether one or another part of the jungle is right in the food chain; whether such behaviour of nature is rational or not".

[4]   Namely, Vera Matrosova and Nikolay Poyarkov, PhDs in biology. Their knowledge in zoology and field experience in studying animals, supplemented by general awareness in biology issues, guaranteed creation of interesting and consistent in-game science.

Pandora living world included several types of organisms: non-motile plants, fungi, insects and higher animals, performed by the special team of non-player characters (NPCs). The NPCs performed higher animals of various species according to prescribed behaviour patterns. They lived a full-featured night-time life, completely independent from humans and full of sounds, movement in the dark, etc. They behaved according to their own rules having internal logic, as habits of animals and their lifestyles were closely related to their role within the ecosystem. Large animals were divided into herbivores and carnivores. Herbivores were aimed at gathering feed and looking for mates for breeding, carnivores sought prey. Therefore, during the game our group of organizers successfully implemented living nature which was completely independent from the characters playing scientists and was of interest for observation and research.

Similar to the object of research, the scientists' community was not simple. Scientific activity included "space zoology" – study of animal species at the planet Pandora. The figure 2 shows the complicated system of scientific professions implemented at the game. Scientists' activities were closely connected to the play of the living nature.

Each plant or animal had a paper tag with a short DNA code in letters. Having killed an animal, scientists received the code. Fungi, animals and plants codes could be processed in the laboratory. DNA code interpretation allowed to incorporate the species in question into the system of already studied organisms of Pandora and to clarify the phylogenetic tree. Therefore, the scientists had an opportunity not only to describe the animals habitus and behaviour, but also to compare them to organisms evolution on the basis of DNA analysis. Thus the scientists could perform full-scale systematization of species, in the way it is done in biology science. Several simple computer programs were developed by organizers in order to facilitate the research.

Certainly, such biology model had some limitations. For instance, from the very beginning we decided to spare simulation of morphology (internal constitution of animals), as it would require vague procedure of post-mortem and more advanced props. The biology at "Pandora" proves that a model of real science can be rather narrow, but still relevant and consistent.

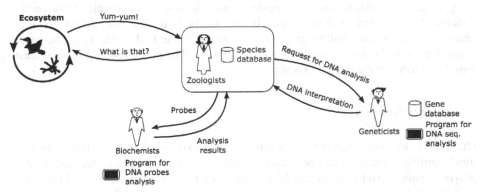

Fig. 2. The structure of scientific activities in the game "Pandora"

Often games are looked false and imitative for the participants. In a live simulations it could be connected with the presence of teachers and organizers who embody the outside world and the constrains of the simulation. We found that it is of importance that all the scientists' activities required no immediate organizers participation. The players interacted with the active living nature, studied its laws, and did not play face to face with an organizer (only with the in-game NPCs). The laws of the implemented living nature, stated by the organizers before the game started, did not change and shift in the players' sight, thus allowing the players to regard nature as a true object of research.

The result of the game was quite obvious. All the participants noted that the science became more understandable for them. The students noted and discussed many aspects of science activity during post-game reflection guided by the game organizers.

The success of the game allowed us to make several conclusions about reproducing scientific activity. Firstly, we managed to state the following essential requirement to scientific storyline composition. In-game research must be heterogeneous: it must include simple riddles, as well as more complicated, complex problems, and, may be, even insoluble paradoxes. Then players will be able to follow their characters through a series of ups and downs and experience the essence of a scientist's work. The game organizers should carefully calculate and balance the time the players need to solve scientific problems.

Secondly, we could state that the object or process, most interesting for research, should live its own life and develop independently from the will of the scientist players. The more data of various kind the scientist can get from the object of research, the more interesting and exciting the science will be.

Certain attention should be paid to in-game organization of scientists' work, including research, exchange of results and discussion of discoveries. If this issue is left in complete control of the players, the community may fall apart, and interesting results just will not be achieved. Personal features of the lead researchers inside the game are of most importance in this case, meaning not only skills in organizing the work but ensuring productive communication between scientists.

At last, game designers should decide if in-game science is completely or partly fictional (e.g., science activity – models and methods remain real, while research object is fictional), or it will be grounded on a real science. In the latter case, the game organizers should carefully select or prepare players. The players should have at least base knowledge in the particular science.

5   Conclusions

Our experience shows that the very complicated activity – scientific activity – and its most significant elements can be simulated and reproduced inside an educational role-playing game. Activity theory can be a framework for the experimental and theoretic activities to be integrated into a game and become temporary real for the participants. The educational results of these games allow this method to be used for the introduction science to schoolchildren and students.

The ideas presented in this paper can be extended to the social aspects of scientific activity. For instance, one can incorporate contradicting theories, scientific conflicts and revolutions (Kuhn, 1996) into the education role-playing game, or recreate the model of the modern relationship between "the ivory tower" and the real world: the necessity of funding, writing reports, innovating, etc. Thus, the scientific activity can be reconstructed at three successive levels: the level of individual scientists who set experiments and clarify theories; the level of scientific groups debating on the truth; and the level of society interacting with science as an institution. These ideas also can be extended to the related human activities, we are considering not only science but humanities as a potentially good targets for such educational games. These topics and methods were proved by a series of educational role-playing games created by our team in 2009-2012. The results of these researches will be published in the future.

References

1. Crookall, D., Oxford, R., Saunders, D.: Towards a Reconceptualization of Simulation: From Representation to Reality. Simulation/Games for Learning 17(4), 147–171 (1987)
2. Davydov, V.V.: The Mental Development of Younger School Children in the Process of Learning Activity (Contd.). Soviet Education 30(10), 3–36 (1988)
3. Davydov, V.V.: Types of Generalization in Instruction: Logical and Psychological Problems in the Structuring of School Curricula. In: Soviet Studies in Mathematics Education, vol. 2, National Council of Teachers of Mathematics (1990)
4. Davydov, V.V.: The content and unsolved problems of activity theory. Perspectives on Activity Theory, 39–52 (1999)
5. Elkonin, D.B.: The psychology of play. Journal of Russian and East European Psychology 43(1), 11–21 (2005)
6. Engeström, Y., Miettinen, R., Punamäki, R.L. (eds.): Perspectives on activity theory. Cambridge University Press (1999)
7. Fedoseev, A.: Educational role-playing games as a way of reconstructing scientific activity in schools. V International Scientific-Practical Conference Theses, Ulianovsk University (2010)
8. Fedoseev, A.: Live-action role-playing games as an educational technology. International Scientific Conference "Interactive Education" Theses, Lomonosov Moscow State University (2011)
9. Fedoseev, A.: The problem of including students into the scientific sphere. The experience of using game educational technologies. International Scientific Conference "Interactive Education" Theses, Lomonosov Moscow State University (2012)
10. Gromyko, Y.: Thought-activity pedagogics. Minsk (2000)
11. Henriksen, T.D.: Moving Educational Role-Play Beyond Entertainment. Teoría de la Educación - Educación y Cultura en la Sociedad de la Información 11(3), 226–262 (2010)
12. Hyltoft, M.: Four Reasons why Edu-Larp Works. In: Dombrowski, K. (ed.) LARP: Einblicke, pp. 43–57. Zauberfeder, Braunschweig (2010)
13. Kant, I.: Critique of pure reason. Cambridge University Press (1999)
14. Kaptelinin, V., Nardi, B.A.: Acting with technology. MIT Press (2006)
15. Klabbers, J.H.: The magic circle: Principles of gaming & simulation. Sense Publishers (2006)

16. Kuhn, T.S.: The structure of scientific revolutions, vol. 2. University of Chicago press (1996)
17. Lainema, T.: Perspective Making: Constructivism as a Meaning-Making Structure for Simulation Gaming. Simulation & Gaming 40(1), 48–67 (2008)
18. Leontiev, A.N.: Activity, consciousness, and personality. Prentice Hall, Englewood Cliffs (1978)
19. Luria, A.R.: Cognitive development: Its cultural and social foundations. Harvard university press (1976)
20. Nardi, B.A. (ed.): Context and consciousness: activity theory and human-computer interaction. MIT Press (1995)
21. Polanyi, M.: Personal knowledge: Towards a post-critical philosophy. Psychology Press (1962)
22. Popper, K.R.: The logic of scientific discovery. Hutchinson, London (1959)
23. Schedrovitsky, G.P.: Underlying philosophy of training and development analysis within the framework of activity theory. "Training and Development" symposium theses, Moscow (1966)
24. Schedrovitsky, G.P.: Pedagogy and Logic, Moscow (1968)
25. Schedrovitsky, G.P.: Organisational activity games, Moscow (1983)
26. Strugatsky, A. & B.: The Snail on the Slope. Bantham, New York (1980)
27. van der Veer, R., Yasnitsky, A.: Vygotsky in English: What still needs to be done. Integrative Psychological and Behavioral Science 45(4), 475–493 (2011)
28. Vygotsky, L.S.: Thought and language. MIT Press (1986)
29. Whitton, N.: Learning with digital games: A practical guide to engaging students in higher education. Routledge (2009)

Achieving Game Goals at All Costs?

The Effect of Reward Structures on Tactics Employed in Educational Military Wargaming

Anders Frank

Swedish National Defence College

Abstract. A key motive in using gaming for educational purposes is to enhance user motivation and involvement to the subject matter. Within military education, games have always been utilized as a means to think clearly about military operations. However, some research results have shown that gaming, regardless of what the game is supposed to portray, is a meaningful activity in itself, and this can distract the learner away from the educational objective. Playing the game, then, becomes similar to competition, such as in sports where the objective is to *only* win the game. The player directs actions to achieving game goals even though some actions are inappropriate from a learning perspective. To shed light on the discrepancy between playing a game to win and playing a game to learn, we conducted an experiment on cadets playing an educational wargame. By varying the conditions of the game, playing with or without points, while still in line with the learning objective, we were interested to see what impact it had on the tactics employed by cadets. The results showed that adding reward structures, such as points, changed the outcome of the game, that is, groups playing with points played the game more aggressively and utilized the military units more extensively. These findings suggest that changes in the game design, although educationally relevant, may distract learners to be more oriented towards a lusory attitude, in which achieving the game goals becomes players' biggest concern.

1   Introduction

Educational gaming is an experiential exercise in which the purpose is to learn from this experience (Gredler, 1996). A motive in utilizing games in education is to enhance user motivation and involvement. However, gaming can also introduce artificiality to the learning activity as users make an effort to achieve the game goals. Although these goals are designed with the learning objective in mind, there is no guarantee that players will exhibit a behaviour in line with the purpose of training. Eagerness to reach game goals can lead to a player behaviour that jeopardizes the learning objectives (Rieber & Noah, 2008), as gaming becomes a meaningful activity in itself regardless of the reality it represents.

In the military, games have been used for centuries as a means to think clearly about military operations (Smith, 2010). In educational wargaming, officers are challenged with real-world problems by facing an adversary in the game. Wargames

S.A. Meijer and R. Smeds (Eds.): ISAGA 2013, LNCS 8264, pp. 13–20, 2014.
© Springer International Publishing Switzerland 2014

are not used to enhance user motivation or engagement, although they may afford participants a great deal of satisfaction (McHugh, 1966). The purpose is to stimulate officers into tactical thinking and decision-making that corresponds to real-world situations without paying the real-world penalties (Perla, 1990; McHugh, 1966).

Despite the military's long tradition of using games, the unwanted behaviour of gaming only to win also occurs there occasionally. The artificial and safe environment provided by wargames may lure players to behave differently compared to the real world, which is exemplified by being over-aggressive and a tendency to take higher risks (Lind, 1985; Rubel, 2006). The safe environment where players do not need to suffer real-world consequences seems to influence them into higher risk tendencies. Furthermore, the game environment appears to shape player behaviour in unwanted directions, as they want to overcome their opponents by using tactics not in accordance with military doctrines.

Consequently, educational wargaming requires more from its learners than just playing a game. Players need to take on two coexisting attitudes towards the activity. First, they must act and think as officers and take on a professional attitude towards the activity. Second, as wargaming involves playing a game, the user must also take on a lusory attitude (Suits, 2005) towards the activity. A lusory attitude involves committing to play the game in ways defined by the game rules and can be seen as a social contract that articulates the restrictive use between players and the game. From an educational perspective, playing wargames, thus, means that officers must maintain a balance between these attitudes throughout the game or else there is a risk that both the learning experience and the gaming experience get compromised. Gredler (1996) warned about this kind of mix between experiential simulations, where participants take on serious roles, and games, which place them in direct competition with each other. According to Gredler, this will create a mixed-metaphor problem, in which two conflicting messages will be sent to the learner. The learner is supposed to play out the roles, but a focus on who the winner is in the end may distort the simulation experience and become detrimental to the learning process.

We wanted to explore this delicate balance between lusory and professional attitudes in an experiment among military cadets by focusing on the competition aspect. We manipulated the computer wargame by adding educationally relevant game points to the scenario to see whether this feature change had any effect on how the operations were conducted, that is, what tactics were employed. Specifically, the objective was to see if the tactics employed were a result of a change in balance between professional and lusory attitudes. As in any learning situation, learning is dependent on many various factors, and a player's behaviour can be corrected by close facilitation and debriefing. However, in this experiment, we focused on a single factor, the game design, and asked ourselves what effect game-like features have on player behaviour as we argued that player behaviour not in line with educational goals is less desirable and creates unnecessary difficulties. Furthermore, it is very common that commercial games used for educational purposes are equipped with reward structures, so our interest on effects to player behaviour addresses a wide audience. The setting was an undergraduate course where cadets used a commercial wargame to learn about combat at battalion level. In this sense, the educational setting was normal with the exception that half of the course participants played an altered version of the computer wargame.

2   Method

2.1   Participants

Eighty-one cadets (8 women and 73 men, aged 22 to 36 years) from the Swedish Military Academy participated in the study as part of an eight-week course in war sciences. The participants had served in all branches of the Arm.

2.2   Game and Scenario

The experiment used a commercial strategic turn-based game, THE OPERATIONAL ART OF WAR (Matrix, 2005). The game was chosen for this course, as it contained all the necessary attributes associated with battalion combat, was fairly easy to use, and enabled training of the whole class simultaneously. The game map consisted of hexagons, and in every turn, the player gave orders to subordinate units. When players were done, the turn was evaluated, and the results of the players' actions were displayed on the screen. The results were then sent to the opponents who started their next turn.

The game allows the instructors to create customized scenarios. The scenario for the course, Operation Pajazzo, was created to match the learning objective and cadets' prior planning phase. Operation Pajazzo was made as a head-to-head battle (at battalion level) with comparable forces on the Blue and the Red sides. Blue's mission objective was to take and hold a valley south of Rome to prepare later advancement towards Rome. Red's mission was to block this advancement. Both sides controlled a mechanized battalion, but because the Blue side had an offensive task they were provided with more companies vis-a-vis the Red side to balance out potential disadvantages. The challenge for both sides was to command their units in tactical ways to take control of the valley. This meant, among other things, to move units in such ways that local supremacy could be reached, coordinate indirect and direct fire, keep the supply chains intact and maintain the combat effectiveness of the troops.

2.3   Design and Measurements

The experiment utilized a between-subjects design. The independent variable was the explicit reward structure in the game, whether if the game was played with or without victory points.

The participants were randomly assigned to teams of two or three people and then each team was randomly assigned to one of the two conditions. For the experimental group, some of the hexagons on the game map were associated with points, that is, victory points. The scoring hexagons were selected in line with the mission objectives for each side, with certain vital hexagons in the central valley resulting in points. A hexagon's score was awarded to the side that possessed the hexagon at the end of a turn. The overall score for each side was calculated between the turns and was only made visible to the player at the beginning of a turn. The control group played without points. As the computer game normally used scoring to keep track of which side was winning, playing without victory points meant that the game could only provide players with information that the game was a tie. Although the experiment group played with points, they were given same instruction as the control group. They were both told that the objective of the game was specified in the military orders.

We were interested in measuring the effect that victory points had on the tactics employed, if we could see indications of a change in balance of a player's lusory and professional attitudes. One way to analyse the tactics employed is to observe how the players make use of the military units, especially the players' choice of maintaining unit strength, readiness, and health. The *Unit Health* in the game represents "…an average of the unit's supply, readiness, and a fraction of assigned vs. authorized equipment" (Matrix 2005). Health is, thus, a result of how much the unit has been engaged in combat, subjected to indirect fire, moved, or provided supplies. A low value means that the unit has been utilized extensively, and this can be a sign of a lusory attitude for two reasons.

First, in games, generally, players adopt a strategy that exploits the rules to achieve game goals. Earlier results from educational wargames (Frank, 2012) indicate that players utilize all military units at player disposal to achieve the game goals, even if this use is in conflict with military doctrines. Examples include giving a support unit (engineers, headquarter, artillery, medical and logistics units) with limited fighting capability an offensive attack order against a superior enemy, or to expose military units to unnecessary risks just to gain victory points in the game. This is generally not advisable from a tactical perspective and will decrease the health value. Measuring and comparing *support units'* value will help expose this issue.

Second, Operation Pajazzo is only a small part of a larger military operation that the cadets need to take into account when they plan and conduct the operations. A risky tactic is to exhaust units within the time allotted, possibly just to fulfil the game goals for Operation Pajazzo, but neglecting the fact that the units are to take part in the next stage of the operations. Measuring the Unit Health among *all units* will help reveal whether or not players are keen on preserving strength.

Furthermore, military doctrinal rules emphasize the importance of *sustainment*, which means that own forces need to maintain combat readiness over time. Consequently, the military units' state at the end of a game session, especially units' health value, will mirror the players' ability in addressing sustainment and how keen they were in following these doctrinal rules. Thus, the dependent variable is the mean of the Unit Health among all units and support units that we assumed would reflect the tactics employed during the game round.

3   Procedure

The wargaming session was the last phase in the advanced course of military tactic. Prior to the gaming session, cadets were separated into groups to plan Operation Pajazzo using predefined planning procedures and to learn about the units in a battalion. Prior activities also included field exercises that taught the cadets how the terrain must be taken into account in tactical thinking. Thus, cadets were familiarized with the terrain and with the capacities of the military units as well as the task of Operation Pajazzo. Before playing the Operation Pajazzo wargame the cadets were given 2 to 3 hours to play a tutorial scenario to learn how to play the computer game.

After training the experiment began. The participants played the game in groups of two to three people in duels – Blue side against Red side. Each group played the same scenario for three rounds, shifting sides between Blue and Red after each game. This meant that half of the groups played Blue twice and Red once, and the other half played Red twice and Blue once. Between each game the opposing team was shifted so no team met the same team twice. This was done to avoid getting familiar with opponents' strategies and tactics. After each game round, there was a debriefing and reflection phase assisted by instructors to discuss lessons learned.

4 Results

To measure Unit Health after each game round, the file containing the last move was loaded into the game. Each and every unit was measured and given a point corresponding to current health status. In the game, the Unit Health is indicated by different colours, green to red, and these colours were converted into numbers, zero to five, where zero indicated an evaporated unit and five a unit with full health.

A mean value was calculated for each side using the scale provided above. However, we were also interested in knowing how each team made use of support units. Therefore, a separate mean value was calculated, which only included engineers, headquarter, artillery, medical, and logistics units. Though it was tempting to compare the mean values of the two sides, problems arose due to the close dependency within a duel. The Blue side's actions would affect the Red side's responses, which in turn would affect Blue's next turn. Therefore, to obtain independency between measurements, a mean value was calculated for each match, including both Red and Blue sides. Additionally, as the same participants were included in all three game rounds, separate analysis was performed for each game round. Table 1 below summarizes the results.

Table 1. Comparison of Unit Health values in wargaming matches with and without points

Game session	All units		Support units	
	Without points	With points	Without points	With points
First round	n = 5	n=10	n=5	n=10
M	1.39	1.17	1.62	1.21
SD	0.26	0.35	0.32	0.29
Second round	n=9	n=10	n=9	n=10
M	1.31	1.18	1.42	1.12
SD	0.23	0.29	0.21	0.34
Third round	n=9	n=10	n=9	n=10
M	1.42	1.06	1.34	1.05
SD	0.31	0.22	0.31	0.22

All units. For each game round, an independent two-sample t-test was performed. Results showed no significant difference for first and second game rounds (t=1.26, df=13, p=0.23) and (t=1.02, df=17, p=0.32), respectively. The number of observations in the first round was fewer (n=5) compared with other rounds, as four matches were disqualified because they did not finish all eight turns within the time allotted. The results for the last round showed a significant difference between matches with or without points (t=2.94, df=17, p=0.01). Effect size (Hedges' g) for all three rounds ranged from medium effect size (0.7 and 0.5 for first and second rounds, respectively) to large size (1.4 for third round). The results suggest that even though there was no significant difference in first and second rounds, there was an effect of health decrease in all rounds when playing with points.

Support units. The independent two-sample t-test conducted showed significant differences in support units' mean health in all three game rounds. The first round generated values of t=2.44, df=13, and p=0.03, between the group that played with points and the group that played without. The second and third rounds also yielded results that were significantly different at similar level between the groups – (t=2.26, df=17, p=0.04) for the second and (t=2.36, df=17, p=0.03) for the third. An estimate of the effect size yielded the following values: d=1.33 for the first round, d=1.04 for the second, and d=1.08 for the third round. Hence, the effect size was large in all game rounds.

As a result, all game rounds played with victory points had, on average, lower health status among units compared with groups who played without victory points. Even though this difference was marginal in the first and second rounds, when comparing all units, the third game round produced a large difference. Furthermore, there was a large effect and significant difference in all three game rounds when comparing support (non-fighting) units between groups. In summary, playing with points had a negative influence on all military units' Unit Health, which supported earlier results that players expose units to risks, such as attack and move orders, when playing with points. This was particularly true to support units, suggesting that players employed tactics not in line with doctrinal rules.

5   Discussions

In this experiment, we investigated the effects of tactics employed when manipulating underlying reward structures in a wargame used for an educational purpose. By comparing game matches, played with or without victory points, our focus was whether or not there was a difference in how the military units were utilized. After each game round, the health status of each military unit was measured, with the assumption that this value represented how the unit was utilized during a game round. Results generated in comparing matches between the conditions showed a large difference in mean values of the units' health status. Reward structures and receiving points for conquering vital hexagons resulted in significantly lower Unit Health mean values, providing evidence that different tactics were employed as compared with matches where no reward structures were used. One explanation of the extensive use is that players with reward structures are being more aggressive and, therefore, utilize their units to a larger extent. In addition, as the support units yielded low Unit Health values, the results indicated that players with reward structures did not differentiate between combat and support units. This confirms results from earlier studies (Frank, 2012) that players, who get carried away by wargaming, disregard what the support units in the game are meant to represent and use them as generic fighting units.

As players in these cases do not prioritize unit rest, recovery, and strength, the results can be interpreted that the players are more aggressive because they are more oriented towards achieving the game goals. They are employing a tactic where they are willing to pay a much higher prize to achieve their goals. Whether or not this is desirable depends on each individual situation. However, this high-risk tendency is a result of a change in balance between lusory and professional attitudes and, therefore, suggests, in general, a non-admissible behaviour.

Arguing that players will employ a different tactic when the game is modified might be trivial. However, we focused on modifying the game in ways that the added reward structure was congruent with the mission objective and, thus, was educationally relevant. Strategic and vital regions on the game map associated with victory points, and yet, this minor modification, in line with the overall task, generated a change of how the units were treated. Players seemed to adopt a different interaction pattern when victory points were introduced in the game. This adaption becomes clear when we observe game round three, in which there is a significant difference between the conditions. Furthermore, in game round three, the standard deviation was among the lowest for the groups playing with points, while the spread fluctuated more in the other condition during all three game rounds. This suggests that the victory points shaped players' behaviour into a gaming-specific interaction pattern; they learned a specific way how to treat their units. Possibly, additional game rounds would shed some light to this observation.

This study confirms warnings from Gredler (1996) to mix experiential simulations (role playing) with games (competition) to its participants. However, warfare is by nature a competition between the fighting sides where the objective is to overcome the opponent. Training warfare with wargaming must, therefore, include techniques to balance players' attitudes. Better design, such as elimination of victory points, is one such aspect supported by the results from this paper, but another solution is to have instructors nearby to monitor the gaming process and steer players' reasoning into the right directions as it happens. Although this is perhaps the most efficient remedy to the problem, there are practical obstacles, such as the availability of instructors required. Often in learning situations, as in our experiment, instructors are a limited resource, especially considering having enough to closely monitor every game round.

Furthermore, this study suggests that wargaming with explicit reward structures becomes a meaningful activity in its own right, potentially suppressing the relation between game and the real world. Instead of being a representation of real military units where doctrinal rules regulate on how to make use of them, they became game pieces in an activity only to be won. Winning the game by points was never mentioned prior the game sessions, the only instruction given to the groups was to follow the military orders. But the indication that the experiment group followed an objective to win the game by points suggests that the game goal were more powerful than to follow doctrinal rules. From a game perspective this is perfectly sound. Salen and Zimmerman (2004) argued that games create their own meaning and provide their own goals. However, from a learning perspective, the results are not in perfect line with Cordova and Lepper (1996) arguments that congruent learning and gaming goals should result in increased learning.

Caution must, therefore, follow ambitions when using commercial games in military training, as these games are designed for entertainment and generally equipped with explicit reward structures. Well-designed games do not guarantee that the tactics employed by the players are in line with the learning objective.

References

1. Cordova, D.I., Lepper, M.R.: Intrinsic motivation and the process of learning: Beneficial effects of contextualization, personalization, and choice. Journal of Educational Psychology 88(4), 715 (1996)
2. Gredler, M.E.: Educational games and simulations: A technology in search of a (research) paradigm. In: Jonassen, D.H. (ed.) Handbook of Research for Educational Communications and Technology, pp. 521–539. MacMillian Library Reference, New York (1996)
3. Frank, A.: Gaming the Game A Study of the Gamer Mode in Educational Wargaming. Simulation & Gaming: An Interdisciplinary Journal 43(1), 118–132 (2012)
4. Lind, W.S.: Maneuver warfare handbook. Westview Press, Boulder (1985)
5. McHugh, F.J.: Fundamentals of wargaming. Naval War College, Newport, RI (1966)
6. Perla, P.: The Art of Wargaming. Naval Institute Press, Annapolis (1990)
7. Rieber, L.P., Noah, D.: Games, simulations, and visual metaphors in education: antagonism between enjoyment and learning. Educational Media International 45(2), 77–92 (2008)
8. Rubel, R.C.: The Epistemology of War Gaming. Naval War College Review 59(2), 108–128 (2006)
9. Salen, K., Zimmerman, E.: Rules of Play Game Design Fundamentals. The MIT Press, Cambridge (2004)
10. Smith, R.: The long history of gaming in military training, in. Simulation & Gaming: An Interdisciplinary Journal 41(1), 6–19 (2010)
11. Suits, B.: The Grashopper: Games, Life and Utopia. Broadview Press, Ontario (2005)
12. THE OPERATIONAL ART OF WAR – A CENTURY OF WARFARE. Matrix Publishing LLC (2005)

Transcoding Pattern and Simulation Games in Learning Geometry – A Research in Primary School

Angela Piu[1] and Cesare Fregola[2]

[1] University of Valle D'Aosta
a.piu@univda.it
[2] University of L'Aquila
cesare.fregola@univaq.it

Abstract. The paper, starting from the analysis of Italian students' difficulties in Maths learnings, presents a quali-quantitative research carried out with some groups of pupils attending the 4th year of the Primary School in Formia (LT), Italy, in the school year 2011/2012. The aim of the research is to verify if the simulation game about the isometries, designed according to a specific theoretic frame and some methodological choices, with particular reference to the transcoding pattern, can: foster and facilitate the learning of geometrical concepts and their retention over time; affect social and scholastic self-efficacy as well as the motivation to learn. The quantitative analysis, carried out with ANOVA, comparing the simulation game to the traditional lesson, shows significant results in the learning for both groups. As far as motivation and social and scholastic self-efficacy are concerned, instead, no meaningful differences have been recorded. The in-depth analysis of the learning and its retention over time carried out through the qualitative analysis has shown the efficacy of the game with regards to both the concepts comprehension and the achievable abstraction levels.

1   Motivation and Reference to Related Literature

The idea underlying the research arose on the one hand from the analysis of Italian students' critical results in mathematical learnings (TIMMS, 2011), as they emerged from both national surveys and the comparison to international results, and, on the other, from the investigation of the simulation games potentialities as learning environments for Maths in primary school and low secondary school, carried out according to the most recent achievements in the psychopedagogical research.

On the basis of the analysis of such situation and having recognized the crucial role of mathematical learning in the citizens education in the society of knowledge, the research started with a preliminary analysis of the simulation games literature that, in its general lines, has shown, on the one hand some potentialities of the simulation games, on the other, from the research methodological point of view, some critical aspects.

As a matter of fact, the simulation games have proved to be effective at: - reinforcing concepts, facts and disciplinary principles; - demonstrating some basic theories application; - developing superior cognitive abilities, related to problem

S.A. Meijer and R. Smeds (Eds.): ISAGA 2013, LNCS 8264, pp. 21–28, 2014.

solving; -making decisions and creative thinking; - developing communicative and interpersonal research skills; - achieving objectives in the affective area [1]. Also, when compared to conventional education, the results of several researches point out the change in the attitude, the increase in motivation and the improvement in retention [2, 3, 4].

As far as the research methodology is concerned, what emerges from the reports in literature, instead, is the difficulty to analyze and compare the examined researches because of the lack of a learning epistemology, a definition, of common and/or simulation game explicit structural characteristics and different design models. All these factors make it hard to compare and generalize the achieved results.

Taking into consideration such criticalities and on the basis of the potentialities of the simulation games, the most recent research achievements in the learning theories have been identified. Such achievements made the background for the simulation games designing. More specifically, we made reference to those theories that acknowledge connections among the following aspects: affective-motivational, cognitive, metacognitive and of context [5], maintaining the focus on the process of construction of language [6] and mathematical concepts, their representation [7], the role and the function of conceptual and procedural knowledge and the explicit link with the existing concepts [8]. The research was also based on the significant and socially shared experiences that use support materials and instruments, in order to make individuals able to understand the meaning and the learning objective they are going to achieve, starting from concrete aspects [9], defined not only in terms of real world physical characteristics, but also according to significant connections that can be discovered, created or applied, by putting into relation other mathematical concepts and situations.

In the range of such knowledge, rooted in psychopedagogy, the research has defined the reference theoretic frame and the methodological choices that are the groundings for the designing and realization of Cartolandia [10], the experimentation of which is presented in the paper.

2   Theoretical Frame and Methological Choices

The design of Cartolandia was developed starting from a first general definition of simulation game [1] and from some theoretical and methodological choices related to the simulation games "grammar" [11].

Cartolandia is a simulation game on the introduction to the Isometries, created for pupils of the 4th year of Primary School. It is set in a city made up of paper, whose inhabitants are upset because someone has stolen the map of the city, kept in the museum. The contestants of the game, playing the role of paper-detectives, have the following tasks: to retrieve the map, to find out the thief and to inform the paper-general about how the investigation is carried out. In the paper-lab the contestants can analyze the clues: the visitors' prints on the paper-carpet, that is the floor of the paper-museum room where the map was kept, and their figures, that is the pictures of the people who visited the museum and/or got closer to the map. The rules of the game are the following: the pupil can:- let the figures or the prints, drawn on the tracing paper, "slip" on one side, or back and forth, without sticking out the paper from the floor; - "rotate" them pointing a pin on the tracing paper corner; -"overturn" them - the important is that the figures and prints have the same distance from the edge of the sheet; -"slip" the print or figure on one side, back and forth, and then make it rotate, pointing a pin on the sheet corner. Moreover, during the game the children decide all together the way to tell the paper-general about the search of the thief and the "code" to use to explain the facts.

The knowledge of the limits of human working memory elaboration capacities and the conception of learning as a mental schemata construction [12] led to the definition of the reality model and the ways children would interact with it. In particular, the model reproduces some elements of a specific reality, remaining faithful to the original but reducing its complexity, through a functional representation focused on the learning task and on the mathematizable aspects of reality. So, the model creates situations, perceived as different, which are able to represent the same concept.

On the basis of this model, the simulation game is set up according to the principles of the guided discovery learning and of the transcoding pattern. The transcoding pattern: - organizes the language and the learning environment of the task, by defining gradual paths on different levels of abstraction in order to facilitate the construction of an accessible and "usable" language [13], to be used as the basis for the formal mathematical language construction; - proposes a problematic situation aimed at provoking a need to represent and communicate the thought organization in order to foster the discovery of concepts, rules, structures and the construction of the related representations in a gradually formalized code in logical-mathematical language.

The transcoding pattern is close to the substantial mathematics conception, that considers it a language, mainly seen in its semantic aspect, interested in the meaning underlying the symbols, and considers Mathematics formal conception the arrival point of the teaching-learning process.

In the teaching/learning relationship, the different levels of meanings that teacher and pupils attribute- on the basis of their knowledge and experience and during the moments of interaction - make it possible to build up intermediate and shared codes and to create the conditions so that children can: -feel a sense of adequacy in accessing to the code that is being used and built up; - understand the relationship between the words used and their meanings; - acquire the mastery in using a gradually more formal code, closer and closer to the mathematical code.

The condition to be satisfied is that, during the transcoding process and the construction of the mathematical language, a substantial rigour is maintained, by preserving: the object of communication, its structure, the concept that is intended to be discovered or formalized and the rule applied.

Therefore, the concrete model proposed and the gradual path create the conditions to provide children with an intuitive support, able to lead them towards a meaningful symbolic representation of the mathematical concept, so that they can understand the importance of the representation both in the comprehension process and in the communicative one [14].

During the game, pupils are involved in a set actions they have to carry out making use of structured materials, the body, the hands and the gestures. The game objectives imply the necessity to describe what happens throughout the game.

The debriefing, that follows the game, is aimed at reporting the experience and, above all, at fostering the conceptualization of what has been discovered, as well as its systematization and generalization. The teacher acts as a facilitator and, at the same time, stimulates and orientates the language use awareness.

3   Research and Experimentation

The research hypotheses are referred to the simulation game that, differently from the traditional lesson, can: facilitate the learning of knowledge and skills of mathematical thinking; facilitate knowledge retention and mathematical thinking skills consolidation; improve the motivation in mathematics learning; improve perceived social and scholastic self-efficacy.

The experimental plan implied the formation of some experimental groups, that were proposed Cartolandia, and some control groups, that were proposed the traditional lesson. The groups were formed within the same class; each class was divided in groups of 6-7 pupils each, according to the multiple intelligences test [15]. The answers to the test were analyzed through a cluster analysis, a data multivaried analysis technique that clusters cases or variables according to measures of similarity in order to create similar groups that, in their inside, with regard to intelligence profiles, are as diversified as possible.

The groups were administered pre-tests and post-tests about: social and scholastic self-efficacy [16], the motivation to learn geometry [17] and the learning assessment [18]. Moreover, the same test on learning retention skills, was administered after 30 days.

In order to have an in-depth analysis of mathematical concepts comprehension, in addition to the close-ended test, the children were also given an open-ended test in which they were asked: "Imagine you have to explain to a pupil who is not in your same class the meaning of the following words: isometry, translation, rotation, simmetry. Write what you would say".

Both the experimental and the control groups had the same curricula and the two different learning environments were run by the teachers- previously specifically trained- according to specific guidelines. The game contents concerning the Isometries had not been dealt with by the teachers before the experimentation.

The research involved 179 children of 8 and 9 of the 4th year of the the primary school, 1° Circolo Didattico in Formia. The teachers who took part in the experimentation were 12, one for each class.

In sum, two groups were formed: an experimental one, made up of 87 pupils and a control one, made up of 92 pupils. The tests of the children who missed even just one of the pre-test or post-test phases were not counted in the data analysis and in the comparison of results.

As far as the assessment test is concerned, the data analysis was carried out only for those pupils who completed the entire process established by the research protocol. In this case the valid tests were 56 for the experimental group and 48 for the control group, for a total of 104 valid tests.

3.1   Results Description: Quantitative Analysis

The assessment tests results were analyzed by using the one-way repeated measures variance analysis (ANOVA one-way). Through this type of analysis it is possible to compare two or more data groups, resting upon the idea of the total variance into two components (internal to groups and among groups) and supposing that the possible differences could be attributed either to the administered intervention or to the independent variable introduced, that is, in our case, the simulation game or the lesson.

From the results in the close-ended test (fig.1) it is possible to observe a remarkable increase in the post-tests scores for both groups (experimental and control) and a decrease in retention tests, due to the students normal tendency to forget part of the previously acquired knowledge (average scores of experimental group: pre-test 11,1; post-test 15,9; follow-up: 15,3; average scores of control group: pre-test: 9,7; post-test: 17,9; follow-up: 16).

The application of the ANOVA to the results obtained in the three phases (pre-post and follow up), leads to the rejection of the null hypothesis (H0), according to which the differences between the two groups were due to chance, with the consequent acceptance of the alternative hypothesis (H1), according to which the differences were due to the intervention (game/lesson). In both cases, the value of F obtained, with a confidence interval of 95% (significativity level: p-value=0,05), is greater than the theoretical value expected (experimental group: $F(0,05; 2,165)=18,89$; Control group: $F(0,05; 2,14) = 37,58$).

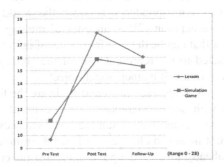

Fig. 1. Chart of the results of the learning assessment tests

From the in-depth analysis of the results variations, obtained comparing the post-test and the follow-up, it emerged how the decrease recorded for the control group proves to be faster than in the experimental group. Such results lead to further considerations, as it is possible to hypothesize, according to the ANOVA applied, that for the experimental group only, the decrease can be due to chance and not to the time elapsed, which is the main oblivion factor in the retention process (experimental group: $F(0,05; 1,110) = 0,48$; control group: $F(0,05; 1,94) = 4,35$).

The variance analysis (ANOVA one-way) was also used in the comparison of the results obtained from the data about the motivation in learning Geometry and those concerning the social and scholastic self-efficacy. In the three cases analyzed, the results led to accepting the null hypothesis, in compliance with which the differences between the averages in the further data collections of the single constructs were due to chance for both the simulation game group and the lesson group.

3.2   Results Description: Open-Ended Assessment Test Qualitative Analysis

With the aim of getting a deeper analysis and further evaluation elements, the open-ended test analysis was carried out. Considered the peculiarity of the transcoding pattern, in order to individuate the criteria for the answers analysis, we proceeded inductively taking into account the learning objectives related to concepts, which were later connected to the abstraction levels and the meanings expressed by children's sentences. In this way, through the analysis of the recurring elements in the sentences, it has been possible to individuate the criteria regarding the concept comprehension and the abstraction levels, presented as follows, together with the descriptors.

For the concept comprehension: - clarity of expression: the pupil formulates the sentence precisely, without leaving room for ambiguities and-or doubts; - coherence among terms: the pupil puts into relation the terms of the sentence (logical and semantical connection) to express-represent the concept; - completeness: the pupil throughly individuates the common characteristics; - pertinence of terms: the pupil chooses and uses the terms in a proper, precise and punctual way.

As far as the abstraction process is concerned, five levels have been identified, according to the degree of correspondence between the world represented and the world generating the representation [7], in an interval ranging from sentences with few references, sentences that can be defined fragments of information and show only few, vague elements related to the representation of the concept itself, to sentences that express the concept in terms of mathematical object.

With regards to the levels of abstractions, the criteria are the following: level 1: the pupil makes sentences with some references to the concept (e.g. isometry: same meter); level 2: the pupil makes some examples or sentences which refer to the concept (e.g. translation: it means to change position, for example the car was behind the other and now it is ahead); level 3: the pupil expresses the concept relating it to a motor-sense level: actions, manipulations of everyday life objects (e.g. translation: when something changes place and remains the same); level 4: the pupil expresses the concept using the references to the reality from which the concepts are generated (e.g. isometry: equal distance between two points of a figure even if it moves); level 5: the pupil expresses the concept using mathematical objects (e.g. isometry: movement that mantains the distances among the points of the figures).

With regards to comprehension, it has been decided to attribute grades (0-3), while for the levels it has been decided to indicate only the level the pupils belonged to. At the end of this phase, we proceeded with the verification of the reliability of the test, measuring to what extent the three members of the research group, who would correct the tests and who carried out the research, agreed (the agreement proved to be higher that 90% of the total of the examined answers).

The analysis shows that the answers of the pupils who participated in the game are more articulate and written in an understandable and coherent way. The answers make reference to examples/actions and concrete contexts evidently elicited by the game (e.g.: sentence on the meaning of translation: " it means that when we take a sheet of paper and turn it, what changes is not the surface but the direction and this happens on the plane"), while the mathematical terms used with little coherence in the sentences, are used by the pupils who participated in the lesson (e.g.: "movement that happens on the plane"). Regarding the levels of abstraction, it can be seen that the participants in the game express sentences that can be referred to level 3 (e.g.: "have a plane advance forward, on the right and on the left) and also to level 2, while in the sentences of those pupils who took part in the lesson, the level 3 doesn't appear and there are lots of sentences of level 1 (e.g.: "It is the distance that there is on the plane"), that is with some references to the concept.

4   Conclusions

Summing up, with regards to learning, the quantitative analysis results show the didactic efficacy for both the simulation game and the traditional lesson, while the qualitative analysis results point out the simulation game efficacy in the comprehension and the achievable levels of abstraction, even over time. Currently, the experimentation has not shown significant differences with regards to motivation constructs and social and scholastic self-efficacy.

The complex articulation of the contents as well as of the experimentation, has highlighted that, due to the molteplicity of variables that can escape the quantitative control, it could be necessary to develop more structured and qualitative analyses so that it could be possible to put in mutual relation cognitive, metacognitive and socio-relational variables.

References

1. Ellington, H.: Games and simulations – media for the new millennium. In: Saunders, D., Smalley, N. (eds.) The International Simulation and Gaming Research Yearbook, vol. 8, pp. 13–32. Kogan Page, London (2000)
2. Pierfy, D.A.: Comparative Simulation Game Research: Stumbling Blocks and steppingstones. Simulation and Games 8, 255–268 (1977)
3. Bredemeier, M.E., Greenblat, C.S.: The Educational Effectiveness of Simulation Games: A Synthesys of Findings. Simulation Gaming 12, 307 (1981)
4. Randel, J.M., Morris, B.A., Wetzel, C.D., Whitehill, B.V.: The effectiveness of Games for Educational Purposes. A Review of Recent Research 23, 261 (1992)
5. Pellerey, M.: Le conoscenze matematiche. In: Pontecorvo, C. (ed.) Manuale Di Psicologia Dell'educazione, pp. 221–241. Il Mulino, Bologna (1999)
6. Fregola, C.: Methodological Proposals for Simulation Games: The Transcoding Pattern. In: Piu, A., Fregola, C. (eds.) Simulation and Gaming for Mathematical Education: Epistemology and Teaching Strategies, pp. 83–111. Idea-Group Inc., Hershey (2011)

7. Gagatsis, A.: Comprensione e apprendimento in matematica. Un Approccio Multidimensionale. Pitagora, Bologna (2003)
8. Anderson, J.R.: The architecture of cognition. Harvard University Press, Cambridge (1983)
9. Dienes, Z.P.: Le sei tappe del processo d'apprendimento in matematica. Firenze, OS (1971)
10. Piu, A.: Design of a simulation games for the learning of mathematics. In: Piu, A., Fregola, C. (eds.) Simulation and Gaming for Mathematical Education: Epistemology and Teaching Strategies, pp. 112–130. Idea-Group Inc., Hershey (2011)
11. Duke, R.D.: Gaming: il linguaggio per il futuro. Edizioni La Meri-diana, Bari (2007)
12. Sweller, J.: Evolution of human cognitive architecture. In: Ross, B. (ed.) The Psychology of Learning and Motivation, vol. 43, pp. 215–266. Academic Press, San Diego (2003)
13. Castelnuovo, E.: Pentole, ombre, formiche. In Viaggio Con La Matematica. La Nuova, Italia Firenze (2001)
14. Vergnaud, G.: Le rôle de l'enseignement à la lumière des concepts de schème et de champ conceptuel. In: Artigue, M., Grass, R., Laborde, C. (eds.) Vingt ans de didactique des mathématiques en France, pp. 177–191. La Pensée Sauvage, Grenoble (1994)
15. Mc Kenzie, W.: Intelligenze multiple e tecnologie per la didattica. Erickson, Trento (2006)
16. Caprara, G.V.: La valutazione dell'autoefficacia. Erickson, Trento (2001)
17. Rheinberg, F.: Valutare la motivazione. Strumenti Per l'analisi Dei Processi Motivazionali. Il Mulino, Bologna (2006)
18. Fregola, C., Piu, A.: Simulandia. Giochi di simulazione e ambienti di apprendimento della matematica. Giornale Italiano Della Ricerca Educativa 6, 59-80 (2011)

Serious Games, Remote Laboratories and Augmented Reality to Develop and Assess Programming Skills

Mariluz Guenaga, Iratxe Menchaca, Alex Ortiz de Guinea, Olga Dziabenko,
Javier García-Zubía, and Mikel Salazar

DeustoTech – Deusto Institute of Technology – University of Deusto
Avda. Universidades 24, 48007 Bilbao, Spain
{mlguenaga,iratxe.mentxaka,alex.odg,olga.dziabenko,zubia,
mikel.salazar}@deusto.es

Abstract. The project "Serious Games for Education–Programming Skills"
presents an innovative technology that integrates serious games techniques with
remote laboratories and augmented reality. The flexible and scalable technology
is designed with a three layer structure: (1) the physical layer - ROBOT
(hardware and communications) remotely manipulated; (2) AR and instruction
interface middleware; and (3) end-user game application including game
interface. This design enables multiple pedagogical objectives and context of
use. In the first prototype we have developed a serious game, the third end-user
layer, to develop and assess programming skills, algorithmic thinking and
debugging.

Keywords: Serious games, remote laboratories, Augmented Reality,
programming.

1 Introduction

"Serious Games for Education – Programming Skills" (SG4Edu-PS) is a project that
comes from an evolution of a previous analysis about the possibility to merge remote
experiments with a game environment [1]. While developing the hardware for the
experiment we came with the idea of applying Augmented Reality (AR) to create a
game world, which could give us the flexibility to adapt themes and scenarios. Such a
solution reduces the layout and hardware costs and significantly improves the game
balance of the original design [2].

Even if the merge of AR and serious games (SG) is widely used in gaming and
programming courses [3], the synergy of remote laboratories, serious games and
augmented reality is an innovative technological approach.

This technological infrastructure is useful for several educational objectives. Since
team members include programming teachers and software developers, we focus the
learning objective in the development and assessment of logical thinking skills,
oriented to students of first grade of engineering studies. They face the difficulty to
solve problems that require logical and systematic thinking, following a set of
instructions described by programming languages.

S.A. Meijer and R. Smeds (Eds.): ISAGA 2013, LNCS 8264, pp. 29–36, 2014.

This paper presents the results of a project where Augmented Reality and remote laboratories have been put together to develop and assess skills needed for programming: solving problems applying logical thinking and algorithms.

2   Games for Programming

There are attempts to recreate the programming experience through games [4] [5]; from life-like programming activities to abstract graphical approaches separated from the traditional act of programming [6], but which help to introduce basic elements of programming. From the richness of programming games we would highlight those related to the project. Prog&Play is a set of bindings to programmatically control game elements in a real-time strategy setting. It is being used to enhance engagement of learners in university classes. Robomind [6] consists in writing programs in a language developed for the game, called ROBO, which guides a robot through different levels in a virtual world. Lightbot [7] and Cargobot are similar in conception to Robomind, but they use instructions or code blocks instead of a programming language.

There are games that mix virtual elements with physical ones. In this category Lego and derivatives are the reference. Lego Mindstorms NXT [8] is a series of kits that contain elements to develop programmable and customizable robots. Electronic Blocks [9] and 3DU Blocks are physical blocks that integrate technology in the proper block to enhance gaming experience and learning for children. 3DU Blocks is a framework for mixing Lego-like blocks with AR to develop games that mix physical manipulation of construction blocks and videogames.

3   SG4Edu-PS, Development and Assessment of Logical Thinking

SG4Edu-PS has both pedagogical and technological objectives. From a pedagogical point of view the game aims to support programming learning, integrating an innovative tool as a complement for teaching and learning basic programming at the Engineering Faculty of the University of Deusto. This game aims to develop and assess skills related to thinking in terms of algorithms, strict set of rules, logic of code writing and debugging.

The programming subject in engineering degrees at the University of Deusto has three specific competences that are:

1. Specify, design and implement algorithms in an object oriented programming language, using efficient, systematic and organized problem solving methods.
2. Write correctly, compile and execute programs in Java.
3. Use data-structures efficiently in algorithms.

The game SG4Edu-PS focuses in the first competence. It does not cover the whole curriculum because it has been designed to develop algorithm design not linked to any specific programming language. We propose a didactic integration combined of a logical processing experimental methodology with the serious game. In addition, the serious game pedagogical approach is based on simple functions managing to move forward progressively at various levels, and gradually increase the level of complexity of functions.

From the technological perspective the objective is to develop such a framework that allows deploying new game scenarios on the base of existing software and hardware infrastructure. In order to achieve this challenge the game is structured in three layers: (1) the physical layer - ROBOT (hardware and communications) remotely manipulated; (2) AR and instruction interface middleware; and (3) end-user game application including game interface (see Fig. 1).

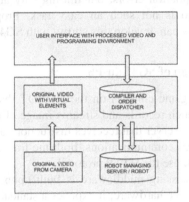

Fig. 1. Software layout of SG4Edu-PS

3.1   Pedagogical Basis

The game takes place in a science fiction world where ROBOT has had an eventful landing. It has to overcome some challenges to recover or fix broken pieces and leave this planet.The adventure starts with easy challenges; simple scenarios with limited number of movements (e.g. rotate left/right). As the player advances challenges get more and more difficult, elements to interact with appear in scene, as well as enemies that hinder the progress of ROBOT.

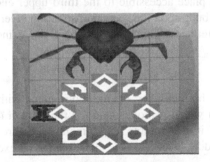

Fig. 2. SG4Edu-PS scenario with eight possible actions and an enemy

The objective, as when students program, is not only to achieve the objective of each level, but to do it in an optimal way. When teaching programming we insist that obtaining the expected result is not enough, the solution has to be the best in terms of resources, i.e. CPU time and memory. In the case of our game, resources are the number of instructions used, energy of the robot, time needed to get a correct solution, and number of non-successful test runs. These results are shown to the player as part of their final score, constituting our main assessment indicators used by the teacher in the classroom.

A very valuable skill for programmers is to know how to debug programs. It is relatively easy to fix compilation errors, but finding why an algorithm does not do what it is supposed to do is not such an easy task. Programmers must control debugging practice and they can develop this ability with SG4Edu-PS.

3.2   Technological Design of SG4Edu-PS

The physical layer of the game consists on the ROBOT that moves on a restricted surface and the camera, which records and streams image of this ROBOT to the end-user. The computer acts as a server that receives instructions and transmits them to the ROBOT over Bluetooth. All communications, both the frame-by-frame video stream and the control instructions, use the HTTP protocol.

AR and instruction processing middleware is built upon the first physical layer. This second layer abstracts the hardware; it exposes a standardized set of instructions for the game level and overlays AR elements on the real video stream. The middleware builds a virtual environment from a map description, projecting the robot video on it and rendering with Unity3D. The set of 3D models that comprise this virtual environment is configurable to accommodate different target users as well as narratives (e.g. simple environments for children or sophisticated life-like industrial settings). On this layer, an instruction queuing system and an execution service ensure proper ROBOT operation.

The second layer is designed in such way that in case the remote experiment is not available it can also operate without a video source eliminating AR. Once the second layer processes the video received from the remote experiment camera, the resulting frames are exposed in a place accessible to the third upper end-user layer. The end-user application layer is built upon the second abstraction layer and presents a typical game graphical user interface. This layer is where the game cycle is set up and executed.

3.2.1   ROBOT

Three elements form the bottom layer: (1) the robot, along with its control server, (2) the physical platform on which it moves, and (3) the camera that gives us the video stream; we might call it the remote experiment hardware. This layer receives instructions from the middle layer and is responsible for its execution, error handling and loading.

The ROBOT base is made of low cost commercial components. The chassis is a robotic kit "Rover 5" of "Dagu Electronic". This kit is sold fully assembled and provides a solid structure and a displacement on stretchy rubber treads which offers great control of an engine maneuver. The ROBOT controller is "Wild Thumper", from the same manufacturer. It provides an AVR ATmega168 microcontroller loaded with the Arduinobootloader and main control code to manipulate the robot movements. This module also features dual FET H-bridges 15A with fuse protection which covers the experiment requirements of power electronics and battery charging management. Four "QRE1113" analog line sensors breakouts from "Sparkfun Electronics®" are connected to the ROBOT to control the displacement on the board. A bluetooth module connected to the controller via the serial UART (Universal Asynchronous Receiver Transmitter) has installed to receive displacement orders.

Functionally ROBOT operates five basic commands: move forward one square, back, turn 90 degrees to the right and to the left and restart the experiment. Each command the ROBOT must send an acknowledge signal after the execution is finished. When the battery charge level is below 20% an indicating warning is produced. If the battery charge level is lower than 5% the ROBOT returns autonomously to charging point. In the first prototype all movements are performed on the area of 2.4 m wide by 1.80 m long divided into squares with 30 cm side. The panel provides 35 squares aligned in a 5x7 pattern. Black ribbon bounds in the squares supply the accuracy required for AR using the line sensors.

3.2.2   Weblab-Deusto – Remote Laboratory

The ROBOT is deployed under the WebLab-Deusto platform so SG4Edu-PS integrates remote laboratories. WebLab-Deusto Server performs administration tasks such as authentication, queue management or user tracking and provides scalability, flexibility and security to the ROBOT game [2] [10]. In order to manipulate of the user's interaction with the ROBOT, a custom Laboratory Server has been deployed, which is also responsible for managing the communication with the ROBOT [11]. The Laboratory Server brings to the user the client interface for interacting with the game, including the controls induced the movement of the robot, the video captured by the Webcam, and the graphical user interface.

3.2.3   Augmented Reality (and beyond)

Originally coined by Tom Caudell in 1992 to define the seamless integration of virtual objects into a physical (real) environment, the term "Augmented Reality" is nowadays often –incorrectly– used to define any composition of real of virtual objects. However, by preserving the idea of the Mixed Reality Continuum [12], we are able to present a broader spectrum of user interactions.

In this continuous scale, ranging from the physical environment to a completely virtual world, it is possible to define different degrees of fusion between real and virtual objects. In the model defined by SG4Edu-PS, all the game entities have a dual nature (a real object that the computer can recognize and a three-dimensional virtual model), enabling our users to define in real-time whether they prefer to see an enhanced version of the real world (Augmented Reality) or a virtual environment in which they can integrate the real objects (Augmented Virtuality).

Although at this point we are only using one real element on top of a virtual world, and it could be argued the experience is not greatly enriched by the inclusion of this real element, this innovative approach allows us to provide more engaging user experiences, both in direct and remote interactions. For example, a user could physically manipulate the game scenario by using special markers to add or remove obstacles, while remote users have to adapt their strategies to the new conditions. This kind of collaborative experiences empower the learning process.

3.3   User Interface – Radial Menu of Instructions

As teachers of programming courses we know that programming language is a tool, the key is to describe the algorithms. When designing the game we have chosen a set of graphical instructions instead of including real code. The instructions are selected from a radial menu that pops from the square in which the user clicks.

The spatial interface is an interface where interactions occur on the same "board" in which game elements are moving. The spatial interface approach is beneficial as it allows keeping in sight ROBOT movements and code execution simultaneously; it avoids the two-pane problem-code separation. This kind of interface is not completely new[13], although it is unusual due to the hardships and constrains. It helps to build an immersive sensation, avoiding the need to focus on two different tasks: (1) identifying spatial elements, and (2) translating them into code [14]. We are aware that this method separates the game from real coding practices; on the other hand it simplifies the comprehension of general programming concepts and logical thinking, which is the aim of the game.

The robot moves in a 5x7 squares matrix. Not all squares are available, so the player has to find the best way to achieve the challenge, as per indicators previously discussed. The available instructions depend on the level of the game.

4   Discussion

SG4Edu-PS means both a pedagogical and technological innovative contribution. From the didactic perspective it represents a motivating tool to develop programming skills in an environment different than traditional authoring tools. It can be applied not only to engineering courses, but as it is an easy game and challenges can be adapted to different levels, it can be used in primary and secondary schools. The sense of immersion, one of the most valuable characteristic of remote laboratories, is a contribution not seen before in this kind of games. The narrative and the connection with a real element such as ROBOT offer an additional incentive.

From the technological point of view the integration of remote laboratories and AR has been a challenge. Augmented Reality is the instrument that can solve a number of problems such as the single user nature of remote laboratories. Combining the real and the virtual world we can offer multi user capabilities to remote experiments, what is very difficult to implement in a totally physical experiment. The software design in three layers allows the reuse of the lower two for different purposes. Changing the upper layer we can develop games with totally different pedagogical objectives using the same infrastructure (ROBOT, virtual world and AR), they can increase or decrease in difficulty depending on the target users and also scenarios may change so we can adapt to different preferences.

There are still challenges to be addressed, such as the integration of other programming concepts in the game (e.g. data structures); limitations in the type of puzzles to be developed due to hardware constraints; the game architecture and developed technology could be used for other subjects and levels of education, but content development and graphical redesign is needed; and finally, even if the game implies more experimental learning, closer to student's context and, ultimately more meaningful, there is not a complete approval of teacher to introduce games as a tool in formal learning scenarios.

5   Conclusions and Future Work

We can merge remote laboratories with Augmented Reality to create serious games for education that benefit from the technological contributions of each technology for learning. A proper architecture design allows the future development of different games based on the hardware and middleware of lower layers, with particular pedagogical objectives. It is flexible and scalable enough to provide a big set of possibilities. Developed technology is suitable to develop and assess basic programming skills; algorithm thinking that is the main challenge that engineering students face in their first year of studies.

In future testing we will evaluate the impact of this kind of games in programming teaching and learning, as well as students' satisfaction and motivation, apart from developing a model of automated assessment. Research areas open to new areas that exploit capabilities of virtual reality and serious games in learning. The aim is to profit the success of simulations in the understanding of cognitive processes, combining virtual and real world.

Acknowledgments. This project has been carried out thanks to the support of the Regional Government of Biscay and its programme Bizkailab.

References

1. Dziabenko, O., Zubia, J.: Remote experiments and online games: How to merge them? In: IEEE EDUCON (2011) ISBN: 978-1-61284-641-5
2. Dziabenko, O., Garcia-Zubia, J., Angulo, I.: Time to play with a microcontroller managed mobile bot. In: IEEE EDUCON 2012, Morocco (2012) ISBN: 978-1-4673-1457-2
3. Muratet, M., Torguet, P., Viallet, F., Jessel, J.P.: Experimental Feedback on Prog&Play: A Serious Game for Programming Practice. Computer Graphics Forum 30(1) (2011)
4. Best free ways to learn programming (Acc. February 12, 2013), http://www.techsupportalert.com

5. Kiili, K.: Digital game-based learning: Towards an experiential gaming model. Internet and Higher Education 8, 13–24 (2005)
6. Introduction to the ROBO programming language (Acc. February 2013), http://www.robomind.net
7. Armor Games, "LightBot", http://cache.armorgames.com (accessed September 2012)
8. Lego Mindstorms, http://mindstorms.lego.com (accessed February 2013)
9. "Aprender programando: Motivaciones y alternativas", Cuadernos Red de la Cátedra Telefónica de la Universidad de Deusto
10. García-Zubia, J., Angulo. I., Orduña, P., Hernández, U., Irurzun, J., Ruiz, J., Castro, M. & Sancristobal, E.: Easily Integrable platform for the deployment of a Remote Laboratory for microcontrollers. In: IEEE EDUCON 2010 (2010) ISBN: 978-1-4244-6570-5
11. Orduña, P., García, J., Irurzun, J., López-de-Ipiña, D., Rodriguez, L.: Enabling mobile Access to Remote Laboratories. In: IEEE EDUCON (2011) ISBN: 978-1-61284-641-5
12. Milgram, P., Kishino, F.: A taxonomy of mixed reality visual displays. IEICE Transactions on Information and Systems 77(12), 1321–1329 (1994)
13. Zachtronics Industries, SpaceChem, http://www.spacechemthegame.com (accessed July 2013)
14. Csikszentmihalyi, M.: Flow: The psychology of optimal experience. Harper Collins, New York (1990)

EfeU: Decision Making Concerning Company Strategy

Gabriele Hoeborn and Jennifer Bredtmann

University of Wuppertal, Interdisciplinary Centre of the Management of Technical Processes,
IZ3, Gaußstraße 20, 42119 Wuppertal, Germany

Abstract. Decision making concerning company strategy (German: Entscheidungsfindung für eine Unternehmensstrategie) EfeU, originated by Jennifer Bredtmann (2008) and designed further on by Jennifer Bredtmann and Gabriele Hoeborn (2012) is a management game being developed especially for university education in engineering degree courses. EfeU is a business game offering the experience and training of decision making and co-operation processes in groups. The awareness of the decision making process, its impact and the handling of the group are the main elements of the game. The authors carried out case studies to observe and evaluate the influence of gender and cultural background on the students' attitudes toward this game and on the learning output as well.

1   Introduction

EfeU is a business game focusing on the simulation of complex processes in and between companies. Dealing with information and knowledge and its transfer into a strategic approach is the focus of the training. The specifications of the game offer the possibility to simulate different company processes. The complexity of reality is simplified by pre-set system boundaries and various input. The students have to make intertwined decisions and to recognize downstream consequences.

2   Setting of Game

This serious game is applied in engineering lectures using a mixed learning concept. It includes four separate lectures.

Firstly, the students meet for an introduction lecture about different management systems as well as decision making theories. Teachers and students get into contact with each other. At the second meeting, the first round of the game starts. The students are free to organize themselves and the distribution of roles. At the third appointment the students play the second round of the game by knowing about the results of their first turn. During the last session an intensive feedback is carried out by reflecting on the game rules and flow, as well as the individual input of knowledge into the game. This phase leads to the identification of problems, important incidents, and decisions concerning communication, risk management and decision making. Therefore, this part combines cognitive and constructive learning paradigms by taking

S.A. Meijer and R. Smeds (Eds.): ISAGA 2013, LNCS 8264, pp. 37–43, 2014.

the two elements of problem based and experimental learning into account. Participation and contributions from all students are requested as a necessary condition to generate learning output. When the play is completed the final result is advised to the students. The span of time between the four meetings depends on organizational circumstances.

This serious game is not offered online. It is described within the following paragraphs and it is applied regularly within lectures, business consultancy and management talks. The following shows the information and communication slides given to the persons concerned:

- You are leading a company which produces and sells bicycles.
- Your sales market is limited to Germany, it is not expandable.
- You and your company are in a dynamic company environment offering various possibilities and information.
- Aim to steer the processing, the requirements on the company and the product by clever decision making.
- Determine the approach to be applied in the next business year by taking all requirements into consideration, and thereby influence the future of your company.
- Be careful and consider all information and the different requirements when making decisions.
- All companies have the same sales market.

After an introduction into the procedure and the division of at least three groups of five to ten persons the game starts. If possible each group has access to its own private space for the opportunity to discuss strategy undisturbed. The game is split into two big phases as already described; it can be expanded for a third and fourth period. Each gaming period symbolizes a business year. And each period includes three gaming parts as *part A*, *forum*, and *part B*.

During *part A* the students get necessary business information such as company key figures, sales figures, and capital on hand as well as additional information by letters including offers of suppliers, of products, investments, and costumer information. This whole package of information influences the decision making process of the business year. The duration of *part A* is 30 minutes.

These are the instructions the students get:

- Split into three equal sized groups.
- Arrange yourself into the separate rooms so that you do not disturb each other.
- Each group gets information about its company. Please, read this carefully.
- Create a name for your company. Define tasks and roles like CEO, production manager, marketing manager.
- Planning should be based on the business data of the last year; received money can be spent (as per document provided). Project your next business year: investments, selling prices, human resources, purchase of material e.g.
- Additionally your planning is based on the given information as weather conditions, notice of machine manufacturer, notice of selling point, announcements and offers.
- Decisions should be made by the team.

The *forum* follows immediately after part A, and offers the possibility to be in contact with representatives of different companies. Information can be shared; networks and co-operation can be built up. The students can acquire information by being in touch with different companies. The application of this offer is up to the students. In general it is possible to meet one different company or two at different times or to meet all different companies at the same time. The duration of the *forum* is 20 to 30 minutes based on the activities of the students.

These are the instructions the students get:

- Application of *forum*: Two gamers of one company may enter the *forum* to meet representatives of different companies. You may invite one or more companies to meet you, at different times or at the same time.

Part B starts immediately after the forum, and its duration is 20 minutes. During this part the information gained at the forum can be advised to the group and included in the decision making process. All decisions have to be finalized, and a decision form has to be filled in. This form records the decisions about the number of bicycles to be produced, sales prices and projected investments. The end of *part B* finishes the first gaming period.

These are the instructions the students get:

- Make up your decisions and come to your final planning.
- Fill in the decision form and submit it.

The application of the second gaming period is very similar to the first one. Again the students get the necessary business information and company key figures, sales figures, capital e.g. for decision making and planning as well as additional information by letters including offers of suppliers, of products, investments, and costumer information. They also get information about the results of the decision reported at the end of the first period e.g. number of bicycle sales, market share, and acquired capital which they may spend within the second period. This whole package of information influences the decision making process of the business year. The *forum* can be used as well. The duration of the second period is as long as period 1.

The final results and the evaluation of the decision making process are discussed during the following meeting. As a first step the calculation success and results of the different companies are offered. In a second step the considerable information for decision making is analysed. The dealing with information and their consequences are evaluated by decision criteria leading to marks which influence the final results of the groups.

3   Handling of the Implicit Learning Goal

The economic gains are only apparently the focus of this serious game; to a greater degree it focuses on the levels of awareness and the experience of decision making processes and their consequences. The accounting profit of a group is not the most important evaluation criterion, on a second level the getting of decision marks is the bigger success. The implicit learning is not expressed to the students explicitly.

But they are told that their decisions lead to impacts concerning the economic success of a company. Not the economic success itself but the awareness about the impact of decisions and of team work on decision making processes define the valuation of a group. Sometime not just one winner appears, but more than one. The game aims to assist practicing decision making processes in teams and to examine the correlation between decision and impact.

4   Observations

EfeU has been used since 2008 by the authors in very different engineering student groups, in Bachelor and Master Courses, in German and International degree courses. There have always been coeducational groups showing a strong underrepresentation of women students. Additionally mostly in international degree courses students having different national and cultural backgrounds participated. The instructions, as shown before, are offered to the students via power point slides. There is an allocated time for asking and answering questions and then the game is started. During all the case studies this procedure was carried out in the same way. All lecturers are female.

The observation of the students focused on:

- General attitude towards the game: Are there gender or cultural differences?
- The role the different students take within the group (choice of role, involvement in the decision making process): Can a gendered or cultural influenced leadership and/or decision making be recognized?
- And solving of tasks and consequences of decision making process: Do the students get the implicit goal of the game and is this awareness influenced by gender or culture?
- Consideration of impact and decisions within in the game: Are there gendered or cultural influenced characteristic features noticeable?
- Behavior of students towards *forum*: Are there gendered or cultured differences perceivable?

All observations were carried out by at least two observers, mostly by three or four. All results were recorded and compared after finishing the game. Finally the students attended focus group discussions about their feelings and experiences within the game. The results of the observation were discussed with the students as well. The results of the different case studies are summarized and focused on the four research questions mentioned above.

4.1   General Attitude towards the Game

In general the students face the game open minded without any resentment to participate in independently to their gendered or cultured background. The students knew the lecturers in advance and they already played another game with them. This leaded to an atmosphere of trust and confidence. The game was evaluated as valued and amusing.

The participants tried to generate creative and unexpected solutions. They even solved tasks they did not get at all and showed a lot enthusiasm right from the beginning of the game. Partly the women students seemed to be annoyed by their male classmates. In between coeducational and international groups the attitudes towards the game differed a lot and depended on gendered and cultured background. Some students were rather unsociable at the start of the game while others turned out to be very enthusiastic. It could obviously be perceived that it was quite common for the students to apply serious games as educational methodology and that they liked to let themselves in for the game.

4.2 Roles Students Take within the Group

The gaming groups noticed each other as being competitive and lived this competition consciously. These groups conceived themselves as a team and acted as a team, but it turned out to be very difficult for the women students to control and to settle the enthusiasm of their male classmates. This excitement definitely supported the gaming character of this educational methodology and led to carelessness towards game rules and their application. For example most of the students translated an Italian letter to contact an Italian company even though the market was limited to Germany.

Women students were not appointed to leadership positions and leadership positions were mostly offered to male classmates. The women students did not complain. Female participants had to struggle repeatedly to be included in decision making processes.

Concerning international degree courses it could be noticed that the groups tried to smooth cultural differences and worked on the integration of introverted members by explicitly inviting them to become engaged. But it has to be mentioned that these students were master students.

4.3 Consideration of Impacts and Decisions within in the Game

Finding of designated target, decision making, and discussion of impact took place within the entire group or within a part of the groups, this behaviour depended on the group itself. The impact, the consequences of the decisions, was discussed intensively over all groups. All groups aimed at getting a high benefit for the business year and aligned their planning on this designated target. Decision making processes and their arrangements were not focussed on.

It turned out that the women students repeatedly tried to discuss the impact while their male classmates made decisions much faster than they did without taking consequent impacts into consideration.

In between intercultural groups obvious differences were noticed concerning decisiveness and dealing with the impact. These master students had already practiced their soft skills so they had a higher awareness of the implicit tasks of the game. Therefore, they discussed the decision making process itself and its impact intensively.

4.4 Behavior of Students towards Forum

The *forum* and its possibility to get into contact with the competitors was an unexpected challenge for the students. Even though networks, affiliations and co-operations had been discussed during previous lectures no student decided to co-operate with another company. The representatives of the different groups, who were appointed by their groups, met in the *forum* but they were neither aware of possibilities nor their roles. Even their body language signalled defence and uncertainty. Polite forms of address were neglected. For example the students did not look for any real exchange of information concerning their company, they even told lies to their competitors and did not trust their competitors and the information they offered. Therefore, no co-operation or network was founded. The students who used the *forum* complained about being excluded from the discussion in their group, because the group kept on discussing and making decisions while two of their representatives were in the *forum*.

No gendered or cultured differences were noticed. But it cannot be denied that existing differences were not addressed by anyone due to an apparent unwillingness for further discussions. This was also observed in the focus group discussions.

5   Focus Group Discussion

The students enjoyed playing the game, but they regret that there was more than one winner. They complained and insisted games just have one winner. Concerning the decision marks all students agreed with the lecturers but at the same time they asked for a more obvious way of evaluation by just taking financial benefit into consideration. The students expressed their doubts concerning the *forum* by admitting their missing trust and confidence in each other and they confirmed that they did not think at all about networks, affiliations and co-operations.

6   Factors of Influence and Identified Barriers

Serious games are to be found rarely in higher education and, therefore, they are a challenge by themselves due to the methodology.

Various case studies lead to the following factors influencing knowledge transfer and learning output:

- *Learning atmosphere and trustful learning environment*: The students have to trust their lecturers; they have to recognize that the application of serious games is a learning concept offering just the chance to win. They have to feel confident and to know that they could not lose their face and that they would never be made look a fool. Games have to be applied in a sheltered [safer] space.
- *Gaming experience*: If the students have a positive gaming experience, the barriers to enter into new games are considerably lower and the enthusiasm increases obviously. A serious game is anticipated joyfully.
- *Apparent content of game*: That the content of the game is familiar determines their motivation to get themselves into the game. The hidden learning effect is not, or only partly, perceived during the learning situation, and, therefore, it does not influence the motivation of the students.
- *Trust of students in each other*: The extent to which students know each other influences their behaviour towards co-operation and competition. A lack of

confidence and high competition destroys the basis of the games which are based on co-operation within the group or with different groups.

- *Mono-education*: Especially for women students in engineering degree courses a mono-educational learning environment generates a confident area offering the possibility of creativity and experimenting. The attitudes of women students are much more held back, less creative, and less happy to try out new things in coeducational groups.
- *Comprehension of subordinated objectives:* The difference between Bachelor and Master Students is obvious concerning recognizing and gathering of subordinated learning objectives. Master students already practiced their soft skills and management skills in different lessons, and they reacted more sensitive on non-explicitly expressed tasks and expectations.
- *Handling diversity:* Gendered as well as cultured differences in and between groups were smoothed – but only in the Master Groups, and especially in international degree courses.

7   Summary and Conclusions

Serious Games are a new methodology of knowledge and competence transfer and are a didactic supplement for higher education. Problem based learning scenarios offer new learning processes. Gaming and learning of competences are connected in the simulation. The learners are intensively involved, challenged and exhibited active concern with their lines of action without being afraid of individual consequence or failure. There is no doubt that engineering students need to practice management competences like decision making, communication, and team building (Wöhe 2008; Windhoff, 2001). At the same time two main barriers to getting involved into games turned out to be: gender and culture. There are still very few approaches to take these factors into consideration. Therefore, the authors recommend focusing more precisely on gendered and cultural influences on the learning output. This should help to reduce the impact of these barriers on the use of serious games.

References

1. Hoeborn, G., Bredtmann, J.: Anwendung von Serious Games in der Universitären Ausbildung, Gender und Ingenieurwissenschaften, IZ3, Winterworks Verlag (2013) (in print)
2. Schwesig, M.: Development of a web based management simulation of knowledge exchange in networked manufacturing organisation. Bremer Schriften zu Betriebstechnik und Arbeitswissenschaft, Nr.54, Verlag Mainz (2005)
3. Windhoff, G.: Planspiele für die verteilte Produktion. Entwicklung und Einsatz von Trainingsmodulen für das aktive Erleben charakteristischer Arbeitssituationen in arbeitsteiligen, verteilten Produktionssystemen auf Basis der Planspielmethodik. Dissertation, Bremen (2001)
4. Wöhe, G.: Einführung in die Allgemeine Betriebswirtschaftslehre, Auflage, Wahlen, Berlin, vol. 23 (2008)

VEERKRACHT 2.0

Embodied Interactions in a Servant-Leadership Game

Rens Kortmann, Els van Daalen, Igor Mayer, and Geertje Bekebrede

Delft University of Technology, Faculty TPM, Jaffalaan 5, 2628 BX, Delft, The Netherlands

Abstract. *VEERKRACHT* is a game for servant-leadership development. Although the first version of the game already provided a rather authentic environment for professional training, some players reported that it did not sufficiently provide the rich and meaningful interaction required to practice leadership skills. To revise the game we took inspiration from the literature on embodied cognition and added embodied interactions with non-player characters. An evaluation of the revised game, *VEERKRACHT 2.0*, yielded significant increases in some of the learning effects when compared to the original game. Further analysis showed that the increased learning was to a large extent due to the revised (embodied) interactions in the game. We concluded that, although some questions remain unanswered, embodied cognition seems a promising area of research for improving game designs and game design theories.

1   Introduction

Interaction with virtual, non-player characters (NPCs) in games is often disappointingly limited and meaningless: in many games players do not feel emotionally connected to virtual, computer-generated characters and are not encouraged to interact with them as they would interact with real people. For instance, some players of the leadership game *VEERKRACHT* (Kortmann et al., in press) reported that their interaction with the virtual employees in the game was very superficial: "I had no strong feelings with my virtual followers" or "I felt no urge to interact with my people properly"[1]. As a result, the potential for practising leadership in that part of the game was very limited.

In this paper we aim to show that embodied cognition is a promising area of research for improving interaction with NPCs in games. We demonstrate how it helped us alleviate the problem identified in the *VEERKRACHT* game described above. As our scientific methods we chose a literature study to inform our new game design and a quasi-experimental method to evaluate the revised game. As a starting point we recalled that good games induce embodied experiences: a mix of cognitive, affective, and sensory-motor processes in a game player (Gee, 2008; Klabbers, 2009). Some mechanisms that mediate embodied experiences can be found in the literature on embodied cognition (cf. Clark, 1997; Shapiro, 2010). Therefore, we used this body of knowledge as a source of inspiration to revise the interaction design in our game.

---

[1] Quotes from players have been translated from Dutch.

S.A. Meijer and R. Smeds (Eds.): ISAGA 2013, LNCS 8264, pp. 44–51, 2014.

The paper's structure is as follows. Below we introduce the original VEERKRACHT game (Section 2) and provide the results of our literature study on embodied cognition and interaction (Section 3) before we continue to present the revised design (Section 4) and our evaluation (Section 5). The conclusions and discussion of the research are presented in Section 6.

2   VEERKRACHT

VEERKRACHT (pronounced [vɪ ː rkrɑxt]) is a game for servant-leadership development in *Rijkswaterstaat*, a governmental agency that manages the Dutch motorways and waterways (Kortmann et al., in press). In the game, players are the management of a fictitious organisation that resembles a scaled-down version of *Rijkswaterstaat*, working on their production targets while the organisation is going through changes. Each player has a budget and a list of production targets, such as the construction of a motorway. He/she needs to meet these targets on schedule and on budget whilst keeping their (virtual) subordinates satisfied. Moreover, the organisational changes have to be implemented completely by the end of this one-day game. Players are challenged to reach their objectives using a servant-leadership approach and receive feedback on this during the game.

Fig. 1. Personalised screen for interaction with virtual employees. Shown are a list of the player's production targets (left) and business cards of the virtual employees (right).

At the start of the game each player receives a personalised tablet computer to manage their virtual, computer-generated employees. Also, the tablet lists and monitors the player's production targets. Finally, it enables the player to assign the various tasks and projects on this list to the employees in his/her team.

The original VEERKRACHT game was evaluated in April 2012 during a full-scale test session with our target group: *Rijkswaterstaat* management (see Kortmann et al., in press, for a full description of the test). We evaluated the game's design and its learning effectiveness by means of in-game observations, group discussions, and questionnaires. From the observations and discussions it became clear that the game represented the production aspects of *Rijkswaterstaat* very well and encouraged the players to be engaged in the game. Some players, however, reported they had insufficient opportunities to really practice leadership skills due to the limited interactions with their virtual employees. These interactions merely consisted of reading context-dependent, pre-programmed statements from the employees and responding by selecting one of a number of pre-programmed responses on the tablet PC. For instance, a virtual employee could complain about too much work. In response, the player could lower the workload which, in turn, would increase the employee's satisfaction and productivity. Players experienced this type of interaction as very mechanistic, devoid of emotion. They enjoyed reverse engineering the dialogue system, but were not encouraged to practice feedback and motivation skills. For more background on the game, its purposes, its design, and its learning effectiveness we refer to (Kortmann et al., in press). We concluded that, although *VEERKRACHT* provided a rather authentic picture of *Rijkswaterstaat*, it failed to facilitate certain players in practicing leadership skills through interaction with their virtual employees.

3   Embodied Cognition and Interaction

We took inspiration from the literature on embodied cognition to design richer and more meaningful interactions in our game. Embodied cognition is a branch of cognitive science that studies the role of the body and its interaction with the physical environment in intelligent behaviour (cf. Clark, 1997; Kortmann, 2001; Shapiro, 2010). Embodied cognition aims to present an alternative to the *cognitivist* tradition in cognitive science (cf. Newell and Simon, 1961; Fodor, 1975).

The cognitivist tradition views intelligent behaviour as the result of symbolic reasoning in the mind. It describes the mind as an executor of perceive-plan-act cycles: our sensory systems, *e.g.*, eyes and ears, build and store symbolic representations of the outside world; the mind reasons about those representations; and finally a plan for action is sent to our motoric systems: our limbs, mouth, etc. In this view our sensory and motor systems are passive components that are controlled by a disembodied mind.

In contrast, embodied cognition views intelligent behaviour as an active process in which the body (both sensors and motors) plays a vital role (cf. Noë, 2004). According to embodied cognition, much of our intelligent behaviour is not the result of calculated plans, but the execution of direct perception-action couplings found in the inner parts of our brains that resemble brain regions found in many 'lower' animals as well (Damasio, 1994; LeDoux, 1998).

Recently, studies have been conducted on the role of embodiment in social cognition: our ability to understand and interact with others in complex social situations. Interestingly, this is also the domain of many games for professional training, policy development, etc. Embodied social cognition states that our capacity for social cognition is not primarily grounded in symbolic reasoning about others. Instead, it poses that "what underlies our ability to understand and interact with others is the capacity for more basic, non-mentalistic, interactive embodied practices" (Spaulding, 2012, p. 433). For instance, the phenomenon of primary intersubjectivity, the ability to understand others through the perception of body movements, facial expressions, voice timbre, gestures, etc. is innate and does not require the ability to form and manipulate symbolic representations of those perceptions: even small infants can interact with others (e.g., imitate faces and respond to bodily cues) without being able to reason symbolically. In adults, embodied cognition claims, these innate, non-symbolic types of understanding are fundamental to complex social behaviour as well (Gallagher and Hutto, 2007).

Therefore, we believe that what is needed for rich, meaningful social interaction in games is more than just the exchange of textual, symbolic information between players and NPCs as happened in the original *VEERKRACHT* game. More than this, embodied interaction enables people to optimally employ all of their social cognitive abilities to understand and interpret others. For example, players reported to us that they prefer face-to-face situations when talking to subordinates. They benefit from the ability to perceive facial expressions, voice timbre, gestures and other body movements of their conversation partner. Potentially, other types of sensory stimuli, *i.e.*, taste, smell, and touch, play an important role as well.

Concluding, the theory of embodied cognition informs us about the importance of non-symbolic, embodied interaction for intelligent behaviour. In particular, we noticed that many of our social cognitive abilities are rooted in innate embodied practices. Therefore, to enable players in the leadership game *VEERKRACHT* to optimally use these abilities and to engage in an optimal learning experience, we learnt that embodied interaction is of great importance. In the remainder of this paper we report on our design and evaluation of embodied interactions.

4 *VEERKRACHT* 2.0

In the period following the first test session, a new version of the game, *VEERKRACHT* 2.0, was developed. The revised design mainly aimed to alleviate the lack of meaningful interaction between players and their virtual followers. From our game evaluation and the literature on embodied cognition sketched above, we concluded that embodied interaction would be vital for a good learning experience. For this reason, and considering our time and development budget, we chose to employ human actors to play out some of the virtual employees that had been modelled in the game software. In this way, the game players could engage in private, face-to-face interactions with the employees they knew from their tablets.

Since we wanted the game context to resemble the actual organisation we needed the actors to be knowledgeable about the actual organisation. This is why recently retired *Rijkswaterstaat* staff members were recruited as actors. We developed a software application that enabled actors to send meeting requests with players according to a pre-defined schedule. A player received those requests through his/her tablet PC which then provided the player with a short briefing for the meeting.

For instance, when a player was told to meet with one of his employees to evaluate his/her work, the briefing could say that the employee had failed to fulfil his/her task. After each meeting, the actors were asked to answer a carefully designed set of questions about how he/she had experienced the meeting. Also, they provided written feedback on the meeting. Actors entered their answers and written feedback on their laptops. The software then calculated a leadership score from the actor's answers and reported this score, plus written feedback, to the players on their tablet PCs. The leadership scores provided by our actors also affected the state of virtual employees in the tablet: higher leadership scores yielded happier and more productive employees.

Our actors received half a day of training to prepare them for the situations they would encounter and for the questions they needed to answer after each meeting. We not only trained the actors to understand and convey the factual content of the meetings; we also prepared them to express suitable non-verbal behaviour, such as facial expressions, gestures, etc. as was described by the literature on embodied cognition. Doing so, we considered, would provide players with a rich and meaningful interaction when meeting with their employees to practice leadership skills.

5   Evaluation

We evaluated the revised *VEERKRACHT* 2.0 game in another full-scale test session with four players from the previous test and sixteen new players. A questionnaire was used which consisted of a subset of the items used in the original game's questionnaire. Using a non-parametric statistical test for independent, small samples we found significant increases ($p < 0.05$) in the average response to two items in the questionnaire as depicted in Table 1 below.

Table 1. Significant differences between the average response to two items in the questionnaires conducted after the test sessions of the original and revised games. Possible responses ranged from 1 (completely disagree) to 5 (completely agree). Due to our small sample, significance was tested using the non-parametric Mann-Whitney U-test for independent samples ($p < 0.05$).

Item	Average response after original game (N = 13)	Average response after revised game (N = 13)
After playing the game I have a better understanding of the organisational changes in *Rijkswaterstaat*	2.46	3.38
After playing the game I have a better understanding of how my followers feel about the organisational changes in *Rijkswaterstaat*	2.77	3.77

To explain the differences found we analysed written comments that players had jotted down during the test session and we conducted semi-structured interviews with four players who had participated in test sessions of both the original and revised game. We arrived at the following explanations. First, *Rijkswaterstaat* has prepared many of the changes in their organisation during the period between the two test sessions. This led to better understanding of those changes in the game. Second, in the revised game most players were asked to assume roles that did not correspond to their job description in real life. The switching of roles between the real world and the game world led the players to view the organisational changes from different perspectives than they would in real life which led to a deeper learning experience than before. The third and, according to the interviewees, most important explanation is that the use of real persons to act as employees of game players rather than just virtual employees in the tablet has led to a richer and more meaningful interaction. This enabled players to better understand the employees' concerns with the upcoming organisational changes. The suggestion that the second test group was simply more sensitive to game-based learning was not reported by the interviewees as a viable explanation in the increased learning; neither was it supported by the (non-significant) changes in other learning effects in the game.

From the written feedback and the semi-structured interviews we derived that the interaction with human employees in the revised game resulted in a higher learning effect, pertaining to understanding employees' feelings about the reorganisation, due to:

- More profound conversations between players and their employees: players received unexpected answers, had to resort to creative problem solving, etc.
- Higher (emotional) impact of the meetings with and feedback from the employees on the players: "I feel left alone", "this is scarily real", etc.
- A higher sense of urgency with the players to pay attention to their employees' problems and questions: players did not as easily ignore a question from a real person as they had done with the virtual employees
- A more balanced focus on production targets and leadership issues: practising leadership became much more important in the revised game.

The interviewees explained that, whereas the interactions with their subordinates in the first version of the game felt rather mechanistic, those in the revised version of the game were very similar to what they experienced in their daily life as a manager.

6   Conclusions and Discussion

From the evaluation of the revised leadership game VEERKRACHT 2.0 we concluded that some learning effects increased significantly when compared to the first version of the game (Section 5). Interviews with four players who had tested both versions of the game suggested that this increase was mainly due to the fact that in the first version players interacted with virtual, computer-generated NPCs in a rather emotionally devoid way, whereas in the second version, the interaction with human NPCs resulted in a richer and more meaningful user experience that much more resembled the players' natural interaction with their followers in real life. Those players indicated that the rich interaction experience in the second version of the game allowed them to better practice leadership behaviour and better understand how their followers felt about the upcoming changes in the organisation.

This conclusion and these observations are in line with the literature on embodied cognition and support the idea that embodied interaction is fundamental to intelligent social behaviour (Section 3). Although humans are able to express intelligent social behaviour through non-embodied, symbolic interaction, *e.g.*, purely text-based as was designed in the first version of the game, the literature points out that many of the mechanisms in our brains for social interaction primarily use non-symbolic cues (voice timbre, facial expressions, gestures, etc.) for which embodied interaction is vital. Therefore, not to design embodied interactions in a game seems to reduce the opportunities of players to fully utilise their cognitive capacities for social behaviour. This, in turn, will reduce their opportunities for (tacit) learning from the game (see also Klabbers, 2009).

Following this line of reasoning we consider that embodied cognition as a scientific field of study provides valuable insights into the design of interactions with (virtual) NPCs in games. For instance, primary intersubjectivity theory tells us that we perceive much of other people's intentions and feelings through their body movements, eye directions, and facial expressions. This means that, in order to induce meaningful experiences in games, it would be equally or even more important to model in detail the non-verbal communication of NPCs than the symbolic information exchange between player and NPC. As one of our interviewees expressed: "I prefer written communication, with a virtual character that also shows genuine non-verbal communication (*e.g.*, body movements, facial expressions), over advanced, speech-based communication with a virtual character that looks and sounds like an inanimate object."

However, embodied cognition is not an answer to all game interaction design issues. For instance, we think that current insights may not explain what some call the 'tamagotchi effect': people growing emotionally attached to 'virtual pets' such as the Japanese Tamagotchis from the 1990s. Although little in the way of body movement or facial expressions seems to take place in the interaction with – especially the first generation of – these toys, many owners grow emotionally attached to their virtual pet (Chesney and Lawson, 2007). Also, another interviewee reported that having a conversation with a virtual NPC that resembles a discussion with a real employee is more important to him than watching an NPC's face and limbs move naturally: "it could be an animated teapot talking to me and I would still experience natural conversation." This challenges the conclusion and consideration above that stressed the importance of non-verbal behaviour.

The challenges to embodied cognition mentioned above are worth serious study. Nevertheless, embodied cognition may provide a suitable theoretical framework to study embodied experiences in games. We feel that embodied cognition is a promising area of research for improving our game designs and game design theories.

Acknowledgements. We greatly appreciate our collaboration with Rijkswaterstaat and Dorfl leadership development: Leonie de Vree and Chiel van der Linden. Also, we thank two anonymous reviewers for their helpful comments.

References

1. Chesney, T., Lawson, S.: The illusion of love: Does a virtual pet provide the same companionship as a real one? Interaction Studies 8(2), 337–342 (2007)
2. Clark, A.: Being there: putting brain, body, and world together again. MIT Press, Cambridge (1997)
3. Damasio, A.R.: Descartes' error: emotion, reason, and the human brain. Putnam, New York (1994)
4. Fodor, J.: The language of thought. Harvard University Press, Cambridge (1975)
5. Gallagher, S., Hutto, D.D.: Understanding others through primary interaction and narrative practice. In: Sinha, C., Itkonen, E., Zlatev, J., Racine, T. (eds.) The Shared Mind: Perspectives on Intersubjectivity. John Benjamins, Amsterdam (2007)
6. Gee, J.P.: Video Games and Embodiment. Games and Culture 3(3-4), 253–263 (2008)
7. Klabbers, J.H.G.: The magic circle: principles of gaming & simulation, 3rd edn. Sense Publishers, Rotterdam (2009)
8. Kortmann, R.: Embodied cognitive science. In: De Back, W., Van der Zant, T., Zwanepol, L. (eds.) Proceedings of the First Dutch Symposium on Embodied Intelligence. Utrecht University Preprint Series, Robo Sapiens (2001)
9. Kortmann, R., Bekebrede, G., Van Daalen, E., Harteveld, C., Mayer, I., Van Dierendonck, D.: VEERKRACHT - a game for servant-leadership development. In: Proceedings of the 43rd Annual Conference of the International Simulation and Gaming Association, Cluj-Napoca, RO (in press)
10. LeDoux, J.E.: The emotional brain: the mysterious underpinnings of emotional life. Phoenix, London (1998)
11. Newell, A., Simon, H.: Computer simulation of human thinking. Science 134, 2011–2017 (1961)
12. Noë, A.: Action in perception. MIT Press, Cambridge (2004)
13. Shapiro, L.S.: Embodied cognition. Routledge, Abingdon (2010)
14. Spaulding, S.: Introduction to debates on embodied social cognition. Phenomenology and the Cognitive Sciences 11(4), 431–448 (2012)

A Serious Game Design Combining Simulation and Sandbox Approaches

Heide Lukosch[1], Roy van Bussel[2], and Sebastiaan A. Meijer[3]

[1] Delft University of Technology
Jaffalaan 5
2600 GA Delft, The Netherlands
[2] Kenteq b.v.
Olympia 6-8
1213 NP Hilversum, The Netherlands
[3] KTH Royal Institute of Technology
Teknikringen 72
114 28 Stockholm, Sweden

Abstract. Research has proven the usefulness of serious gaming for learning and advancing motivation by a combination of visuals, audio, text, and entertaining elements. Nevertheless, a broadly accepted, practical instructional design approach to serious games does not yet exist, especially when focusing on vocational edu-cation. The authors introduce a new instructional design model developed for this massive field of education, and argue some advantages compared to other design approaches. The first application is presented in mechanics mechatronics edu-cation to illustrate the close match of timing and provision of information that the instructional design model prescribes and how this has been translated to a rigidly structured serious game design. The structured approach answers the learning needs of applicable knowledge within the target group. It combines advantages of gaming simulations related to the transfer of knowledge from and to the workplace with a sandbox approach, an integrated fun-part of the game, which is aiming at motivating the students in in the best possible way.

1 Introduction

Traditional e-Learning environments, which are packed with a huge amount of (theoretical) learning content, often fail to attract and motivate students using the material [1]. Especially at vocational levels of professional education, students are typically very practice oriented. Theory, in their perception, is only there to apply in 'the real job'. Overcoming the motivational challenges, gap between theory and practice and soloist behavior regularly observed amongst these students would benefit not only the students, but also society at large as the number of students in this type of education greatly outnumbers university students. Applications of serious gaming at this level of teaching are less common. Often they are a derivative from the approaches in higher education. However, simulation games seem to be more effective than other instructional approaches because they address learner's affective

S.A. Meijer and R. Smeds (Eds.): ISAGA 2013, LNCS 8264, pp. 52–59, 2014.

and cognitive processes at the same time [2]. They work intrinsically motivating [3] and support knowledge transfer from the virtual to the real world when designed as a so-called "there-reality" including a high level of physical fidelity [4]. Transfer research emphasizes that transfer is effective when the trained skills have similar logical or deep structures in virtual and in real world [5], which is referring to functional fidelity. Failure to achieve the 'right' level of realism holds the risk that the player adopts a 'wrong' or different strategy than needed in real life [4]. Furthermore, serious games increase motivation when designed as problem-centered trainings. A problem-solving approach compels learners to think about the content, to organize and use the information through actively constructing meaning. Furthermore, it helps building long-lasting memories [6].

In the Netherlands, as it is in many European countries, professional education comes at different levels of training. Much focus in the literature has been on game-based learning at the university and for professional education level, where students typically have to acquire insights into real-world systems, get familiarized with and sensitized for bodies of theory and need safe experimentation environments, typically in the business and management domain [7], [8].

This paper describes a design approach developed for serious gaming for vocational education based upon the four components instructional design (4C/ID) framework by Merrienboer et al. [9], [10] that handles what is called 'Complex Learning'. This framework is ideally suited and widely accepted in the area of vocational education for technique-based professions. It furthermore discusses advantages of simulations and sandbox approaches in serious games and shows why and how we combined both approaches to design a motivating learning experience.

2   Design Approaches of Serious Gaming in Vocational Education

There are a number of definitions of serious games, the much broadest one includes all games with more than only the purpose to entertain, e.g. to train, support decision making or situational awareness processes. For many researchers and designers the term serious game has thus become an umbrella term for educational games, including simulation, business or policy games [see e.g. 11]. Serious games used for learning and training purposes transport instructional content that the learner should use in order to achieve intended learning goals, and that can be classified into four types: facts, procedures, concepts, and principles [12]. For our case, facts and concepts are the most important, but knowledge of physical principles is also needed. Games offer a friendly environment where students are able to play, probe, make mistakes and learn [13]. Serious games have some advantages compared to other technology-enhanced learning environments. Traditional e-Learning environments, which are packed with a huge amount of learning content, often fail to attract and motivate students using the material [1]. The dropout rates of some systems were enormous. As a result, new web technologies, first of all Learning Management Systems [14], were introduced to foster technology-enhanced learning by offering communication mechanisms, interactive and multimedia content, and context adaptive settings [15]. Serious games make use of visual, textual and auditory channels for feedback, challenges, and further components. They enable the player to enter fantasy worlds [6], together with the opportunity of a strong relationship to the real world.

Serious games are often applied in higher education and in business trainings, for example in health or safety settings [16]. The game described here is developed for technical vocational training, taking into account the specific target group of mechanic mechatronics. Typically, a mechanic mechatronics has to undergo a two years initial vocational training at secondary level. One of the important issues of designing the game is thus to keep it interesting and motivating over a period of two years. The students typically are around 16 and 17 years old and male (percentage of female students: 1,4). The daily work of a mechanic mechatronics is quite technical, and requires practical experience as well as profound knowledge of basic principles of mechanics and electronics. We assume that practical experience of machine use and crafting is best trained in practical settings, so the serious game developed is meant to complement the theoretical parts of the vocational training. For using the right machines in the optimal manner, mechanic mechatronics have to adopt and construct knowledge patterns, which are based on procedures and practical tasks. The game will cover different knowledge areas within different projects or levels, which are designed along the four components instructional design (4C/ID) model for complex learning. We choose this design approach instead of other recent game design approaches because of the specific challenges of the game setting we have to deal with, especially the transfer of theoretical knowledge to a very practice-oriented target group as well as the aim to keep the group motivated to play the game over a period of two years.

Other recent game design approaches were analyzed, but did not seem sufficient to tackle those prepositions identified for our case. One of these game design approaches, the triadic game design model [17], [18] focuses on the three dimensions of reality, play and meaning of a serious game and illustrate why design dilemmas and trilemmas between these dimensions make it difficult to balance a serious game. For our own project, this design approach seemed to us to be too abstract to put a game into practice. The work of Kriz and Hense [7] discusses design and evaluation issues of simulations and games. Although they introduce a logic model of a serious game with input, process and outcome-variables, the model is very much focused on the ex-post evaluation of a game, seen as an intervention. Its aim is to gain evaluative knowledge on one particular gaming simulation [7], but the model does not contribute to an instructional design model for a serious game. The contribution of van Staalduinen and de Freitas [19] presents an overview of game elements and their contribution to learning. Furthermore, a game-based learning framework is introduced, which serves as "a checklist and a reminder for designers of serious games" [19]. The framework shows aspects as learner specifics, pedagogy, representations and context, but it does not prefer any specific instructional approach. Eventually, it has not been tested yet.

In summary, the 4C/ID instructional model for complex learning provides answers to the specific needs of our target group and learning goal. In the following, we describe the fundamental design approach of the game, based on the 4C/ID model, before we show how this is combined with a sandbox approach for fostering motivation and support knowledge transfer.

3   Complex Learning

Not only professionals, but also trainees in vocational education experience the increasing need of a strong relationship between theoretical knowledge and practical work. Work related and practice oriented learning and training asks for specific design of instructional interventions to support the application of knowledge on practical tasks. The field of constructivist learning design with focus on problem solving [20] and the work on design principles of instruction by Merrill [21] are examples for instructional approaches as answers to these particular learning needs. The approach of complex learning, with its so-called 4C/ID model [9], [10] addresses three deficits of other instructional design models, which was the reason for us to choose this model as design guideline for the serious game.

First, this model focuses on the integration and coordinated performance of task-specific skills rather than on knowledge types, context or presentation-delivery media [9]. Starting from task-specific skills is a well-suited approach for vocational education in the technological domain. Second, the model provides a difference between supportive information for routine actions and just-in-time or procedural information, focusing on the performance, not on knowledge [9]. In designing a learning system like a serious game, one can use this distinction for embedding distinct types of information into the system, adjusted to the different needs of the learner. Third, the model recommends a mixture between more simple part-task and complex, whole task practice to support whole-task learning [9]. By following this advice, a combined approach of simple and complex problem solving is achieved with the main aim to support complex learning skills.

The idea of combining different levels of activities and learning is the basis of the 4C/ID-model of complex learning. It indicates that different skills are related to each other. The horizontal and vertical relationships between tasks of the same or a different difficulty level have to be taken into account when designing an instructional intervention like a serious game. In general, the design model for complex learning described here, delivers three essential components for the design of learning environments, namely learning tasks, supportive information and procedural information, and part-task practice [9], [10].

4   Design Approach of a Serious Game Based on Complex Learning Principles

The game developed is meant to continue for 2 years, to be played during the full vocational education curriculum with 400 hours for playing the game within the two years. The first domain for application is the mechatronics program, a coherent program with components from metal works, electronics, pneumatics, hydraulics and logic/programming. Typically, the students find work as construction or service operation employee. The current curriculum is a combination of theoretical classes, taught in traditional classroom setting by a teacher, and practical classes in a learning work shop setting that has all machines available. The game will replace a large part of the traditional theoretical classes by providing an active virtual environment in which the student will get the different sources of information at the right time and in the right format. The practical classes will not be replaced at all, but will be enriched with content from the game. The main idea is that the student first makes an assignment in the game and after successful completion in the game will go to the physical learning workshop to accomplish a comparable task in real life. Therefore the game design does not only involve the game environment, but a full learning environment, including coupling with reality to actually facilitate the knowledge transfer. The three crucial components of the 4C/ID model are applied to our game design as follows.

First, the 4C/ID model focuses on the integration and coordinated performance of task-specific skills rather than on knowledge types, context or presentation-delivery media [13]. In our design we translate this to a focus on what the student has to do to successfully finish a construction assignment. We created a nested approach in which any construction assignment can be split up to singular actions of the order of magnitude like 'select the correct size of bolt' or 'screw bolt X on screw Y'.

Second, 4C/ID provides a difference between supportive information for routine actions and just-in-time or procedural information, focusing on the performance, not on knowledge [9]. In the game design there is a plethora of sources of information available. At the level of the Project, Task and Assignment, the player can get supportive information for routine actions. At the Procedure and Step level the player can get just-in-time and procedural information. In the definition of the procedures and steps the game designers set links to an existing expert system for the mechatronics sector, so that currently available and validated information can be re-used in the game. The aim of the combination of this part of the 4C/ID approach with knowledge patterns provided by the expert system is to "teach" the players to think like an expert. With the combination of supportive and procedural information, the user will get "just enough" information just-in-time, which is prerequisite to the learning and performance of the students [9] and where information can best be understood and used in practice [13].

Third, 4C/ID recommends a mixture between more simple part-task and complex, whole task practice to support whole-task learning [9]. In our game design method this is implemented through the nested approach, where in the game-play the participant navigates up and down through the complexity levels. Both automated (through recognition of the level of the participant) as well as manually, the player can pursue procedures in a step-by-step or in an unguided fashion.

5   Simulation and Sandbox Approach in Serious Gaming

In addition to the complex learning model, our approach to game design combines advantages of educational simulations with strengths of sandbox approaches of serious games. The more educational, or simulation part of the game, represents a work place of a mechanic mechatronics. The environment is situated in a machine hall, containing all machines, tools and materials a real workplace also includes.

It shows a high level of physical and functional fidelity. In the workplace, the students have to accomplish the projects that are designed along the 4C/ID-model of complex learning.

Strongly connected with this is the sandbox part of the whole system. In our understanding, the sandbox part of the game represents an area where the students are rewarded for their work in the educational/simulation part of the game. It is an area where students can play around, have fun with the game and share what they are doing. Using the term metaphorically, sandboxes are good for learning: if learners are put into a situation that feels like the real thing, but with risks and dangers greatly mitigated, they can learn well and still feel a sense of authenticity and accomplishment [6]. Students can use the work pieces tailored in the workplace. With accomplishing a task in the workplace, students will get a work piece or a reward to be used in the other "fun" machine hall to build up a rollercoaster. Rewards can be used to buy additional underparts or to try out other students' attractions. This combined design approach is meant to answer the need of high functional and physical fidelity of a simulation game, simultaneously combined with a motivating fun-part of the leisure park. Students always can enter and individually create own content, thus turning into producers of the game instead of remaining simply consumers of any learning content [13]. The useful rewards are working as immediate feedback and thus also foster the motivation of the students [6].

In summary, the main purpose of the simulation game is to provide the mechatronics students with theoretical knowledge needed for education and later in daily work. A challenge of designing the game is to keep the students motivated to play the game over a period of two years. The design decision we took as an answer to these two prepositions is to design the whole game as an integrated combination of a simulation game and a sandbox approach, which will keep the students engaged while designing their own game environment.

In the following, we describe how we translated the complex learning approach into game mechanics for the two parts of the serious game developed in more detail.

Supportive and procedural information is made available in time and in place in a structured way that has proven to be beneficial in other learning materials built upon the 4C/ID method. This pushes the gameplay more to Virtual Reality-like simulation, and therefore needs to be balanced not to lose the game play. By providing the information in a structured, consequent and predictable way the student will not get out of his flow of play. Rewards are coupled to the structure of the assignments in the virtual workshop. Therefore there is a direct and recognizable system for earning game rewards. Given the structured simulation part of the project, the value of the rewards will pay off in the sandbox part of the game. This way rewards will have the temptation that is so powerful in gaming but is the incentive system coupled to direct learning results. Scores come from rewards, from other players who can contribute to, and play in your sandbox, and from teachers who score the student-players on their motivation and skills both playing the game and doing assignments that first have been made in the simulation also on real machines in the educational workshop. This means that scores are more than the result of game-play, but also include the learning and social environment.

Through these mechanics the game couples fun to learning in a way that is different from existing game design methods. Using the 4C/ID way of describing learning elements, it has already proven to be effective to make the often complex coupling of gaming with an existing community of teachers. Schools have shown great interest in providing their learning material for the game, and have made first efforts to structure it in the right format. This has proven natural to the teachers involved. After field trials of the first mechanics mechatronics game a more formal evaluation can follow.

6   Conclusions and Further Research

The authors introduced a game design framework developed for vocational education application of gaming simulations. The design is based upon the 4C/ID framework by van Merrienboer [9], [10] which has a proven value for vocational education design. The close match with timing and role of knowledge and information that 4C/ID prescribes translates to a very structured game design. The framework is expected to yield games that have a closer alignment with the vocational learning goals of the teaching method(s) that a game might replace. The clear structure and recognizable tasks, steps and actions should lead to fast acceptance of a game amongst teachers, even if they are not familiar or positive about gaming for education in general. The lessons organized around a game based upon our framework can have a clear delineation, something that is often hard to do with current games. The combination of a simulation and a sandbox approach in the game as an answer to learning and engagement or motivational needs, represents one possible answer to balance the phenomena of gameplay and learning within a serious game and to foster motivation amongst the target group of mechanic mechatronics students.

The first game prototype was built in Summer 2012. An evaluation model has been developed, based on Millers pyramid of competence assessment, for the simulation game. It has been tested within a semi-experimental setting with more then 70 students within a three-days workshop. Observation and evaluation of the test have been conducted. The proper analyses of the results are done at the moment and will show how effective the game is at transferring the needed knowledge in mechanics mechatronics education.

Acknowledgments. This work could have been realized with support of Kenteq b.v., The Netherlands.

References

1. Levy, Y.: Comparing dropouts and persistence in e-learning courses. Computers & Education 48(2), 185–204 (2007)
2. Sitzmann, T.: A meta-analytic examination of the instructional effectiveness of computer-based simulation games. Personnel Psychology 64, 489–528 (2011)
3. Malone (1981)

4. Chalmers, A., Debattista, K.: Level of Realism for Serious Games. In: IEEE Proceedings of 2009 Conference in Games and Virtual Worlds for Serious Applications (2009)
5. Lehman, D.R., Lempert, R.O., Nisbett, R.E.: The effects of graduate training on reasoning: Formal discipline and thinking about everyday-life events. American Psychologist 43, 431–442 (1988)
6. Greitzer, F.L., Kuchar, O.A., Huston, K.: Cognitive Science Implications for Enhancing Training Effectiveness in a Serious Gaming Context. ACM Journal Educational Resources in Computing 7(3), article 2 (2007)
7. Kriz, W.C., Hense, J.U.: Theory-oriented evaluation for the design of and research in gaming and simulation. Simulation & Gaming 37, 268–285 (2006)
8. Meijer, S.A., Hofstede, G.J., Omta, S.W.F., Beers, G.: Trust and Tracing game: learning about transactions and embeddedness in the trade network. Journal of Production Planning and Control 17(6), 569–583 (2006)
9. van Merrienboer, J., Clark, R., de Crook, M.: Blueprints for Complex Learning: The 4C/ID-Model. ETR & D 50(2), 39–64 (2002)
10. van Merrienboer, J., Kirschner, P.: Ten Steps to Complex Learning. A systematic Approach to Four-Component Instructional Design. Routledge, New York (2007)
11. Woods, S.: Loading the Dice: The Challenge of Serious Videogames. Game Studies 4(1) (2004)
12. Yusoff, A., Crowder, R., Gilbert, L., Wills, G.: A conceptual framework for serious games. In: Proceedings of the 9th IEEE Conference on Advanced Learning Technologies, pp. 21–23 (2009)
13. Gee, J.P.: What Video Games have to teach us about Learning and Literacy. Palgrave Macmillan, New York (2003)
14. Mayes, T., De Freitas, S.: Review of e-learning theories, frameworks and models. JISC e-learning models study report (2004), http://www.jisc.ac.uk/elp_outcomes.html
15. Moreno-Ger, P., Burgos, D., Torrente, J.: Digital Games in eLearning Environments: Current Uses and Emerging Trends. Simulation & Gaming 40(5), 669–687 (2009)
16. Zyda, M.: From Visual Simulation to Virtual Reality to Games. Computer 38(9), 25–32 (2005)
17. Harteveld, C., Guimaraes, R., Mayer, I.S., Bidarra, R.: Balancing Play, Meaning and Reality: The Design Philosophy of Levee Patroller. Simulation & Gaming 41(3), 316–340 (2010)
18. Harteveld, C.: Triadic Game Design. Springer, Heidelberg (2010)
19. van Staalduinen, J.P., de Freitas, S.: A Game-Based Learning Framework: Linking Game Design and Learning Outcomes. In: Khine, M.S. (ed.) Learning to Play. Exploring the Future of Education with Video Games, pp. 29–54. Peter Lang Publishing, New York (2011)
20. Jonassen, D.H.: Instructional Design Models for Well-Structured and Ill-Structured Problem-Solving Learning Outcomes. Educational Technology Research and Development 45(1), 65–94 (1997)
21. Merrill, M.D.: Knowledge objects and mental models. In: Advanced Learning Technologies, pp. 244–264 (2000)

Building a Virtual World for Team Work Improvement

Heide Lukosch, Bas van Nuland, Theo van Ruijven, Linda van Veen,
and Alexander Verbraeck

Delft University of Technology
Jaffalaan 5, 2600 GA Delft, The Netherlands

Abstract. Many working tasks in our complex, fast changing world are no
longer to be solved by single workers, but require effective cooperation of a
team of workers. Communication, cooperation and participation are basic skills
needed for a well functioning team, especially in safety-critical domains like
security. In these domains, the ability of a team to cooperate sometimes even
decides about life and death. The development of a shared understanding of a
given situation is a prerequisite for effective teamwork. Traditional methods of
enhancing teamwork related skills are limited due to their lack of flexibility and
their distance to real world challenges. In more general terms, rapidly changing
environments require emerging and creative strategies and tools. Our research
aims at exploring whether and how such a creative tool, namely a simulation
game, can be used as a socio-technological system to support shared situational
awareness. Results from usability tests of various game scenarios show that
realistic virtual environments imply the ability to foster teamwork related skills
like situational awareness and communication.

1   Introduction

Exploring the potential of simulation games to enhance teamwork skills, we approach
simulation games as social systems themselves, constructed out of roles, rules and
resources, with the ability to also emulate real socio-technological systems [1]. With
simulation games, players and teams of players can train and probe actions and reactions in a real-like safe environment, without the risk of real-world consequences.
On the other hand, simulation games provide immediate feedback and help the
players to reflect on their own abilities, skills, knowledge and actions, especially
when a proper de-briefing phase is included in a game [2]. Simulation games seem to
be more effective than other instructional approaches because they address learner's
affective and cognitive processes at the same time [3]. They work intrinsically
motivating [4] and support knowledge transfer from the to the real world when
designed as a so-called "there-reality" including a high level of physical fidelity [5].
Transfer research emphasizes that transfer is effective when the trained skills have
similar logical or deep structures in virtual and in real world [6], which is referring to
functional fidelity. An important aspect of fidelity for immersive virtual worlds for
simulation gaming and training is that the interactions with objects, people, and
colleagues/co-players in the virtual environment of a simulation game need to be
realistic enough to enable the right level of learning to take place. For example, the

S.A. Meijer and R. Smeds (Eds.): ISAGA 2013, LNCS 8264, pp. 60–68, 2014.

military has a long tradition of using simulations for strategy and combat training, because of the chance to clearly illustrate consequences of actions in a safe environment, without risk of injury or other damage [7; 8]. Furthermore, fidelity defines the degree to which a game emulates the real world [9; 10], and has been researched extensively [11; 12]. The results show, contrary to common belief, that there is no linear relationship between level of realism and effectiveness of training. Abstraction and simplification can lead to excellent training outcomes [13]. For safety and security training in urban environments, however, it is not clear how different level of realism and different aspects of realism affect training effectiveness, although certain aspects have already been researched. As an example, Visschedijk [14] researched fidelity guidelines of human emotion expressions for 3D military simulation games. Other research showed that failure to achieve the 'right' level of realism holds the risk that the player adopts a 'wrong' or different strategy than needed in real life [5]. Nonetheless, the effect fidelity actually has on processes of shared situational understanding has not yet been researched properly; to understand this relationship is the major aim of our research. Harteveld [10] defines three criteria for realism in game play: validity, flexibility and fidelity. In terms of validity that he defines as the visual resemblance between reality and virtual worlds for training, much progress has been made in the past decades. With the increasing possibilities of high-speed graphical visualization, the design of simulation games has become more and more realistic. Virtual environments with adequate levels of detail for buildings and objects are readily available. Flexibility can be guaranteed by modular design of the games, the use of scenario editors, and by teacher-led games. Through simulation games, different virtual scenarios can be designed and played. Players can experience taking over different roles in a game, dealing with various social situations, and characteristics of the reference system (the "reality" for instance). Within a game, players can develop alternative modes of action and re-action [2].

This paper describes a design approach for simulation game scenarios for situational awareness training of reconnaissance teams. In the following, we introduce why teamwork is essential in this working field and how we define teamwork. We see shared understanding of a given situation, its interpretation and prediction of its future state as prerequisite for effective teamwork. We show how we designed simulation game scenarios in a virtual environment to explore training possibilities. Finally, we discuss the outcomes and provide a conclusion and outlook on future research.

2   Elements of Effective Teamwork in Reconnaissance Duties

Reconnaissance and close protection of politicians and threatened persons are important security tasks of the police and security services. Our work with experts from the field provided us with deeper insights in the competencies and skills needed in this field. For police officers in reconnaissance and close protection, it is of crucial importance to interact with suspicious persons in a way to gather reliable information. Response to police contact can tell the police a lot about the person and provides hints for further actions. Additionally to this interaction with suspects and other persons in the environment, effective teamwork is of great importance to gather as much environmental information as possible. Interpersonal relation competencies are of crucial significance in the field, as one team member has to trust and rely on the action and information of other team members, for his/her own safety and the safety of other involved persons. Competencies also include analyzing and resolving problems, and adapting to the changing demands of a situation. Very good communication skills are a precondition for proper decision making and action taking. These skills include the interpretation of information, and it's processing. Team members have to recognize and interpret signs and hints in the environment, and have to decide on their importance and the way to proceed the information to other team members, if needed. This also relates to situational awareness skills, a concept extending communication of information with the relation to past (experiences) and future (prediction).

3   The Role of (shared) Situational Awareness in Effective Teamwork

To make effective decisions, team members have to understand and judge a situation based on their experiences in comparable (training) situations. The definition of Endsley [15; 16] of such a conceptualization of a situation as Situational Awareness (SA) is widely accepted. Situation awareness has always been needed to perform tasks effectively [17]. Endsley's definition includes the perception of the elements of an environment in time and space, the comprehension of their meaning and the projection of their statues in the future [15]. This process of perception, comprehension and projection leads to a decision for a certain action. The process reveals two important aspects that characterize expert decision makers. It also includes that experts have a repertoire of relevant cues and patterns that enable them to recognize the situation. Additionally, experts have mental models, which they use to match these relevant cues and patterns. SA includes more than perceiving or attending to information, but also the integration of pieces of information and a determination of the information to a person's goals. In this way, experts are able to mentally simulate possible outcomes of actions and decisions [14]. A real simulation can help team members to increase their situational awareness skills in providing cues and patterns and to develop mental models.

As other concepts of SA, Endsley's model is focused on single persons, not on teams. To increase teamwork effectiveness, the team needs a shared mental model. For our research this means that we have to develop a concept of shared situational awareness (SSA). Commonly, Shared Situational Awareness (SSA) is defined as "shared awareness/understanding of a particular situation", "common operational picture" or common relevant picture distributed rapidly about a problem situation [18]. Nonetheless, those definitions focus on hierarchical command and control systems and organizations. Simulation games can support a SSA process focused on teamwork processes by providing the same experience frame for a group of players.

Furthermore, the information given, perceived and understood not only has to be related to a single person's goal, but to the goal of the whole team. For SSA, the projection of future actions has also to be shared. This last step can also be supported by a simulation game, as it shows consequences of actions and decisions with the same feedback to every player and makes them a shared experience.

4 Design Approach of Game Scenarios to Increase Teamwork Skills in Reconnaissance Work

Training of reconnaissance teams nowadays is an expensive, resource intensive activity. A wide set of skills and knowledge is needed to do a good job in close protection and observation. Traditional training includes use of case material, training on the job and expanded "real world" simulations or role-plays. A lot of organization, planning and human commitment is needed to simulate any relevant event within a "real" environment, which often is near to being impossible. Furthermore, realistic training of safety and security officers in the public space has the risk of raising distress among the general public. As a consequence, the safety and security field recognizes the importance of the use of simulations and simulation games to prepare people for responding to natural disasters or crisis situations.

Between 2010 and early 2013, Agentschap NL, "Pieken in de Delta", and the Municipality of The Hague, financed a project called "CharliePapa" to study the impact of the use of virtual realistic environments in security simulation games, varying from single-player stand-alone versions to trainer-led team play. In the following, we introduce the different scenarios that have been developed and show an overview about how these scenarios have been tested with the target group. As first development step, possible training scenarios have been discussed with experts from the police together with educational experts with experience in the safety domain. As a result, some scenarios emerged, taking place at crucial areas within the city of The Hague, the Netherlands. As second step, several square kilometers of the inner city of The Hague around the parliament buildings were scanned with a high-precision laser scanner, and processed into 3D virtual environments. To achieve a highly authentic experience, streets of The Hague were re-built as realistically as possible, with authentic positions, heights and textures of buildings, streets and objects like plants, tram lines and dust bins [19].

The virtual world was built within the third development step, using two different game development engines, the one aiming at a self-supporting game where players could train their skills without a trainer, the other especially aiming at trainer-lead sessions. In total, three different scenarios have been built and tested with the target group. Within these tests we tried to analyze how important the dynamic, and the quantity and authenticity of the elements of the environments are for the training process. The games were played in an experimental setting out of work context, and extensively evaluated with security professionals to obtain insight into the relationship between the level of graphical realism and training effectiveness. The tests included a pre- and a post-test questionnaire, live observation through two researchers, videotaping and a de-briefing phase that addressed both the content of the simulation game as the process of playing itself. The results of each of the first two tests were brought back into the further development process of the game scenarios. The test-trainings were one element in a participatory design process, which is described in detail in [19].

4.1   First Scenario: Trainer-Lead Team Play in an Authentic Virtual City

The first game scenario was based on a Unity-development. Five experts played a trainer-lead game within the virtual environment. At every game round, two police officers played together in front of two big screens. They formed one team, but were able to navigate their own avatar through the environment. The players could communicate with each other in person, and could use their handheld phone to communicate with the team leader who was located in a different room. One trainer accompanied the team, taking over the roles of virtual persons the team wanted to interact with in the game. Technical staff was on site to help out if technical problems would occur. The players were able to get used to the game and the navigation within a tutorial round. The assignment of the real game was given after the tutorial within a briefing, structurally based on real briefing situations from daily work. The police officers were asked to walk through the virtual city of The Hague along a prescribed route, and to make sure that this route would be safe for a person to be protected afterwards. This means that the police team had to detect suspicious objects and persons. After a short feedback moment, the police team got its second assignment and played a second round within the virtual environment, with a similar objective. The game ended with a de-briefing moment, focused on both the playing experience and the training effect.

Feedback of the test persons regarding game play targeted the flow feeling, which was disturbed by the recurrent switch between in-game action and interaction with the trainer, taking over the role of one of the virtual agents. This also hindered real empathy with the persons and the situation. The movement of the virtual persons has not yet been realistically enough. The virtual agents did not provide enough hints to make any assumptions about the person itself. For example, if police agents approach someone in reality, they can identify patterns of behavior that give them a clue whether someone seems to be suspicious or not. Based on behavioral signs, police agents decide about further actions. These signs and with them a fundamental basis for decision making processes lacked in the game. Furthermore, the whole scenario did not hold enough details to make clear interpretations of the situation. Relationships between objects and persons are important for interpretation, but have not been clear enough in the game. The feedback regarding the training effect of the game included that especially the de-briefing phase was crucial to learn from each other's observations. Situational awareness could be sharpened, but especially based on the cleanness and lack of details of objects and agent behavior it was not seen as an alternative to a traditional training. The outcomes of the first test lead us to the development of a second game scenario, developed with the UDK game engine, and aiming at a self-directed training activity without interaction with a trainer during game play.

4.2   Second Scenario: Self-directed Team Play in an Authentic Virtual City

The second scenario was based on outcomes and requirements from the first test session. To solve the problem that the environment seemed to be too clean and static, the UDK game engine was used for development this time. A first version of this second scenario was built as a single-player game with more objects included. This version was tested in a usability test by six experts from the police. It showed that this version had improved regarding richness of objects and visualization of the environment, but that the single-player version offered no interaction and/or communication skill training. Together with police and instructional experts, a team-training scenario has then been built, too. A slightly different, livelier area of the inner city of The Hague was chosen for the team set-up of the game. The assignment of this scenario was to walk through the environment with three players in a row, each of them confronted with both different and same objects, persons and actions as the other players. Player one had to observe the environment and to pass over information to player two, who had to interpret the scene based on this information and his/her own observations. He/she had to pass over information to the third player, who had to take a decision on an action (whether to let the person to protect walk the observed route or not) based on the information he/she had from his/her colleagues and based on his/her own observations.

Again, 16 experts, 8 from the police, and 8 from a private security organization played this game. While a team of four accompanying researchers could observe differences in the game process between players with experience in computer games and players with less experience, the whole group easily understood the aim and mechanics of the game. Information retrieved from the game was written down on paper and passed over to the next player. Players made use of the information from prior players, e.g. when recognizing deviant behavior of a virtual person. Before interrogating the virtual person, the players used the information from the previous round to gain more insight into the recent situation. This mechanism also served as a quality control of each other's work. The player afterwards had to rely on the information he/she received. Thus, when a player observed properly and was able to process and share the information well, he/she enabled the next player doing his/her job properly, too. Thus, this game scenario was able to address distinct training goals as awareness skills, interpretation and communication skills like information gathering, processing and sharing. As the last player in the row had the task to make a decision on how to proceed, decision-making skill was also included.

4.3   Third Scenario: Trainer-Lead Single Play in a Generic Virtual City

The third scenario was again developed as a trainer-lead scenario, based on the Unity game engine. This scenario did not take place in the city of The Hague, but in a generic Dutch urban space. An open-air concert took place in the area, which was crowded with a huge amount of virtual persons. The assignment of the game was to accompany a person of public interest (VIP) to the event. The game was divided into the three phases of work preparation, observation and execution of the task. 8 police officers and 8 employees of a private security organization played the game. The police officers were focused on protecting the VIP and detecting deviant behavior of other subjects at the sight, while the employees of the private security organization where focused on the security of objects and buildings. This task distribution mirrors the tasks in real security duties of the two organizations. Two teams of two players, one police team and one team of the private security organization, played each round of the game synchronously. The idea behind that was that the teams with different professional background and tasks also could use each other as information source, which actually did not happen within the game. Information exchange within the teams of the own organization worked well. The trainer of the game took over the roles of the virtual persons the players wanted to interact with instead of a user interface. The de-briefing of the game showed that players appreciated the generic, unknown virtual environment, because this made them more alert about the situation. Additionally, the unknown environment forced them to communicate very well with each other, because they could not rely on known mental models or patterns about the surrounding. Different to reality, the players within a team couldn't see each other's faces, which minimized their information and ability of interpreting the situation. In reality, they also use each other's body language and facial expressions for information exchange and cooperation. The environment was very busy, but players still missed clear signs in virtual person's behavior and face expressions. This kind of information is of crucial interest for the situational awareness process in reality. The role of the trainer as dialog partner compensated this lack of information and fostered the flexibility of the scenario, but the players mentioned the fact that this way of interaction always meant a break in game flow.

5   Discussion

The test sessions showed that the way in which the interaction within a simulation game takes place is of the utmost importance. When people talk among themselves in reality, but they are forced to use written text in a game, they feel distracted from showing realistic behavior with respect to other aspects. The realistic virtual environment shows the ability to enhance teamwork skills, especially communication skills. (Shared) situational awareness can be fostered to a certain limit. Virtual objects could be used for awareness training, but virtual agents of the game scenario's still lack realistic behavior and expressions. The decision for man-machine interaction or a teacher-lead approach, where the teacher takes over the roles of the virtual agents, relates to the balance between fidelity and flexibility of the game. While interaction with the virtual agent produces a more realistic feeling and holds the player within the feeling of flow, a teacher-lead approach supports flexibility of gameplay, but cuts in the gameplay. Although the players from the test sessions and the expert observers of the tests were enthusiastic about the game and the playing experience, two fundamental requirements were identified, regarding fidelity and interaction.

First, the virtual environment looked "too clean". To resemble a real city, the number of objects on the streets should have been much higher (e.g. dirt, bikes, parked cars). These are objects that distract attention and that block lines of sight in reality, and therefore are very important for reconnaissance training purposes. Furthermore, the ability for humans to focus attention on an object is present in reality but is hard to resemble in the game as you only have a wide-angle view. In spite of realism of buildings, cars, public transport, and people on the street, and a huge amount of other objects created especially for this game, participants still feel that the fidelity of the virtual environment is insufficient for safety and security training. Secondly, the interaction with people and objects in the game was still too slow and cumbersome, especially in the first two scenarios. Although the user interface for interaction is intuitive, it distracts from being able to keep looking around and continue the observation. The same holds for the trainer-lead version of the game were the flow feeling of the game is distracted by the interaction with the trainer.

6   Conclusions and Further Research

Both requirements described above are related to each other. One of the ways of obtaining a higher "fidelity" is to provide a realistic way of interaction with virtual objects and persons in such a way that it does not distract game play. When reality is used as reference system for the game as proposed, the game represents a dynamic model of reality. The development and game sessions of a virtual training environment for reconnaissance teams described here show that the behavior of, and the interaction with the objects or simulated players in a virtual training environment should have a minimum required level of realism to provide enough hints for decision making processes. Furthermore, the test results illustrate that assignments and tools within the game should also have a high level of fidelity to ensure effective training activities in a virtual environment. The level of fidelity needed in simulation games for training is crucial when multiple players in the same virtual environment have to communicate extensively to create a shared situational awareness, while actively scouting the virtual environment to build their own picture of the current state of the world. Still, little is known about how to reach the optimal balance between fidelity and transfer in designing a simulation game. High fidelity gaming simulation, which emulates the real world helps to create a better understanding and (shared) situational awareness of this reference system. When we define situational awareness as a state of knowledge about an environment, than we see from the questionnaires and the de-briefing, that this state has been changed through the use of the high-fidelity simulation games. The results show that understanding of the situation (the environment), but also the need for information sharing increased. Especially after the de-briefing phase, participants recorded that they developed a different way of viewing the environment through the discussion with colleagues during the de-briefing.

As next steps, relations between simulation game fidelity and (shared) situational awareness should be researched in more depth including game and control groups, and relations between gameplay behavior (log-data) and team competencies, and should be grounded on a sound theoretical concept of shared situational understanding in teams.

Acknowledgments. This work could have been realized with support of The Pieken in de Delta-program and the Municipality of The Hague, The Netherlands.

References

1. Klabbers, J.H.G.: The Magic Circle: Principles of Gaming & Simulation. Sense Publishers, Rotterdam (2006)
2. Kriz, W.: Creating Effective Learning Environments and Learning Organizations through Gaming Simulation Design. Simulation&Gaming 34, 495–510 (2003)
3. Sitzmann, T.: A meta-analytic examination of the instructional effectiveness of computer-based simulation games. Personnel Psychology 64, 489–528 (2011)
4. Malone, T.W.: What makes things fun to learn? A study of intrinsically motivating computer games. Pipeline 6(2), 50–51 (1981)
5. Chalmers, A., Debattista, K.: Level of Realism for Serious Games. In: IEEE Proceedings of 2009 Conference in Games and Virtual Worlds for Serious Applications (2009)
6. Lehman, D.R., Lempert, R.O., Nisbett, R.E.: The effects of graduate training on reasoning: Formal discipline and thinking about everyday-life events. American Psychologist 43, 431–442 (1988)
7. Macedonia, M.: Games Soldiers Play. IEEE Spectrum, 32-37 (March 2002)
8. Bonk, C.J., Dennen, V.P.: Massive Multiplayer Online Gaming: A Research Framework for Military Training and Education, Technical Report, Department of Defense, USA (2005)
9. Alexander, A.L., Brunye, T., Sidman, J., Weil, S.A.: From Gaming to Training: A Review of Studies on Fidelity, Immersion, Presence, and Buy-in and Their Effects on Transfer in PC-Based Simulations and Games. Aptima, Inc., Woburn (2005)
10. Harteveld, C.: Triadic Game Design. Springer, Heidelberg (2011)
11. Feinstein, A.H., Cannon, H.M.: Fidelity, Verifiability, and Validity of Simulation: Constructs for Evaluation. Wayne State University Marketing Department Working Paper 2001-006 (2001), http://sbaweb.wayne.edu/~marketing/wp/008HC.pdf
12. Hays, R.T., Singer, M.J.: Simulation Fidelity In Training System Design: Bridging The Gap Between Reality And Training. Recent Research In Psychology Series. Springer, New York (1988)
13. Toups, Z.O., Kerne, A., Hamilton, W.A.: The team coordination game: Zero-fidelity simulation abstracted from fire emergency response practice. ACM Transactions on Computer-Human Interaction 18(4), Article 23, 37 pages (2011)
14. Visschedijk, G.C.: The issue of fidelity: What is needed in 3D Military Serious Games? Master Thesis, University of Twente/TNO, Soesterberg (2010)
15. Endsley, M.R.: Design and evaluation for situation awareness enhancement. In: Proceedings of the Human Factors Society 32nd Annual Meeting, pp. 97–101. Human Factors and Ergonomics Society, Santa Monica (1988)
16. Endsley, M., Jones, W.M.:: Situation Awareness Information Dominance & Information Warfare. Tech. Rep. February, DTIC Document (1997)
17. Endsley, M.R.: Designing for Situation Awareness in Complex Systems. In: Proceedings of the Second International Workshop on Symbiosis of Humans, Kyoto, Japan (2001)
18. Nofi, A.: Defining and Measuring Shared Situational Awareness. Tech. Rep. 10, Center for Naval Analyses, Arlington (2000)
19. Lukosch, H.K., van Ruijven, T.A.W., Verbraeck, A.: The other city? How to design authentic urban environments for serious games. In: Proceedings of the International Conference on Information Systems for Crisis Response and Management, ISCRAM 2012 (2012)

Developing an Ambient Assisted Living Environment Applying the advanced Learning Factory (aLF)

A Conceptual Approach for the Practical Use in the Research Project A²LICE

Daniel Plorin and Egon Müller

Chemnitz University of Technology
Department of Factory Planning and Factory Management
09107 Chemnitz, Germany
daniel.plorin@mb.tu-chemnitz.de

Abstract. More than ever, companies find themselves in a dynamic market with changing conditions, technological change and increasing competition. Sustainable industrial enterprises have recognized that the development of employee skills is a key success factor for manufacturing companies. However, it is not the easiest to address this topic with the help of a suitable learning environment. In this paper, the concept frame of the advanced Learning Factory (aLF) is introduced and clarified by a special use case out of the research project A²LICE (Ambient Assisted Living In Controlled Environments). In combination with the didactic method of serious game it represents an effective way for learning. Thus, with the serious approach of a playful exchange of knowledge, the respective grievances can be resolved.

1 Introduction

The main issue of this paper is to demonstrate innovative and practical teaching methods in the training and education of students, researchers and industrial users. However, serious gaming has emerged as a very efficient method especially in manufacturing education (Pourabdollahian et al. 2012). Accomplished researches in this area pointed out that the value of this methodology through the practical integration of intrinsic and extrinsic knowledge is clearly visible (Tröger et al. 2011). Thus, an effective knowledge transfer will be guaranteed between the interested parties and teachers. Linked with the concept of the advanced Learning Factory (aLF) a holistic learning environment will be provided (Müller, Plorin and Ackermann 2012).

The aLF is currently being developed at the Department of Factory Planning and Management of Chemnitz University of Technology. It is focused on the holistic education and training of practicing and future engineers. The concept is an essential methodological framework and component for the effective use of the existing Experimental and Digital Factory (EDF). As an exemplary application the research field of the Ambient Assisted Living (AAL) is presented and placed in the methodological environment of the aLF.

S.A. Meijer and R. Smeds (Eds.): ISAGA 2013, LNCS 8264, pp. 69–76, 2014.
© Springer International Publishing Switzerland 2014

2   Concept Framework

The integral parts of the conceptual framework are the concept and the regulatory framework of the aLF, within the didactical method of serious gaming and the application due to the use case of ambient assisted living (figure 1).

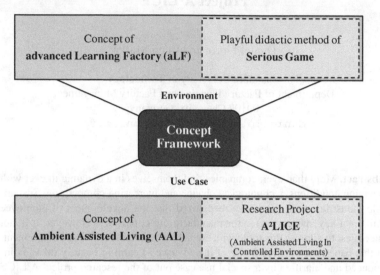

Fig. 1. The concept framework

Within this, the use case of the Ambient Assisted Living (AAL) should be explored through the methodology of the serious gaming and knowledge transfer of experimental research trough researchers and potential users. A²LICE initially isn't in its basic character a part of factory planning and management. However, it offers an interesting experimental and research use case regarding the practical implementation in the laboratory landscape of the Institute of Industrial Management and Factory Systems. In the following, the individual components of the conceptual framework of this article are presented.

2.1   Concept of the advanced Learning Factory (aLF)

Learning methods and strategies in the area of education and training of technically oriented students, trainees and industry entrepreneurs are changing (Lamancusa et al. 2008). Furthermore, problems in research, academia and business are becoming increasingly extensive and complex and must be solved by appropriate qualified staff. With this background the concept of an advanced Learning Factory (aLF) is currently being developed. The concept framework of the aLF is presented in figure 2. This shows an initial approach to the implementation of a suitable digital-real learning, research and training environment for use case-specific analysis of themes like factory planning and factory operation.

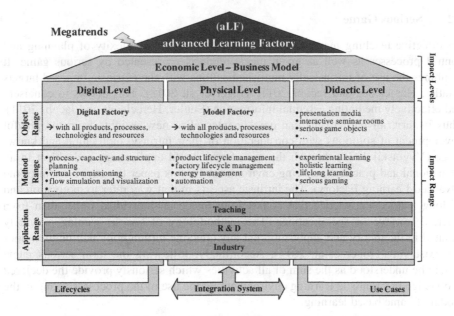

Fig. 2. Concept framework of the advanced Learning Factory (aLF)

The concept framework is divided into 3 main fields, see Figure 2. The object range internalizes all the essential elements of the digital and physical model factory including the digital and physical image of products, processes and resources. The didactic objects are the center point of the transfer of knowledge in the physical and visual level (e.g. versatile conference rooms) (Müller, Plorin and Ackermann 2012).

As shown in figure 2, the methods range contains the methods and procedures for obtaining, storage and processing of knowledge from each individual level (e.g. factory and product lifecycle management, digital manufacturing and logistics, as well as the automation of the power and knowledge management). In relation to the didactic level, the methods of knowledge and expertise exchange are manifested by holistic and experience-based learning (e.g. the Serious Play Tröger et al. 2011). The application range sets the main issue of the aLF. It connects the teaching as well as R&D and industry (see Figure 2). Thus an effective framework and place for the holistic exchange of knowledge, experience and competence in an interdisciplinary way will be given. To ensure an effective transformation it integrates all levels which have already been explained. Furthermore, the application range defines to what extent and in what manner the available supply of the aLF can be used.

The integration system connects all the objects, methods and contents out of the individual lifecycle phases with considered use cases by systematic, parameterized and modularized integration morphology. A use case in that way can be understood as a typical problem or knowledge gap which should have been solved by appropriate models, methods and tools given in the individual levels of the concept framework (see Figure 2).

2.2   Serious Game

An effective teaching method to handle the increasing complexity of planning and control processes as well as given mega-trends is represented by serious game. It combines the use of intrinsically motivated actions with the extrinsic imposed targets (Statler, Heracleous and Jacobs 2011; Tröger et al. 2012). This allows to concisely and effectively mediating essential information (Statler, Heracleous and Jacobs 2011). Thus in turn, all participants can quickly internalize new insights from the playful development of solutions with consideration of their intrinsic motivation and knowledge (Vygotskij 1979) through the use of real world applications and object in an educational and practical inspiring environment (in this paper the environment of the advanced Learning Factory). The intrinsic aspects in that way refer to motivation and lifelong learned knowledge that comes from inside an individual rather than from external rewards or specifications. The methodology of serious gaming is widely situated in the theory and application but any concrete terminology delimitation does not exist yet (Tröger et al. 2011). Accordingly, following the term serious game should be understood as the sum of all activities which seriously provide the declared knowledge in a realistic learning environment by the use of the processes acting in the model of game based learning.

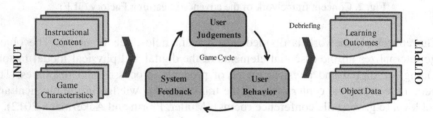

Fig. 3. Extended **game based learning Model, based** on **(Garris, Ahlers and Driskell 2002)**

As figure 3 shows, the original model is extended with the sets of object data. They result from the performed event-driven and everyday life experiments and are essentially determined by the interaction of the users with the objects (sensors and actuators). For example, these data can be furthermore used to make the ambient assisted system more energy efficient due to more intelligent behavioral pattern controlled objectives (Teich 2010).

2.3   Ambient Assisted Living (AAL)

The young research field of Ambient Assisted Living (AAL) is engaged in the exploration of new concepts, services and products that combine modern technology and the social environment with each other. The most compelling objective is to improve the quality of life of all ages with the assistance of appropriate technical systems (e.g. sensors, actors, visualization technologies). A particular focus of research is the advanced period of life of elderly, who are physically or mentally limited. Their daily life should be assisted by a system based environment (in the private and public sector) with the intention to enable independent living and to preserve their mobility. This ensures in a holistic and integrated way that the gap between the domestic private sphere and the healthcare system can be closed (Leonhardt et al. 2012).

Major challenges in the implementation of such technologies and services result from the technology acceptance, the installation and service costs, the availability and reliability as well as the legal framework and requirements. Furthermore, the stigma of the elderly and physical such as mental restricted people represent a large acceptance problem for the use of assistive systems in the medical field. It requires the creation of corresponding real systems which will allow the exploration of AAL environments. This must be done, however, in an appropriate serious and realistic, as well as event-driven everyday life simulation, through the inclusion of personal characteristics (whether physical or mental) and of realistic daily routines. Only this ensures that a gain of knowledge can be established.

The research project A²LICE is funded by the European Social Fund (ESF) and is processed in a group of junior researchers at the University of Applied Sciences Zwickau, Chemnitz University of Technology and the University of Leipzig. The project deals with the closure of the above-mentioned conceptual gap between institutional care and (municipal) housing industry in the health care chain within the research field of the ambient assisted living (Plorin et al. 2012). The main task of the sub-project of the Department of Factory Planning and Factory Management is the methodical examination and representation of potentials for adapting the already researched methods and approaches in the planning of versatile plants in the concept of the AAL environments (Plorin et al. 2012).

3   Implementation Approaches

As already stated the AAL system with its sensors, actuators and visualization media should be explored in a digital as well as physical simulation environment. Therefore, the laboratory landscape of the Institute of Industrial Management and Factory Systems (Spanner Ulmer et al. 2010) offers with the Experimental and Digital Factory (EDF), the project house METEOR and further laboratories an excellent research environment. Initial approaches on how to implement the AAL application with the methodology of the serious gaming concept is shown onward.

At the digital level the use case-specific apartment is mapped into a digital model. It based on modular principles composed by the users. Key elements of such an assisted housing system are the basic elements (e.g. control unit, interactive display or safety related sensors) and the user-specific sensors and actuators (e.g. heart function monitoring sensors or therapy relevant actuators).

At the physical level, the fundamental objects out of the digital model have to be implemented in an experimental environment. In the use case of an ambient assisted environment a partly prepared accommodation unit will be installed with all needed sensor and actor objects. Furthermore, in this level the physical objects needed to create the digital models as described are also arranged. They are represented in the EDF by the Digital Center (DC). An essential method for configuring the use cases in both levels (digital and physical) are the "building blocks for adaptable factory systems" (Müller and Horbach 2011).

At the didactic level different objects can be used. It could be objects within the Experimental Center (EC) or ones of the versatile areas in the project house METEOR. Furthermore, for a more realistic implementation a suit can be used which simulates the physical restrictions of the elderly. So there already exists a wide range of objects in digital, physical and didactical level. Related to the classification shown above, the considered implementation of such an event-driven everyday life simulation game is shown.

The interaction and mechanisms of actions in an AAL system should be experienced via playing a game through predefined daily routines of more or less restricted persons. According to the principles of the PLUG+PRODUCE (Hildebrand, Mäding and Günther 2005) methodology the housing will be created in a digital model by the participants in a first step. This establishes a direct link in mind to the scenario presented. According to the extended game-based learning model shown in figure 3, the main goals and fundamentals of the AAL will be explained to the participants at the beginning, the general scenario for the practical experiment will be provided and the key features of the upcoming simulation will be explained. In this context, the introduction of intrinsic knowledge of the everyday life of the people plays an important role. The target group should be primarily the future users of the systems. This now bring a certain level of acceptance to electronic assistance systems with it.

In a next step, the digital home is created. If it meets the requirements of the given scenario it will be extended to the real environment under the guidance of the experiment conductor. In this, necessary sensors and actuators are being activated in accordance with the defined scenario. Participants will receive a handheld which shows adhoc the events from the daily routine. To accomplish their tasks they must respond and interact with the system. There action including all sensor and actuator activity is recorded permanently. However, the handheld acts as a transfer medium as well as monitoring system in the AAL environment. The participants experience the interaction with the given information and they act with intrinsic and extrinsic motivation. According to the patterns of behavior out of the intrinsic motivated interaction with the assisted environment as well as the recorded sensor data, it is possible to continue and refine the intelligent link of the installed objects, and in perspective to force the acceptance in the use of telemedicine technologies. Furthermore the gained data sets are used to lower the energy consumption in private households as such as residential complexes. For more meaningful data and behavior patterns, the environment of the experiment is changed into other simulation runs under constant input data in its spatial form and sensor technology equipment. Accordingly, deviations can be clearly stated and included in the valuation of the individual configurations.

4   Conclusion and Outlook

The approach to integrate serious gaming in the concept of the advanced Learning Factory (aLF) provides an excellent tool for students, researchers and industry users for an effective and motivated further training in considered use cases. In the specific application of the Ambient Assisted Living (AAL) research project A²LICE, a conceptual approach is demonstrated which allows exploring the research subject in a suitable realistic experimental environment.

With regard to the inclusion of future system users, existing fears and prejudices about ambience systems will be reduced due to playing the experimental game. If this happens in a relevant dimension of the integration of e.g. tele-medical products or security and energy efficiency relevant sensors and actuators, substantial contributions to society can be made. To achieve these requirements, however, further investigations for the implementation of such event-driven and everyday life experiments within the methodology of the serious play are still required. Corresponding objects and other methods have to be identified and integrated meaningfully into valid scenarios. At once, the significant benefit offering patterns of behavior have to be explored out of the collected sensor data. Thus, in turn, intelligent systems for home use can be developed accordingly and bridge the gap in the care and support of restricted people. Both, the researchers and the prospective users can take their benefits out of such serious game based everyday life simulation.

References

1. Garris, R., Ahlers, R., Driskell, J.E.: Games, Motivation, and Learning: A Research and PracticeModel (2002), http://www.hci.iastate.edu/REU09/pub/Main/BiologyInVRBlog/games_motiviation_learning.pdf (accessed January 29, 2013)
2. Hildebrand, T., Mäding, K., Günther, U.: Plug+Produce. Gestaltungsstrategien für die wandlungsfähige Fabrik. IBF, Institut für Betriebswissenschaften und Fabriksysteme, Technische Universität Chemnitz, Chemnitz (2005)
3. Leonhardt, S., Häber, A., Teich, T., Lamprecht, M., Randow, A.: Interdisziplinäre Zusammenarbeit im Forschungsgebiet Ambient Assisted Living zur bewältigung demographischer Probleme im Gesundheitswesen. Szenarienkonzeption und automatische Konfiguration von Gebäudesystemtechnik. In: Westsächsische Hochschule Zwickau, Scientific Reports, 1st edn., Westsächsiche Hochschule Zwickau, Zwickau, vol. 3, pp. 3–10 (2012)
4. Müller, E., Horbach, S.: Building Blocks in an Experimental and Digital Factory. Technische Universität Chemnitz (2012)
5. Müller, E., Plorin, D., Ackermann, J.: Fachkompetenzentwicklung in der advanced Learning Factory (aLF) als Antwort auf den demografischen Wandel. In: Müller, E. (ed.) Demographischer Wandel. Herausforderung für die Arbeits- und Betriebsorganisation der Zukunft; [Tagungsband zum 25. HAB-Forschungsseminar], pp. 3–28. Gito, Berlin (2012)
6. Plorin, D., Ackermann, J., Müller, E., Randow, A., Leonhardt, S.: Ansätze zur Adaption wandlungsfähiger Fabriken im Kontext des "Evolutionären Wohnens". In: Zwickau, W.H. (ed.) Scientific Reports, 1st edn., Westsächsische Hochschule Zwickau, Zwickau, vol. 3, pp. 48–53 (2012)
7. Pourabdollahian, B., Taisch, M., Kerga, E.: Serious Games in Manufacturing Education: Evaluation of Learners' Engagement (2012)
8. http://www.sciencedirect.com/science/article/pii/S1877050912008393 (accessed January 30, 2013)

9. Spanner Ulmer, B., Müller, E., Glöckner, S., Ackermann, J., Keil, M., Börner, F.: Erforschung wandlungsfähiger Produktionssysteme im IBF-Lab unter Berücksichtigung der Interdependenzen zwischen Mensch, Technik und Organisation. Peter Nyhuis (Hrsg.). In: Wandlungsfähige Produktionssysteme (2010)
10. Statler, M., Heracleous, L., Jacobs, C.D.: Serious play as a practice of paradox. The Journal of Applied Behavioral Science 47(2), 236–256 (2011)
11. Teich, T.: Energieeffizienz in Wohngebäuden: Beiträge zum Fachsymposium. In: Energieeffizienz in Wohngebäuden (1st edn, Fachbuchreihe, Vol. 13), Lößnitz: GUC Gesellschaft f. Unternehmensrechnung u. Controlling (2010)
12. Tröger, S., Jentsch, D., Riedel, R., Müller, E.: Serious Games as a Transfer Method in Industrial Management and Engineering. In: Smeds, R. (ed.) Co-Designing Serious Games Proceedings of the 15th Workshop of the Special Interest Group on Experimental Interactive Learning in Industrial Management of the IFIP Working Group 5.7, in collaboration with EU Network of Excellence GaLA, pp. 137–150. Aalto Print, Helsinki (October 2011)
13. Tröger, S., Jentsch, D., Riedel, R., Müller, E.: Ernsthaftes Spielen – Eine paradoxe Tätigkeit. Industrie Management 28(3), 35–38 (2012)
14. Vygotskij, L.S.: Mind in society. The Development of Higher Psychological Processes, 2nd edn. Harvard Univ. Press, Cambridge (1979)

Status and Trends of Serious Game Application in Engineering and Manufacturing Education

Borzoo Pourabdollahian Tehran[1], Manuel Fradinho Oliveira[1], Marco Taisch[1],
Jannicke Baalsrud Hauge[2], and Johann c.k.h. Riedel[3]

[1] Department of Management, Economics and Industrial Engineering
Politecnico di Milano, Milan, Italy
Piaza L. da Vinci, 32 - 20133, Milano, Italy
{borzoo.pourabdollahian,manuel.fradinho,
marco.taisch}@polimi.it
[2] Bremer Institut für Produktion und Logistik, Bremen, Germany
University of Bremen
Hochschulring 20; 28359 Bremen, Germany
baa@biba.uni-bremen.de
[3] Nottingham University Business School,
University of Nottingham
Jubilee Campus, Wollaton Road, Nottingham, NG8 1BB, UK
johann.riedel@nottingham.ac.uk

Abstract. The application of serious game arising from their capability to present learning and entertainment simultaneously has been emerging as a popular learning tool in various domains, although they have not reached to the highest potential yet at least in the manufacturing and engineering domain. One of the main reasons could be an extensive fragmentation among stakeholders including designers, users, teachers, students, players and facilitators. GaLA[1] aims to establish a virtual research center in a scientific way where all research and activities on serious games are gathered, organized, integrated and harmonized to be promoted at the international level. Engineering and manufacturing is one of the special interest groups in GaLA. In this paper the result of our efforts are described and the planned practices aiming to diffuse the understanding of how to design serious games well and also to produce the maximum benefit of serious games' application in engineering and manufacturing is discussed.

Keywords: Serious game, Manufacturing and Engineering, Learning.

1 Introduction

Manufacturing environment has been going to be more complex and complicated due of several global changes and so that they are moving towards novel approaches by

---

[1] GaLA (Game and Learning Alliance) is a 4 years network of excellence on serious games funded by the EU which started in October 2010.

S.A. Meijer and R. Smeds (Eds.): ISAGA 2013, LNCS 8264, pp. 77–84, 2014.
© Springer International Publishing Switzerland 2014

focusing on digital business, extended production, virtual enterprises, and customized production (O'Sullivan et al., 2011). In this situation, industries are challenging to recruit multi skills engineers who are able to behave professionally in the current rapidly changing environment. Therefore, moving to use effective learning methods that are able to answer this critical need of industries is now an issue for engineering curriculum developers. It has been claimed that serious games have been welcomed and integrated in curriculum at several engineering schools (Baalsrud Hauge et al., 2008; Duin and Pourabdollahian 2012; Riedel, 2001; etc.); however, it has not been reached to a maximum diffusion so that it can be concluded that it is still a less known concept at both academy and vocational training. While stakeholders are not enough aware about the invaluable features and capabilities of serious games at the domain, it will not be accepted as a sustain part of engineering curriculum. In this situation, serious games application has been taken in consideration, due of its capabilities to improve engineering knowledge, also technical and soft skills, at GaLA as a Special Interest Group.

In this paper we have reviewed previous efforts to identify the advantages of serious games based on stakeholders' perception. They are aimed specifically to achieve different kinds of learning outcomes (e.g. sustainable manufacturing, new product development, etc.) as well as at three learning outcome categories including knowledge, skill and motivation (Bloom, 1956). In that case the main purpose of this study is to classify games regarding their learning outcomes so that they can be integrated fully and rightly at engineering curriculum or vocational training and to provide some recommendations to design serious games at the domain. For this goal, searching at literature gives us a list of games including the evaluation results as well. In the next step these games need to be again studied at a systematic way so that it makes a comparison of learning outcomes supported by the serious games. Although Inaccessibility is a big challenge to run the games, but we can access free to eight of monitored games by collaboration of project partners involved at game design process.

In following, monitored serious games to be introduced and then the analyze studies to be discussed. In conclusion the result of comparison study is depicted at table 1 and also the best practices to decrease the fragmentation are proposed.

2   Serious Game Monitoring

The main purpose of game monitoring is to identify relevant serious games to engineering and manufacturing. For this goal, collected SGs were studied by experts to indicate different features of each one such as: source, nature, form, users, learning approaches, etc. A short description of the games is given below:

- Sustainable Global Manufacturing game (SGM): it is a single-player and digital game that comes from TARGET[2] project. It aims to introduce students with sustainable manufacturing so that they need to apply their engineering knowledge and business skill to produce a green product.

---

[2] TARGET (Transformative, Adaptive, Responsive and enGaging EnvironmenT) was an integrated project funded by EU, which concluded in October 2012.

- Beer game: it is one of the oldest and most popular games at supply chain management. It is multi-player, free online game that players, in different roles, need to collaborate in order to transfer production from firm to customers as efficient as possible.
- Seconds: it is a multi-player and digital game. The game is designed in order to answer the existing change educational demand in manufacturing and production systems. The main objective of the game is increasing the awareness and understanding of the impact of strategic decision making in distributed manufacturing by simulation of production networks (Baalsurd et al., 2008).
- Plantville: it is an online simulator allowing users to manage a bottling, vitamin, or manufacturing plant. That gives players the opportunity and challenge of running a virtual factory, complete with evaluation of key performance indicators, allocation of scarce capital funds, and the ability to improve process efficiency with the purchase and installation of (naturally) more Siemens equipment.
- SBCE[3]: It is a multi-player board Game aiming allowing players to have a better understanding of "Set-Based Concurrent Engineering Model". It is about how to design an airplane by using LEGO bricks, in order to have less development cost and time according to two different models of product development process. (Kerga et al., 2012).
- Shortfall: it is a multi-player and free online game to teach supply chain management and sustainable manufacturing. Students are assigned to make suitable decisions in trade-off between two incompatible issues in an automobile manufacturer company, economic and environmental (Qualters et al., 2008).
- Cosiga: It is a multi-player digital simulation game designed to tackle the problem of teaching today's engineering and management students the know-how of how to design and manufacture new products, to equip them with the experience of design, and to teach them how to deal with the complexities of the new product development process (Riedel et al., 2001).
- Beware: it is a multi-player digital game implemented in a workshop setting. The application is used as a training medium for companies involved in supply networks covering the issue of risk management. Currently, Beware is designed with two distinct and independent levels (Baalsrud et al., 2012).

3   Serious Game Analysis

Among mentioned SGs, authors were totally or partially involved at design process, except Shortfall and Plantville that those are free online games, and therefore we were permitted to access the games free. We have run some game sessions both at university and industry to evaluate the effectiveness. In the below, the four examples, SBCE, Shortfall, Cosiga, and SGM are used to look at different perspectives in engineering education will be discussed.

---

[3] Set Based Concurrent Engineering game.

3.1   SBCE

Set Based Concurrent Engineering is a concept in new product development by considering lean thinking perspective. It is going to be more diffused in production system, in versus of Point Based, due of its advantage in decreasing the time and cost of production. The aim of this game is to highlight the benefits of applying SBCE concept to produce a simplified airplane. In the first stage, players to be asked to design an airplane regarding both customer requirements and supplier components based on PB (Point Base) and then they will be introduced by SBCE enablers those they need to be executed to design the airplane, with the same given data in the first stage. Finally, players will be informed about their performances and they will be able to observe to what extent applying SBCE decreases the time and cost of the design (Kerga, et al., 2012).

Two studies were done in an Italian company, CAREL, where 36 engineers and project managers participated to evaluate the acquired knowledge and level of engagement. In the first study the participants answered a questionnaire based on 5 point Likert scale to measure to what extent their knowledge improved by playing the game. The results showed that the level of awareness of SBCE enablers is increased by playing the game and they feel that they can apply these enablers to design the airplane (Kerga, et al. 2012). In the second study players were asked to answer 21 questions based on a 5 point Likert scale to assess the level of engagement. The result showed that players had feelings of challenge, enjoyment and control, and also they were satisfied by the different kinds of feedback during the game (Pourabdollahian et al., 2012).

3.2   Shortfall

This game was originally developed as a board game to teach supply chain management and sustainable manufacturing concepts by putting students in an environment where they are assigned to make various decisions in trade-off between two incompatible issues in an automobile manufacturer company, economic and environmental. Later the digital version was designed and lunched by Northeastern University at 2007.

Qualters and others did a study in which 12 students participated at a board game session, and they were asked to answer pre and post-test questionnaires; first, to measure the level of knowledge before and after playing game and second, to identify changing in the level of students' confidence about their responds. Moreover, at the end of the game students responded to a questionnaire about strength and weak points of the game to collect useful information to design digital version. Finally students were invited to take place at a focus group session one week later to discuss about their experiences of shortfall. Quantitative analysis in knowledge survey showed 1) students acquired more knowledge and 2) significant improvement in their confidence to reply the questions. In focus group session three noticeable points were raised, 1) the ability of game to increase the teamwork and communication skills, 2) shortfall can be used as learning method and 3) there was not an agreement among students about the level of enjoyment (Qualters et al, 2008).

3.3   Cosiga

It was designed to tackle the problem of teaching today's engineering and management students the know-how of to design and manufacture new products, to equip them with the experience of design, and to teach them how to deal with the complexities of the new product development process (Riedel, et al. 2001). The Cosiga simulation game was specifically designed for learning how to do 'New Product Development', i.e. how to work in parallel, how to co-operate in a multi-disciplinary and multi-cultural (geographically dispersed) environment. It is a team player game, played by five people in the same room or distributed in different locations. Each person plays a role in the product development process (project manager, designer, marketing manager, purchasing manager and production manager) where they work collaboratively together, using whatever communication means they choose, to specify, design, and manufacture the final product - a type of truck. They will be involved in drawing up market and product specification, designing the product, purchasing components and allocating manufacturing processes. The product's manufacturability will be put to the test in the simulated factory to produce the final products.

The study of effectiveness of Cosiga was done (Baalsurd and Riedel, 2012). They evaluated the game based on different aspects. Analysis of communication showed that most frequent communication type was asking for (mostly specific) information with 37%, followed by offering information (22%), requesting action (17%), while compliments were the least type with only 2%. The results of the communication analysis demonstrated that the games showed the expected communication pattern: information was requested by downstream players (purchasing, production) and given by upstream players (marketing, design). Cognitive analysis was done by pre and post questionnaires which consisted of 19 concepts of product development and each player was asked to rate each one how related to the other 18 concepts on a scale from 0 to 10. The results demonstrated different experience for the different roles, for instance the marketing manager had a good experience, the designer an excellent experience, while it was negative for the production manager. Also the authors stated that the game can help players to improve their decision making skills.

3.4   SGM

This game was designed so that engineering students understand the sustainable manufacturing concepts by focusing on "communication and negotiation skills"; "system thinking"; "ability to see the big picture"; "short versus long term strategies" and "critical thinking". The scenario of the game provides an opportunity for learners to assume a role of sustainable manager in a virtual household appliances producer company to improve both engineering knowledge and business skills. During the game they will confront with different challenges to produce a green coffee machine. The main job is gathering and then filtering relevance data from CEO, Production manager, and Shift manager to define boundaries, complete product flowchart, determine inputs, and clarify outputs in Life Cycle Assessment (LCA) tool.

Two studies did to evaluate the game. First, it was run among 24 MSs students at University of Bremen. They were asked to fill a preliminary questionnaire to collect existing knowledge about LCA. Then, they rated how the performance of three competences improves, and again they played the game and replied to the same questions. Finally students were asked to answer questions to measure the learning outcome and the level of enjoyment. The result showed that the game is an effective method to improve target competences (ability to perform LCA, information gathering, decision making). The second study was carried out at Politecnico di Milano to assess how teachers think to SGM as a useful learning method to teach at class. Nine teachers were introduced about the game and then they watched a video of complete game in which all features of the game were elaborated. Finally they participated in a semi instruction interview to collect background information and evaluate its effectiveness. The result demonstrated that they believed it can be used in class, even though they strongly preferred to play the real one before taking final decision (Duin and Pourabdollahian, 2012).

The evaluation result by focusing on learning outcomes, which is shown in three classes; is summarized at table 1. "Knowledge" represents that engineering or manufacturing content is learnt, "Skill" pinpoints social and professional skills those graduated engineers are expected to have, and "Motivation" raises the emotional outcomes those can make learners to be fully involved at game. Moreover, Each cell shows whether specified learning outcomes are supported or not (i.e. "×" = yes, "-" = no, and "?" = not known).

Table 1. Different types of learning outcomes of Manufacturing Serious Games

	Learning Outcome	Serious Game							
		Beware	Beer Game	Cosiga	Plantville	SBCE	Seconds	Shortfall	SGM
Knowledge	Supply Chain Management	×	×	-	-	-	×	×	-
	Sustainable Manufacturing	-	?	-	×	-	?	×	×
	Factory layout	-	-	-	×	-	-	-	-
	Product Development	×	-	×	-	×	?	-	-
	Engineering principles	-	-	-	×	×	?	-	×
	Business Orientation	×	×	×	×	×	×	×	-
Skill	Decision making	×	×	×	×	×	×	×	×
	Problem solving	×	×	×	×	×	×	×	×
	Communication	×	×	×	-	-	×	×	×
	Team working	×	×	×	-	×	×	×	-
	Conflict resolution	×	×	×	×	×	×	×	×
Motivation	Enjoyment	-	?	×	?	×	×	×	×
	Engagement	×	×	×	?	×	×	×	×
	Negotiation	×	×	×	?	×	×	×	×

4   Conclusion

The analysis results combined with the practical studies and assessment workshops to distil the serious games in engineering and manufacturing have yielded important guidelines that are relevant for designing successful serious games in the domain. The body of work collated, although significant, is not sufficient to consider the resulting guidelines as best practice. Nonetheless, the following guidelines provide important considerations for designing serious games in the domain of engineering and manufacturing.

A key criterion for serious game adoption both in university and industry is whether the game is web based so that facilitate access to the game easily whenever and wherever. However, at some case either losing network connectively or not having connectively is an important barrier to deploy web based game. It is concluded that the benefit and cost of web based game should be studied before taking decision whether to design web based or not.

In the area engineering and manufacturing, the corporate interest is to have high contextualization of the tasks embodied in the serious game design. This is in contrast to the academe approach of generalization, which is less contextualized to a particular corporate environment. The trade-off between high contextualization and generalization needs to be decided early in the game design, involving all the relevant stakeholders. In order to achieve a balanced outcome, user participatory design is recommended to ensure that the expectations of the stakeholders involved are addressed.

The subjects associated to engineering and manufacturing are challenging and complex, which provide the basis for serious games with depth and richness of features. However, it is necessary to avoid the pitfall of over-engineering the game design that leads to a serious game with an overly steep learning curve to handle the game from a user experience perspective. In those cases where the game design is necessarily complex, then the learner should be gradually guided into the complexity allowing them to avoid the burden of building the mental model of the system, which detracts from the learning. This is a common mistake in the many manufacturing and engineering serious games, as in the case of Plantville.

Acknowledgment. The authors gratefully acknowledge the supports of the EU funded network of excellence Game and Learning Alliance - GALA (ICT-2009-258169, www.galanoe.eu).

References

1. Baalsurd, J., Duin, H., Hunecker, F.: Application Areas for Serious Games in Virtual Organizations in Manufacturing. In: Proceeding in Learning and Evaluation in Manufacturing, Innovation Networking IFIP Workshop, Nottingham, UK, pp. 77–84 (2008)

2. Hauge, J.M.B., Pourabdollahian, B., Riedel, J.C.K.H.: The Use of Serious Games in the Education of Engineers. In: Emmanouilidis, C., Taisch, M., Kiritsis, D. (eds.) Advances in Production Management Systems. IFIP AICT, vol. 397, pp. 622–629. Springer, Heidelberg (2013)
3. Baalsurd, J., Riedel, J.: Evaluation of Simulation Games for Teaching Engineering and Manufacturing. In: The Proceedings of the 4th International Conference on Games and Virtual Worlds for Serious Applications (VS-GAMES 2012), In Alessandro De Gloria and Sara de Freitas, Procedia Computer Science, vol. 15, pp. 210–220. Elsevier, Amsterdam (2012)
4. Bloom, B.S.: Taxonomy of educational objectives, Handbook 1: Cognitive domain. David McKay, New York (1956)
5. Duin, H., Pourabdollahian, B.: TARGET Evaluation and Demonstration Analysis; part 5, Deliverable D8.2, TARGET European Commission Seventh Framework Project (IST 231717), 292-344 (2012)
6. Kerga, E., Rossi, M., Taisch, M., Terzi, S.: A Serious Game Approach for Learning Lean Product Development. In: 16th IFIP WG 5.7 workshop, Wuppertal, Germany, June 3-5, pp. 55–65 (2012)
7. O'Sullivan, B., Rolstadås, A., Filos, E.: Global education in manufacturing strategy. Intellectual Manufacturing 22, 663–674 (2011)
8. Pourabdollahian, B., Taisch, M., Kerga, E.: Serious Games in Manufacturing Education: Evaluation of Learners' Engagement. In: The Proceedings of the 4th International Conference on Games and Virtual Worlds for Serious Applications (VS-GAMES 2012), by Alessandro De Gloria and Sara de Freitas, vol. 15, pp. 256–265. Elsevier, Amsterdam (2012)
9. Qualters, D.M., Isaacs, J.A., Culinane, T.P., Larid, J., McDonald, A., Corriere, J.D.: A Game Approach to Teach Environmentally Benign Manufacturing in the Supply Chain. International Journal for the Scholarship of Teaching and Learning 2(2) (2008)
10. Riedel, J.C.K.H., Pawar, K., Barson, R.: Academic & Industrial User Needs of a Concurrent Engineering Computer Simulation Game. Concurrent Engineering: Research & Applications 9(3), 223–237 (2001)

The UCS-Model of Corporate Sustainability

Description, Development and Incorporation in the Simulation Game Napuro

Markus Ulrich

UCS Ulrich Creative Simulations, Zurich, Switzerland
markus.ulrich@ucs.ch

Abstract. The UCS-Model of Corporate Sustainability, developed based on an extensive systems analysis, is a qualitative framework that describes the essential elements of corporate sustainability in a lucid way. It forms the basis of the simulation game *napuro*. For readers interested in corporate sustainability, the paper describes the model, and its validation. For game developers, it describes how the model underlying the simulation game was developed, and incorporated into the simulation game *napuro*, in order to maximise the learning of the participants. The model is transparent and helps participants to experience the components of corporate sustainability, and their dynamic interactions. This constitutes a fruitful basis for an effective transfer of game experience to practical application.

1 Introduction

This paper focuses on one specific aspect of simulation game design, the construction of the model for a simulation game. It describes the simulation game napuro - Corporate Sustainability and, in particular, the underlying model, the UCS-Model of Corporate Sustainability (in short: UCS-Model). This qualitative model is the conceptual framework that supports the operation of the simulation game, and the subsequent transfer of the participants' game experience to practical knowledge. It is a pragmatic framework that structures the fuzzy term "corporate sustainability" and fills it with life.

The paper starts with a brief introduction to corporate sustainability, and the values the simulation game napuro is based upon, followed by a short description of its key specifications. Thereafter, the simulation game, and its model are presented in action, and the UCS-Model is described. The next section sketches the development of the UCS-Model, and its integration in the simulation game. The two last sections describe the validity checks, and the conclusions.

2 Theme of Napuro, Corporate Sustainability

2.1 Introduction to Corporate Sustainability

Corporate sustainability is a management concept for hedging risks and for early detection of opportunities for a company. It brings, in addition to economical factors, also ecological, societal, and other factors to the attention of the company.

S.A. Meijer and R. Smeds (Eds.): ISAGA 2013, LNCS 8264, pp. 85–92, 2014.

Many different approaches are used (Triple Bottom Line [1], Social Responsibility, Corporate Social Responsibility (CSR), Corporate Responsibility, Sustainable Management [2, 3]). The focus can be on ecological responsibility, on clean or efficient production, on stakeholder management, on innovation, etc.

Many standards provide guidance for companies [3]. Among them are GRI (Global Reporting Initiative [4]), ISO 26000 (social responsibility [5]), UN Global Compact (United Nations for sustainable businesses [6]), or AA1000 (Assurance Standard for sustainable businesses [7]). While these standards address all dimensions of sustainability, others focus on environmental (ISO 14001, environmental management [8]; EMAS, European Eco-Management & Audit Scheme [9]) or social aspects (SA8000, socially acceptable practices in the workplace [10]).

Does sustainability pay? It may (see e.g. [11]). According to current research, the question has to be asked differently: Is there a business case for sustainability? Yes, sustainability does not pay by itself, but a company that develops a business case for sustainability has a good chance to outperform its competitors [12].

2.2   Basic Referent System

Values and basic assumptions underlying a simulation game constitute the "basic referent system" [13]. They influence the characteristics of a game, and should be made transparent. napuro is based on a comprehensive notion of sustainable development, abbreviated as B&B. The first B stands for needs (German: Bedürfnisse) of current and future generations. Basic needs such as food and shelter have priority over luxury needs. The second B stands for limitations (Begrenzungen) of the earth to provide resources and to absorb waste. B&B-sustainability provides to all humans, today and in the future, a good life within the planetary limits [14].

The Swiss sustainability monitoring MONET [15] defines the following principle for the economy: "Economic activity should … meet the needs of the individual and of society. The economic framework should be shaped in such a manner that it promotes personal initiative, thus putting self-interest to the service of the common good and ensuring the welfare of the present and future population" [16]. napuro is based on this principle. It implies that seeking profit is not a goal in itself, but a means to provide a valuable service to individuals and society.

3   Specifications of *napuro* and the UCS-Model

Corporate sustainability often appears as a nebulous concept. The simulation game napuro was developed to overcome this shortcoming. Participants should become familiar with the components of corporate sustainability, and experience their dynamic interaction. They should learn to identify such components within their company, and to actively contribute to their development.

The game lasts 4-8 hours, including debriefing. It can be run with 6 to 24 participants. Target audiences are managers and employees of companies and administrations, as well as students of sustainable management. Major characteristics of sustainable management are depicted at a slightly abstracted level. In this way, the game experience can be transferred to different types of companies, while different sustainability standards can be also employed. For clarity, it is also stated what napuro is not. It does not provide a perfect path towards sustainability. It does not claim to reproduce 1:1 real world outcomes, including financial performance.

These requirements demanded a generic, lucid model as an underlying engine and frame for the simulation game. The UCS-Model developed for this purpose includes all major elements of corporate sustainability. These elements are represented in the model on a generic, qualitative level that can be applied to different real-world counterparts. In this way, the UCS-Model serves as a frame, triggering the development of clear mental models by the participants.

4   The UCS-Model in Action during a Game Run

Participants of napuro are asked to assume the role of company managers, and are seated in a big circle, distributed at six separated company tables. The managers have access to exclusive information on the internal company state shown on a game board that is hidden within a box representing the company. They evaluate sustainability measures, described on 51 action cards assigned to the scales of the UCS-Model and can select to implement a subset during each round. Whenever they implement a measure, they update the model by moving tokens on the board.

The internal state is not directly visible to competitors, and customers. They only see the external state of the companies, displayed on top of the company boxes. This includes product type, price, quality, and the sustainability index which equates to the reputation of the company in respect to sustainability – the so-called B&B-level (needs and limits, as explained above).

Events, presented by the facilitator affect the companies depending on their state, and measures already implemented. Events include for instance critical NGOs, young talents searching an attractive company, or resources that become scarce. In addition, companies can *promote* their products with 30-second-advertisements. *Customers*, with different priorities (e.g. price or B&B level) presented by the facilitator, show up. The game is played for three to five rounds.

Debriefing includes a reflection on successes and failures, on the strategies chosen (displayed in the cockpit, see Fig. 1), on corporate communication, and on the interrelations experienced. Outcomes are linked to the participant's company.

5   Description of the UCS-Model of Corporate Sustainability

5.1   Overview

The UCS-Model of Corporate Sustainability distinguishes an internal and external view (or state). The internal view includes all sustainability measures implemented by the company. Outside stakeholders have to rely on the external view of the company, constituted by the company's product, its sustainability reputation, and its corporate communication. The internal and the external view do not necessarily match, and companies operate between these two poles.

5.2   Internal View to the Company

The internal view (Fig. 1) includes the implementation of sustainability within the company by means of specific measures, and sustainability management.

Implementation of Sustainability within the Company

Specific measures to promote sustainability, arranged on six scales (variables V1 to V6):

Governance (V1). Governance and leadership in the company, including internal organisation, transparency, accountability, compliance and handling of corruption.

External relations (V2). Relations to external stakeholders (e.g. clients, suppliers, local community, society, non-governmental organisations (NGOs), media) and their management.

Internal relations (V3). Relations to employees (human resource management, including working conditions, gender issues, career planning, etc.).

Office ecology, facility management, and mobility (V4). All aspects related to sustainable resource and energy use that arise in a similar way in most companies (e.g. office printing, cleaning agents, heating/air conditioning, business travel).

Processes (V5). Design of the production processes of goods and services (including efficient energy and material use, innovative production methods, etc.).

Product sustainability (V6). Sustainability of the product itself (e.g. recycling, impact on society, energy consumption, harmful substances).

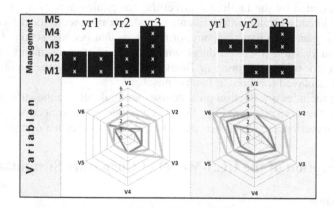

Fig. 1. *napuro cockpit* displaying the internal state of companies. Example shows the development of two different companies over 4 rounds, with the variables V1…V6 (bottom), and sustainability management M1…M5 (top). The company (left hand side) focused on V2 and V3, and a well developed management system M1…M4; the company on the right on V6, and V3, with an incomplete management system.

Sustainability Management

Management tools that align sustainability measures (V1...V6) with the long-term goals of the company, ensuring a maximum benefit.

Mission statement and vision (M1). The mission statement defines the core values of the company. The vision shows the future state to be achieved by the company.

Sustainability strategy (M2). The strategy outlines how to realize mission statement and vision. It provides guidance for decisions taken in daily operations.

Performance indicators and targets (M3). They define quantifiable parameters and target values that measure and document a company's performance and progress.

Systematic management system (M4). This system defines the procedures to be applied by the management, and the necessary management tools.

Sustainability report (M5). The report documents and communicates the company's sustainability performance to external and internal stakeholders.

5.3   External View of the Company

External observers, such as clients or competitors perceive primarily the external view of a company. The product, its type, quality, and price constitute the external state, together with the corporate communication, and the sustainability reputation represented by the company's B&B-level. Its five levels stand for profit, compliance, internal responsibility, external responsibility, and creation of B&B-identity [17]. These B&B-levels can be matched to the levels of Maslow's pyramid of needs [18] and the four sustainability levels of Schwartz and Carrol [19]. The external view is influenced by the decisions of the company and by its stakeholders.

6   Implementation of the UCS-Model

6.1   Development of the Model during Systems Analysis

The UCS-Model combines all essential elements of corporate sustainability in a qualitative way. It was developed in three steps: data collection, development of the conceptual frame, and incorporation into the simulation game.

During systems analysis [13], data on corporate sustainability was collected, using publications [2, 3, 11, 20, 21, 22], case studies [23], and expert discussions [24]. While doing so, the developers took intentionally the perspective of naïve, curious observers. The leading question was: "Where do we see corporate sustainability in the company?" This perspective helped to frame the model in a way that is helpful to the target audience, which often has a nebulous notion of corporate sustainability. In the next step, the information was analysed and categorized. In this process, the basic characteristics of the UCS-Model emerged. The distinction between the inside view and the outside view of a company proved to be essential. The outside view includes both hard factors, such as price, as well as soft factors, such as reputation. The inside view is composed by the concrete actions (V1...V6) and the activities that align these actions to a coherent framework in order to achieve maximum effectiveness for the company (M1...M5).

6.2   Incorporation of the Model into the Simulation Game

The specifications of napuro asked for a lucid model that triggers the development of clear mental models by the participants. Hence, the model is not a black-box but is displayed transparently in the game. The "company building", a box with one open side, shows on its roof the outside view (e. g., price, product). Inside the box, the internal view is displayed on a game board. According to the intended abstraction level, the scales are qualitative. The internal and external states change over time, according to implemented action cards, or events. Action cards and events correspond to real situations. A company may, for example, implement video conferences using an action card, with a positive effect on scale V4 and possibly further dependent variables. An event may involve an NGO that checks whether the internal state corresponds to the B&B level. Products sold generate the earnings required to implement further action cards in the next rounds. Participants obtain feedback from the model, the events, the competitors and the market. In this way, they obtain valuable information to improve their strategy over time.

Thanks to this transparent approach, participants experience the components of corporate sustainability, the conceptual frame of the model, and the dynamic interactions in the game. This constitutes a fruitful basis for an effective transfer.

7   Validity Checks of the UCS-Model

The validity of the model was verified by the feedback of participants, and by comparison with established standards and real companies. In two surveys, participants assessed the statement "The simulation game has practical relevance and can be applied to a company" with an average of 1.7 (n=15) [25], and 1.8 (n=17) [26] on a scale of 1 (best)...6 (worst). First evidence of a systematic comparison to three established sustainability standards (GRI, Global Compact, ISO 26000), currently underway, shows that the model can be successfully mapped to these standards. A study that tested the UCS-Model in seven Swiss companies operating in different sectors concluded that the UCS-Model can be applied to these companies [27]. In another study the UCS-Model served as a conceptual framework for the analysis of the sustainability strategy of a large Swiss furniture store [28], which indicates that the UCS-Model is valid beyond the simulation game.

8   Conclusion

The project napuro started with the vision of creating a simulation game that conveys corporate sustainability in a comprehensive, lucid way. Experience gathered so far shows that this goal was achieved. The transparent model approach helps participants to capture the multifaceted corporate sustainability in a well structured mental model that is helpful for everyday application. The validity checks confirmed that the UCS-Model represents the core elements of corporate sustainability adequately, and in a way that is helpful for the transfer of the game experience to the work situation. It seems that the UCS-Model of Corporate Sustainability may be applied in the future beyond the simulation game napuro.

Acknowledgments. *napuro* would not have been possible without the creative and practical support of many colleagues and friends. A big *thanks* goes to Sybille Borner, Marieke de Wijse-van Heeswijk Sonja Eser, Andrea Frank, Yves Gärtner, Adrian Mallon, Till Meyer, Thomas Reinhold, Simon Schwarz, Rita Volpers, Herbert Winistörfer, Reto Zeller.

References

1. Elkington, J.: Cannibals with Forks: the Triple Bottom Line of 21st Century Business. Capstone Publishing (1997)
2. Schaltegger, S., Herzig, C.H., Kleibner, O., Klinke, T., und Müller J.: Nachhaltigkeitsmanagement in Unternehmen – Von der Idee zur Praxis: Managementansätze zur Umsetzung von Corporate Social Responsibility und Corporate Sustainability. Bundesministerium für Umwelt, Naturschutz und Reaktorsicherheit, ecosense, Centre for Sustainability Management der Leuphana Universität Lüneburg (2007)
3. Winistörfer, H., Perrin, I., Teuscher, P., Forel, A.: Management der sozialen Verantwortung in Unternehmen – Leitfaden zur Umsetzung. Hanser, München (2012)
4. Global Reporting Initiative (February 19, 2013), http://www.globalreporting. org
5. ISO 26000 – Social responsibility (February 18, 2013), http://www.iso.org
6. UN Global Compact (February 19, 2013), http://www.unglobalcompact.org
7. AA1000 principles-based standards (February 19, 2013), http://www.accountability.org
8. ISO 14001 – Environmental management (February 18, 2013), http://www.iso.org
9. Eco-Management and Audit Scheme (EMAS) (February 18, 2013), http://ec. europa.eu/environment/emas
10. Social Accountability SA8000 Standard (February 19, 2013), http://www.sa-intl.org/index.cfm?fuseaction=Page.ViewPage&pageId=937
11. Buried Treasure – Uncovering the business case for corporate sustainability, Report published by SustainAbility (2001) http://www.sustainability.com/library /buried-treasure#.USJZr6XrAsw (February 18, 2013)
12. Schaltegger, S., Lüdeke-Freund, F., Hansen, E.G.: Business cases for sustainability: the role of business model innovation for corporate sustainability. Int. J. Innovation and Sustainable Development 6(2), 95–119 (2012)
13. Duke, R.D., Geurts, J.L.A.: Policy games for strategic management – Pathways into the unknown. Dutch University Press (2004)
14. Wachter, D.: Nachhaltige Entwicklung – Das Konzept und seine Umsetzung in der Schweiz. Rüegger Verlag (2012)

15. The MONET indicator system (monitoring of sustainable development in Switzerland) (February 17, 2013), http://www.bfs.admin.ch/bfs/portal/en/index/themen/21/02/01.html
16. Principles of sustainable development, including Economic efficiency/General principle (February 17, 2013), http://www.bfs.admin.ch/bfs/portal/en/index/themen/21/02/ind9.approach.905.html
17. Ulrich, M.: Planspiel napuro: UCS-Modell für unternehmerische Nachhaltigkeit (Version FHNW). Internal report (2012)
18. Maslow, A.H.: A theory of human motivation. Psychological Review 50(4), 370–396 (1943)
19. Schwartz, M., Carroll, A.: Corporate Social Responsibility: A Three-Domain Approach. Business Ethics Quarterly 13(4), 503–530 (2003)
20. Hildesheimer, G., und Marchesi, M.: Das Unternehmen in der Gesellschaft – Die soziale Dimension der Nachhaltigkeit in Theorie und Praxis – Was leisten Schweizer Unternehmen? ÖBU-Schriftenreihe SR26 (2005), http://www.oebu.ch/de/publikationen (February 19, 2013)
21. Kommission der Europäischen Gemeinschaften (2001). Europäische Rahmenbedingungen für die soziale Verantwortung in Unternehmen (Grünbuch) (February 19, 2013), http://eur-lex.europa.eu/LexUriServ/site/de/com/2001/com2001_0366de01.pdf
22. Argyris, C., Schon, D.A.: Organizational Learning II: Theory, Method, and Practice. Addison Wesley (1996)
23. Case studies, documented in the database ("Infothek") of the Internet online service ProofItfor small and medium-sized companies, German, French (February 17, 2013), http://www.proofit.ch
24. Personal communication with various entrepreneurs, managers, and experts (2011/2012)
25. Ulrich, M.: Workshop with simulation game napuro – Questionnaire for participants. MBA Sustainability Management/HCD. Leuphana University, Lüneburg (2012)
26. Ulrich, M.: Workshop with simulation game napuro – Questionnaire for participants. Evonik, Essen (2012)
27. Roux, S.M.: Praktische Umsetzung der unternehmerischen Nachhaltigkeit – Der Praxisbezug des Planspiels napuro am Beispiel von ausgewählten Unternehmen. Vertrauliche Einzel-Bachelor-Thesis at the University of Applied Sciences in Business Administration (HWZ), Zurich (2013)
28. Wegmann, L.: Nachhaltigkeit als Megatrend in \der Schweizer Möbelbranche am Beispiel Micasa. Vertrauliche Einzel-Bachelor-Thesis at the University of Applied Sciences in Business Administration (HWZ), Zurich (2013)

Effects of a Game-Facilitated Curriculum on Technical Knowledge and Skill Development

Roy van Bussel[1], Heide Lukosch[2], and Sebastiaan A. Meijer[3]

[1] Kenteq b.v., Olympia 6-8, 1213 NP Hilversum, The Netherlands
[2] Delft University of Technology, Jaffalaan 5, 2600 GA Delft, The Netherlands
[3] KTH Royal Institute of Technology, Teknikringen 72, 114 28 Stockholm, Sweden

Abstract. Education in the European Union is one of the key factors to safeguard our competitiveness in the globalising economy. Based upon the Knowledge Triangle, the EU and its member states are working on improving the quality of education, the connection with research for transfer of new knowledge and the connection with industry to bring innovations. Within this paradigm, there are a lot of initiatives targeted towards higher and professional education to work on new teaching methods that implement the knowledge triangle better, especially for learning about complex systems and complex questions in society. From an economic point of view, however, the base of craftsmanship in society is key to keep up our productivity and ability to produce new and more advanced products, in times where most simple production activities get outsourced to developing countries. Vocational education is therefore arguably equally or even more important than higher and professional education. Unfortunately, vocational education is not yet functioning optimally. Our work represented in this paper aims to contribute to improve the outcomes of vocational education by exploring the use of gaming simulation that is already successful in other forms of education.

1 Introduction

Dropout in vocational education in the Netherlands and many other European countries is high (Verstegen & Severiens, 2007a, 2007b; van der Steeg, van Elk, & Webbink, 2013). Recent research describes three assumptions that contribute to this large dropout rate. First, discrepancies exist between students' daily life environment and the school environment. Students live in a flexible and networked world in which they have free access to the Internet and social media via smart phones, tablets and other mobile devices (Veen & Vrakking, 2006). They do not only have free access but they also connect to each other and become more and more both consumers and producers of content (Gee, 2003). This enables them to have a continuous availability of information, have frequent contact with their peers and to do entertainment activities on their own demand. Contrary to this daily life environment the school environment over all is still dominated by the use of paper-based materials, theoretical lessons and fixed year groups. The curriculum usually exists of a set of fixed courses or modules with only implicit relationships between each course and module (Veen & Vrakking, 2006).

S.A. Meijer and R. Smeds (Eds.): ISAGA 2013, LNCS 8264, pp. 93–101, 2014.
© Springer International Publishing Switzerland 2014

Secondly, there is a lack of coherence between form and content of tasks within the curriculum on one hand and the tasks performed in professional practice during work placements or internships on the other. Students often have difficulties employing the curriculum-based knowledge in to performance in real-life tasks and in practical problem solving skills. To students, the curriculum often has an unclear relevance of what they are supposed to learn for their future professions (van Merriënboer & Kirschner, 2012). Thirdly, participation of students who dropout often has been low in a quantitative way (non-attendance) and in a qualitative way (van der Steeg, van Elk, & Webbink, 2013). Students who drop out do not feel connected with school or the school-attended curriculum and show low involvement with teachers and peers (van Veen, 2006; Verstegen & Severiens, 2007a, 2007b).

A game-facilitated curriculum might help to solve these problems. It could diminish the gap with students' daily life since most students will be familiar with gaming and spend considerable time playing. Educational games could provide access to a wide variety of online resources where traditional materials often fail. Educative games could also provide opportunities for social learning activities.

In a recent meta-analysis, Sitzmann (2011) examined the instructional efficacy of computer-based simulation games in proportion to a comparison group. The data suggested that simulation games have the potential to enhance the learning of work related knowledge and skills. Learning was maximized when trainees actively (rather than passively) learned work-related competencies during game play, when trainees could choose to play as many times as desired and when simulation games were imbedded in an instructional programme (rather than serving as stand-alone instruction). Ke (2008) studied the efficacy of computer based instructional games for learning. Sixty-five studies were included in a meta-analysis. Most game design studies indicate significant effects. In terms of results, 34 of the 65 game efficacy studies reported significant positive effects of the computer-based game. Seventeen studies reported mixed results. The instructional games facilitated a trend in learning outcomes towards a significant level. Twelve studies reported no difference between computer games and the conventional instruction. Only two studies reported conventional instruction as more effective than computer games. Further analysis showed that instructional supporting features like teacher guides and support are a necessary core element in instructional games. Without this instructional support, learners will learn to play the game, but will not adopt the domain specific knowledge embedded in the game.

Much focus in literature has been on game based learning at university settings and in professional education settings. However not only university students or professionals have a need for a safe experimental game-based simulation environment to practice skills. More practical types of education also have an explicit need for such an environment. This type of education (e.g. senior secondary vocational education) consists for a large part of practicing skills in real task environments such as workshops or learning company settings. However in these real task environments (e.g. business-related environments) it is often difficult or even impossible to provide the necessary support or guidance to learners. Real task environments also make it difficult to present all the needed tasks (e.g. practicing with intermittently occurring technical problems) and can lead to dangerous or life threatening situations or loss of materials (e.g. incorrect use of machines) (Roobeek & Mandersloot, 1998). Safety training and emergency management therefore are more and more trained in gaming and interactive simulations (Meijer & Poelman, 2011; Lukosch et al, 2012). Furthermore real task environments may confront learners with a level of detail and work stress that interferes with learning itself (van Merriënboer & Kirschner, 2012). Thus it is worthwhile to use game-based simulation task environments that can offer a safe and controlled environment in vocational education as well, so learners may develop and improve their skills through well-designed practice. To achieve a high level of practicing skills it is necessary to master theoretical knowledge as well. Bolhuis and Simons (2005) state that trainees in vocational education experience an increasing need of a strong relationship between theoretical knowledge and practical work. Work related and practice oriented learning ask for a specific design of instructional interventions to transfer the application of knowledge on practical tasks (Merrill, 2002). Van Merriënboer and Kirschner (2012) have developed such a specific design. Their approach of complex learning, with its so-called Four-Component Instructional Design (4C/ID) focuses on the integration and coordinated performance of task-specific skills. This design is already widely used in competency-based vocational education in the Netherlands and abroad.

A game-facilitated curriculum for vocational education would make it possible to combine a demonstrated effective instructional design, such as the 4C/ID model, with a safe game-based simulation environment. In this environment students are encouraged to master theoretical knowledge and directly practice this knowledge in to performed tasks. A game-facilitated curriculum could set learning tasks that first can be practiced inside the game and secondly can be practiced in school. This way, students are well prepared for real-life tasks that must be performed outside school at a workplace. Nevertheless a broadly accepted effective instructional design approach for such a game-based simulation environment does not yet exist in vocational education.

2   Designing a Game-Facilitated Curriculum

This research is connected to a game development project that is coordinated by and built for Kenteq (a centre of expertise in technical vocational education), Little Chicken (a game design company) and Delft University of Technology. A team with members of these organisations developed a first prototype called CRAFT (Lukosch, van Bussel, & Meijer, 2013). The prototype is targeting the education in the mechatronics domain. CRAFT (www.kenteq.nl/craft) contains a game-based simulation environment (GBSE) and a game-based entertainment environment (GBEE). Both environments are strongly connected with each other through a portal and exchange of parts and results. The GBSE represents a workplace of a mechanic mechatronics and is situated in a virtual machine hall. This machine hall contains all machines, tools and materials that are also available in a real workplace (Figure 1). Students have to accomplish tasks in the GBSE that are designed in CRAFT along the 4C/ID model of complex learning.

Fig. 1. GBSE in CRAFT   **Fig. 2.** GBEE in CRAFT

The GBEE represents a leisure park and is added to increase student's intrinsic motivation. In this part of CRAFT students are free to create their own attractions built with their tailored work pieces made in the GBSE (Figure 2). In the GBEE the player becomes a creator instead of a consumer (Gee, 2003). The game-facilitated curriculum also contains a real life practice environment (RLPE). The RLPE is a workplace facilitated in schools or in learning company settings. In the RLPE students have to accomplish the same tasks as in the GBSE, again along the 4C/ID model of complex learning. With accomplishing tasks in both the GBSE and the RLPE students can earn credits. These credits can be used in the GBEE to buy upgrades for the leisure park. The credits work as immediate feedback and therefore foster the motivation of the students (Jallade, 1989). The instructional design in CRAFT, based on the 4C/ID, foresees a nested design of project, task and assignment to guide the actions a student needs to do to successfully finish a learning task.

CRAFT is structured along a nested design of projects, tasks and assignments to guide students' actions within GBSE in order to successfully complete a learning task. The embedded instructional supporting features are based on the 4C/ID model of complex learning. The ultimate aim in the development of CRAFT is to deliver a game facilitated curriculum that lasts for 2 years, completing the full vocational education curriculum of mechatronics with approximately 400 hours of game time. CRAFT is meant to replace a large part of the traditional theoretical classes and provides a unique opportunity to overcome some shortcomings in current vocational education.

3   Research Design

The research presented here takes the finished CRAFT prototype as a starting point of a game-facilitated curriculum in vocational education. Given that the prototype does not yet cover a full curriculum, the research focuses on the learning that takes place in one module. The aim of the present study is to investigate the efficacy of the developed prototype CRAFT within vocational education. More precisely we ask following research questions:

1. Do students in senior secondary vocational education learn the theoretical knowledge (in mechanic mechatronics) provided by playing CRAFT?
2. Do students' practical skills (in mechanic mechatronics) increase by playing CRAFT?

4   Research Methods

To answer the research questions, a non-controlled semi-experimental pre-test post-test design was conducted to evaluate the efficacy of CRAFT. During pre-test assessment, prior to playing CRAFT, students' prerequisite theoretical knowledge level and practical skills (in mechanic mechatronics) were assessed. Prerequisite knowledge was examined by completing a multiple-choice questionnaire on milling, turning, drilling, safety and machine handling. Two observers examined prerequisite practical skills while students had to complete a practice task on turning, milling and drilling. During post-test assessment (after the intervention of playing CRAFT) students' level of theoretical knowledge and practical skills were assessed again corresponding to pre-test assessment. Students had to complete the multiple-choice questionnaire and were observed while completing a practice task. The test design took place during three working days within one calendar week. The pre-test was done at the first day, the intervention at the second day and the post-test was conducted at the third day.

All 27 schools in senior secondary vocational education (basic vocational training in mechanic mechatronics) in the Netherlands were invited to participate in this study. Thirteen schools were willing to participate, out of which 7 schools met the inclusion criterion of being able to spent 24 hours on this study spread over 3 days within one week for participation this study. The research was carried out over these 7 different schools. The schools were located in 5 different provinces in the Netherlands. In total 71 students ($M = 19.5$ age, $SD = 4.41$; 2 ♀, 69 ♂) were recruited on a voluntary basis.

5   Measuring Instruments

During pre-test assessment, prerequisite theoretical knowledge on milling, turning, drilling, safety and machine handling was assessed with an existing online tool (Kenteqtoets), consisting of 25 multiple choice questions with 4 answering possibilities (http://www.kenteqdemo.nl/kenteqtoets). During post-test the same online tool was used with a similar but slightly different online questionnaire compared to the one used during pre-test assessment. These differences were implemented to control for a possible test effect (Brown, Le,, & Schmidt, 2006).

To examine whether the students' practical skills in mechanic mechatronics increased after the offered intervention, a binominal measurement system was used during pre-test and post-test assessment. With this system it became possible to discriminate between students' intentional behaviour and their actual behaviour while working on a practice task on turning, milling and drilling. The turning and milling tasks offered during pre-test assessment differed from the tasks offered during post-test assessment. The tasks during pre- and post-test assessments however contained the same sub-steps in turning and milling. The drilling tasks are components of the actual turning and milling tasks. So during pre-test assessment students were asked to complete one task each on turning and on milling. The same was asked during post-test assessment.

Intentional behaviour was examined by offering students a developed preparation form of the specific turning and milling task. The preparation form described the different part-tasks that were necessary to complete the total task at a random sequence. Students were asked to set these part-tasks in the right sequence. During pre-test assessment the preparation form on turning contained 14 part-tasks and on milling 13 part-tasks. Because the drilling tasks are components of the actual turning and milling tasks they had no separate preparation form. During post-test assessment the preparation form on turning contained 10 part-tasks and on milling 8 part-tasks.

Actual behaviour was examined during pre-test and post-test assessment by observing students while working on the milling and turning tasks in the workplace facilitated inside the school. Two professionals in turning and milling observed and registered the sequence in which students carried out the part-tasks of the turning and milling tasks.

6   Results

The analyses of the questionnaire related to the theoretical knowledge results done by a paired sampled T-test show that there is significant a difference between pre-test (M = 6.31, SE = 1.07), and post-test (M = 6.73, SE = 1.06), t (67) = -2.549, ρ= 0.013, r = .08. This indicates that theoretical knowledge in mechanic mechatronics increased after the intervention.

For the test on practical skill development, the data set had many missing values. In total 67 students did make a practical work-piece. Not all part-tasks could be observed during this research. After removal of whole and partial missing values, a remaining sample size of 27 players remained that was analyzed with the methods mentioned before.

Still, there is a significant difference between pre-test and post-test outcomes. Pre-test and post-test outcomes on skill-level (intentional vs. actual behavior, intentional behavior vs. ideal method and actual behavior vs. ideal method) and type of work-piece showed a significant difference. Results indicate that the total amount of errors made by students decreased significantly after the intervention. Furthermore, data show that there is a significant decrease in errors between pre-and post-test. This indicates that student's practical skills increase after playing CRAFT.

The first test outcome indicates that students' intentional and actual behavior increase significantly after intervention. Students operational intentions associated with the task are related with their actual behavior while working on this task. The second test outcome shows that after intervention students' intentional behavior increasingly corresponds with the ideal method for solving the task. The last test outcome shows that after intervention students' actual behavior increasingly corresponds with the ideal method to solve the task.

7   Conclusions and Discussion

During this research we were looking for two answers. The first question was if the students would increase their theoretical knowledge with use of the supportive information would provided by CRAFT. The result showed that the use of supportive information during the game is effective. The increase of cognitive knowledge is significant between pre- and post-test. This result should be toned because the used measuring tool had a RIT-value that indicates that this questionnaire could be doubtful. Also the re-use of the questions in the pre- and post-test can have influence on the result. The technical problems with a free internet connections can also have an impact on the results. The most students started with problems during the pre-test and these problems did not occur on the post-test. Taking these error factors into account we still may assume that transfer of the provided theory (supportive information) during the game is effective and that students do learn from playing CRAFT. The second question was if there would be an increase of practical skills during playing CRAFT. The increase of skill-level measured by the three skill-level parts shows that an average growth of 30% in skill-level is achieved. These results should be toned because the differences in work-pieces can be the reason for this increase even with the correction on the outcomes for the work-pieces in the post-test. Another explanation could be the familiarity by the students of the working procedure during the post-test. The observed students knew what to do and what to expect from the observers. This research shows that the basic educational element of the game-facilitated curriculum, the implementation and the use of supportive and procedural information based on 4C/ID principles, works for the application in CRAFT, studied by the target group. Further work should aim at exploring if this approach also works in other domains. During the test sessions at these different schools we experienced that the use and the combination of simulation, gaming (the sandbox approach) and real practice worked as a direct stimulants for learning during the test sessions. Further research is needed to test CRAFT during a longer test period based on the KirkPatrick Levels, including also a control group to explore differences in learning effects between traditional teaching methods and the game facilitated curriculum approach. Also the feedback and assessment methods inside and outside the game should be tested in further research.

Acknowledgments. This work could have been realized with support of Kenteq b.v., The Netherlands.

References

1. Bekebrede, G., Mayer, I.S.: Build your seaport in a game and learn about complex systems. Journal of Design Research, 273–298 (2006)
2. Bolhuis, S., Simons, P.: Naar een beter begip van leren. Retrieved from Archief Universiteit utrecht. (August 26, 2005), http://igitur-archive.library.uu.nl/ivlos/2005-0622-190145/5695.pdf
3. Brown, K.G., Le, H., Schmidt, F.L.: Specific aptitude theory revisited: Is there incremental validity for training performance? International Journal of Selection and Assessment, 87–100 (2006)
4. Chalmers, A., Debattista, K.: Level of Realism for Serious games. In: IEEE Proceedings of, Conference in Games and Virtual Worlds for Serious Applications (2009)
5. Eggen, T.H., Sanders, P.F.: Psychometrie in de praktijk (September 28, 2012), http://www.cito.nl/onderzoek%20en%20wetenschap/onderzoek/psychometrie/publicaties/psychometrie_praktijk.aspx (retrieved from Cito.nl)
6. Feldt, L.S.: The relationship between the distriburtion of item difficulties and test reliability. Applied Measurement in Education, 37–49 (1993)
7. Field, A.: Discovering statistics using SPSS. SAGE Publications Ltd, London (2009)
8. Gee, G.P.: What Video Games have to teach us about Learning and Literacy. Palgrave Macmillan, New york (2003)
9. Girard, C., Ecalle, J., Magnan, A.: Serious games as new educational tools: how effective are they? A meta-analysis of recent studies. Journal of Computer Assited learning, 1–13 (2012)
10. Jallade, J.P.: Recent Trends in Vocational Education and Training; An Overview. European Journal of Education, 103–125 (1989)
11. Ke, F.: A Qualitative Meta-Analysis of Computer Games as Learning Tools. In: Ferdig, R.E. (ed.) Handbook of Research on Effective Electronic Gaming in Education, Research Center for Educational Technology - Kent State University, kent - Ohio, pp. 1–32 (2008)
12. Klabbers, J.H.: The Magic Circle: Principles of Gaming & Simulation. Sense Publishers, Rotterdam (2009)
13. Kriz, W.C., Hense, J.U.: Theory-oriented evaluation for the design and research in gaming and simulation. Simulation & Gaming, 268–285 (2006)
14. Lukosch, H.K., van Bussel, R.H., Meijer, S.A.: A Game Design Framework for Vocational Education. International Journal of Social and Human Sciences 6, 453–457 (2012)
15. Lukosch, H.K., van Bussel, R.H., Meijer, S.A.: Hybrid Instructional Design for Serious Gaming. Journal of Communication and Computer, 69–76 (2013)
16. Lukosch, H.K., van Ruijven, T., Verbraeck, A.: The other city – Designing a serious game for crisis training in close protection. In: Rothkrantz, L., Ristvej, J., Franco, Z. (eds.) ISCRAM 2012 Conference Proceedings; 9th International Conference on Information Systems for Crisis Response and Management, Vancouver, Canada (2012)
17. Meijer, S.A., Poelman, R.: Supervisor: a 3D serious game for hazard recognition training in the oil industry. In: Supervisor: a 3D Serious Game for Hazard Recognition Training in the Oil Industry, ISAGA, Poland (2011)
18. Meijer, S.A., Hofstede, G.J., Omta, S.W., Beers, G.: Trust and tracing game: learning about transactions and embeddedness in the trade network. Journal of Production Planning and Controle, 569–583 (2006)
19. Merrill, D.M.: Knowledge objects and mental models. In: Wiley, D.A. (ed.) The Instructional Use of Learning Objects, pp. 261–280. Agency for instructional Technology & Association for Educational Communications and Technology, Washington, DC (2002)

20. O'Neill, H.: Globalisation, competitiveness and human security: Challenges for development policy and institutional change. The European Journal of Development Research, 7–37 (1997)
21. Roobeek, A.J., Mandersloot, E.H.: LWWL: Leren werken, werkend leren: een kennisnetwerkconcept voor duale leertrajecten. Van Gennip, Amsterdam (1998)
22. Shaffer, D.W.: Hoe Computer Games Help Children learn. Palgrave Macmillan, New York (2008)
23. Sitzmann, T.: A meta-analytic examination of the instructional effectiveness of computer-based simulation games. Personnel Psychology, 489–528 (2011)
24. van der Steeg, M., van Elk, R., Webbink, D. (2013), Does intensive coaching reduce dropout? Evidence from a randomized experiment. CPB Nederlands Bureau for Economic policy Analysis, The Hague. http://www.cpb.nl/publicatie/de-effecten-van-intensieve-coaching-op-voortijdig-schoolverlaten (retrieved from CPB I Economische beleidsanalyse)
25. van Merriënboer, J.J., Kirschner, P.A.: Ten steps to complex learning (2nd Rev. Ed.). Taylor & Francis, New York (2012)
26. Veen, W., Vrakking, B.: Homo Zappiens. Growing up in a digital age. Network Continuum Education, london (2006)
27. Verstegen, D.L., Severiens, S.E.: Succes- en faalfactoren in het beroepsonderwijs en de volwasseneneducatie 2006: Deelrapporten van de zevende meting van het zelfevaluatie-instrument succes- en faalfactoren. RISBO contract research BV, Rotterdam (2007b)
28. Verstegen, D.M., Severiens, S.E.: "Het MBO is totaal anders'Een onderzoek naar de aansluiting tussen vmbo en mbo in de zorg. RISBO Contract research BV, Rotterdam (2007a)
29. Yussoff, A., Crowder, R., Gilbert, L., Wills, G.: A conceptual framework for serious games. In: Proceedings of the 9th IEEE Conference on Advanced Learning Technologies, pp. 21–23 (2009)

Simulation Game as a Live Case Integrated into Two Modules

John Mulenga[1] and Marcin Wardaszko[2]

[1] Accounting Department
[2] Centre for Simulation Games and Gamification
Kozminski University
{jmulenga,wardaszko}@kozminski.edu.pl

Abstract. The desire and need to provide attractive and more effective learning environment for students is one of the main motivators for creating practical oriented tasks and courses. One of the ways to deliver more effective and attractive learning environment is the use of experiential learning methods. This paper follows a long discussion among scholars of design and implantation methodology of experiential exercises into the curriculum e.g. Gentry, McCain and Burns (1979); Butler, Markulis, and Strang (1985); Cannon and Feinstein (2005).

The paper discusses the concept of a double game structure featuring two different courses from two departments yet intertwined on one platform to provide accessibility of data. The first game is a classic start-up management business simulation game played in teams by a class of entrepreneurship course (management students) while the second game is an investment game played by students in the financial analysis course (Finance and Accounting Students). Both courses are conducted by lecturers from respective disciplines, through the use of a live game interaction platform. The investment game draws data from the business game of entrepreneurship course for all investment decisions while the business game in itself maintains the traditional entrepreneurial role of growing a viable business as in the real world.

The financial analysis course independently analyses the data from the first game to make independent investment decisions based on business growth potential. Students from both games receive constant feedback as they move from one quarter to another.

This paper describes an organizational and methodological set-up of both games and their integration in the courses as well as learning outcomes. Among other interdisciplinary learning outcomes or experiential education potential, we highlight the practical approach to ethical issues and dilemmas related to management decision-making process based on existing financial information and transparency issues in reality. The attractiveness of the proposed course module will be the introduction of two business games together and combining them into one larger game structure. The teaching and learning effectiveness come from creating dynamic and realistic learning environment based on the metrics and feedback.

S.A. Meijer and R. Smeds (Eds.): ISAGA 2013, LNCS 8264, pp. 102–109, 2014.
© Springer International Publishing Switzerland 2014

1   Introduction

Today's interdependent global economy has not only redefined the practical approach of business strategies but has also seen a complete paradigm shift of pedagogical approach in higher education and professionalism at large. On one hand, we are seeing unprecedented record numbers of the exchange program agreements between universities, and high records of ERASMUS students. (EuRopean Community Action Scheme for the Mobility of University Students), including dual degree programs. On the other hand, there has been a significant increase in multinational corporations seeking to recruit from "non-traditional disciplines" for their respective businesses. For example, chemical engineers hired in investment banking and psychologist in top management roles.

Introducing early stage interdisciplinary collaboration between departments or faculties in universities is the key approach to preparing students to face today's complex corporate system for "non-traditional roles". This paper presents an interdisciplinary collaborative approach to game simulation between two departments and two courses or modules, and consequently two games implemented simultaneously. The pedagogical approach discussed here, captures the conceptual and operational feature of the learning process, thus, cognition, effect, and behaviour (Gentry, Commuri, Burns, and Dickinson 1998)

The concept of a double game structure is featuring two different courses from two departments yet intertwined on one platform to provide accessibility of data. The first game is a classic start-up management business simulation game played in teams by a class of entrepreneurship course while the second game is an investment game played by students in the financial analysis course. Both courses are conducted by lecturers from within their respective disciplines, through a live game interaction platform, where the investment game draws data from the first game. The entrepreneurship course focuses on growing a viable business while receiving constant feedback while financial analysis course independently analyses the data from the first game to make independent investment decisions based on business growth potential, while receiving constant feedback.

2   Methodology – Teaching and Learning

The authors take into account multiple learning domains following Bloom's taxonomy and stipulate different levels of learning capturing cognition, effect, and behaviour (see Gentry, Commuri et al. 1998). These vary from basic knowledge and comprehension to synthesis and evaluation. Thus, authors are looking for two sources of methodology and inspiration for creating a framework of teaching and learning.

The first source of inspiration comes from the revised Bloom's taxonomy of learning and teaching (Anderson, L.W. and Krathwohl, D.R 2001). In the revised model higher levels of knowledge creation requires more challenging and motivating teaching environment. At the same time, the presence of knowledge and skills at meta-cognitive level and creating critical thinking skills are desired effects of teaching for the future alumni.

Authors recognize the need to deliver both above mentioned effects and at the same time attain objectives set under the assurance of learning quality systems. The notion of how to deliver these follows Cannon-Feinstein dynamic knowledge concept, thus "the knowledge that allows people to manipulate elements of - and interact with - an object system, an actual place of work or other setting where people must make problem-solving" (Cannon and Feinstein 2005 p.348-349)

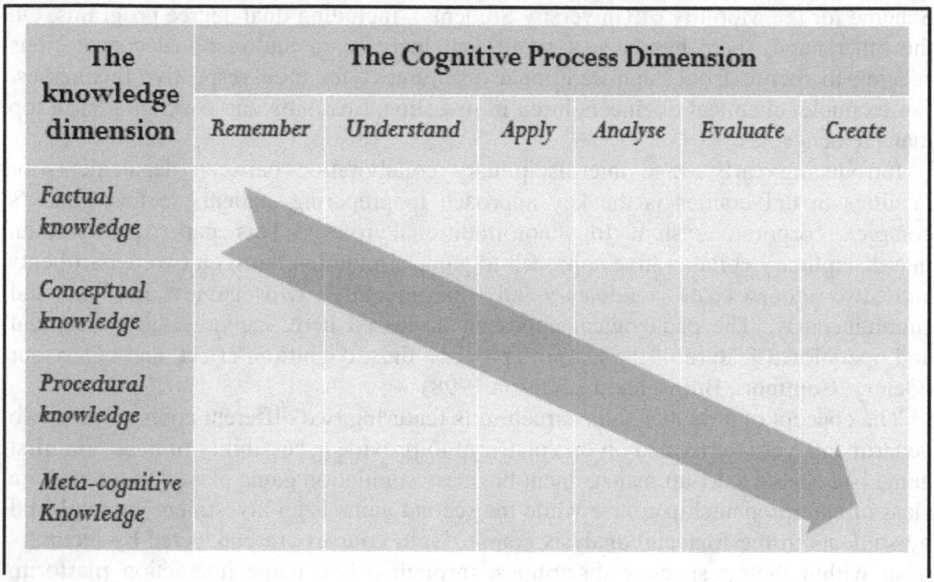

The knowledge dimension	The Cognitive Process Dimension					
	Remember	Understand	Apply	Analyse	Evaluate	Create
Factual knowledge						
Conceptual knowledge						
Procedural knowledge						
Meta-cognitive Knowledge						

Fig. 1. Revised Bloom's Taxonomy - the change of focus in the teaching and learning paradigm Source; *Anderson, L.W. and Krathwohl, D.R (2001).*

Second source of inspiration is the problem of teaching students dealing with complexity and complex systems. The game system offer an extensive experience and teaching methodology of how to deal with complexity in business (Cannon 1995). Games offers high level integration of complexity and evoking information processing mechanisms. Learning of complex systems and dealing with complexity happens, when following activities are introduced:

• Strategic chunking - where players effectively reduce the amount of information they need to process by grouping, or "chunking," a set of related ideas into a higher level, more abstract ("strategic") concepts.
• Sequential elaboration – where players reduce effective complexity by breaking complex thinking into smaller, less complex parts, spreading them out over time.
• Organizational specialization and coordination – where players reduce individual complexity by distributing components of the complex tasks among different members of their simulated organization

Intermediate measures of performance – where games are structured to reward players for successful performance of a component task (such as forecasting or demand creation) in the overall management of a simulated firm. By introducing game mechanisms to both courses, authors provide a more effective and attractive environment in terms of dynamic knowledge creation and complexity management.

3   Business Simulation Course

The business simulation game course is a workshop supported by Marketplace©
computer simulation, offered to the students of the 6th semester of the management and finance majors. The game course follows the standard scenario of a start-up company in 8 decision rounds (Caddote and Bruce, 2008). Students can preferably pick their teams by their own, aiming at teams of 4 or 5. The instructor will intervene only if a student cannot find a team or in a conflict situation; in such cases he will assign students to teams randomly. The team performance is measured in the multi-criteria system: 40% of total score is the game performance measured by balanced scorecard measuring method, 40% is assigned to a written paper in the form of a business plan and 20% is the final report in form of in-class presentation. Students gain points in all three activities and in each of them they receive a budget of points waged by team size. The business plan, which is written in the middle of the game, aims at gaining additional funding from the venture capital fund and it involves:

- Current situation assessment with performance analysis up-to-date
- Strategic and tactical planning for the next year
- Offer to the Venture Capital Fund including financial indicators
- Pro-forma financial statements for next year in quarterly segments

Typically, business plans are graded by game instructors with usage of performance matrix prepared according to the AACSB assurance of learning quality standards. The Venture Capital funds are distributed based on the business plans quality and the offer to the investor made by the business plan team. Business teams can negotiate the proposal from the capital funds but it often requires business strategy improvement.

In the proposed solution, business plans and virtual companies performance will be fed into on-line investment game and will become a live business case for the students from the second course in the financial analysis course

4   Financial Analysis Module

The main aim of the module is to introduce candidates to fundamentals of financial analysis; thus, evaluating the quality of financial information and using the information to reveal the economics of firms. These are core skills for equity and credit analysis, investment banking and advisory or consulting work. The module builds on assumed candidate's knowledge in accounting, finance and statistics. The focus is primarily on accounting and financial analysis, assessing the quality of accounting information, and analysing operating profitability and growth. The module also introduces practical and more rigorous tools and techniques for report writing substantiated with financial and macro/micro economic data.

Students of the investment game from financial analysis course use financial statements and other macro/micro economic data generated from the simulated business game for analysis and investment decisions. Learning outcomes and competences follow AACSB quality standards and are Brocken down as follows;

- Knowledge and understanding
  - Understand the role of financial reporting in capital markets and valuation theory and concepts
  - Acquire an in-depth knowledge of purpose and function of financial analysis,(ratio analysis, forecasting, risk, credit, and accounting analysis)
  - Understand the nature and concept of investment decisions the appraisal process, and capital structure
- Subject specific skills
  - Calculation and interpretation of accounting ratios and trends to give an assessment of an entity's financial performance and position
  - Explain the role of investment appraisal in capital budgeting, and explain and apply concepts relating to interest discounting, risk, return and sustainable growth
- Personal transferable skills
  - Develop the ability to write reports substantiated with evidence of financial analysis critical thinking
  - Identify major and minor problems in the case study setting and apply tools and concepts to the real world issues

The business simulation course is graded on the basis of team performance, and the investment game is based on the individual scores of the participating students. The typical business simulation measures performance based on company value at the end of the game (40%), the analytical papers and strategy formulation paper (40%), and the final presentation of the team's performance with step-by-step strategy analysis (20%). The course takes between 20 to 30 hours to complete. Usually, after the initial enthusiasm fades, students experience a slowing trend in their motivation to continue through the game. Thus, a second game will be brought up, and initially all team-based performance grades will be responsible for 80% of the total score, while 20% will be based on the individual assessment within the investment game

5   Joint Game Mechanics

In order to bring both courses together an exchange mechanisms has to be created and put together with rules from of the game. Business simulation teams will provide the business plans and the business simulator will feed the investment game with financial results. Investment game teams will make investment decisions based on provided data and will provide feedback to business plans of the business teams.

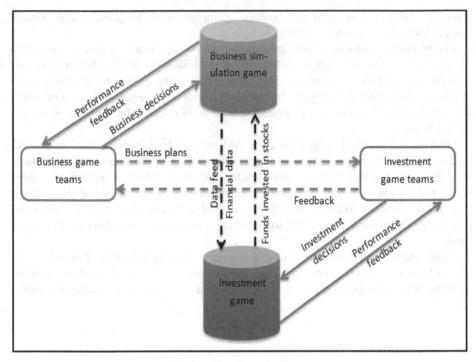

Fig. 2. Joint game mechanics

Investment game teams will be placed in the role of Venture Capital Fund management teams. Each team will receive an investment fund with initial capital of 20 million virtual dollars with goal of maximizing value of their portfolio after the next four decision rounds. The minimum investment they can make into one company is 1 million and the maximum is 4 million. Business game teams are looking for up to 5 million of direct investment from the capital fund, their goal is to receive funding in exchange of the highest possible price per share and lowest number of total shares, which strongly influence their final performance score in the game. Business game teams will also receive written feedback on their business plans, in form of funding offers and quotation. Game masters (both course lecturers) play a role of the "last resort" investor in the case that a worthy business plan dos not receive any offers of funding.

6   Performance Evaluation

One of the obvious challenges with experiential learning is evaluation and effectiveness. One approach we have taken is assess based, which means not only traditional exercise assessment, but continuous assessment, where students will be competing for a good grade depending on the performance on the virtual market created for/by them. This goes for both investment game students and business game students. Authors also want the business game students to present their virtual companies to the investment students

The problem of how to deliver the dynamic knowledge is also a part of interest of the researchers and the experiential learning methodology, where the students are actively involved in acquiring information as the learning environment changes and develops while students' progress in knowledge with experience. This also provides an opportunity for authors to compile the results as data in the multiple game for further research.

Students are assessed using KPIs (Key Performance Indicators) as used in the real investment world, such as return on investment (ROI), capital gains, and investment strategies implemented when picking which company to invest in from the business game. Each team starts the game with an equal amount of borrowed capital to invest which they must use to create wealth. The capital is borrowed in order to assess the risk averse behaviour as in the real world where most of traders/brokers use borrowed funds.

Additionally each team prepares a report substantiated with Financial and Macro/Micro economic data showing application of financial analysis critical thinking while defending the investment position the team took during the entire period.

7   Summary

The paper discussed the concept of a double game structure featuring two different courses from two departments yet intertwined on one platform to provide accessibility of data. The first game is a classic start-up management business simulation game played in teams by a class of entrepreneurship course, while the second game is an investment game played by students in the financial analysis course. Both courses are conducted by lecturers from respective disciplines, through a live game interaction platform, where the investment game draws data from the first game. The entrepreneurship course focuses on growing a viable business while receiving constant feedback, while the financial analysis course independently analyses the data from the first game to make independent investment decisions based on business growth potential, while receiving constant feedback.

The data compiled from the double game will be used for further research in the experiential learning using simulation games. This will also provide an opportunity to further discuss and improve on evaluation issues and assessment.

References

1.   Caddote, E., Bruce, H.J.: The management of strategy in Marketplace, Innovative Learning Solution (2008)
2.   Anderson, L.W., Krathwohl, D.R.: A taxonomy for learning, teaching, and assessing: A revision of Bloom's Taxonomy of Educational Objectives. Longman, New York (2001)

3. Feinstein, A.H., Cannon, H.M.: Constructs of simulation evaluation. Simulation & Gaming: An International Journal 33(4), 425–440 (2002)
4. Cannon, H.M.: Dealing with the complexity paradox in business simulation games. Developments in Business Simulations and Experiential Exercises 22, 96–102 (1995)
5. Cannon, H.M., Andrew, H.F.: Bloom beyond Bloom: Using the revised taxonomy to develop experiential learning strategies. Developments in Business Simulations and Experiential Exercises 32, 348–356 (2005)
6. Butler, R.J., Markulis, P.M., Strang, D.: Learning theory and research design: How has ABSEL fared? Developments in Business Simulation and Experiential Exercises 12, 86–90 (1985)
7. Gentry, J.W., McCain, K.C., Burns, A.C.: Relating teaching methods with educational objectives in the business curriculum. Insights into Experiential Pedagogy 6, 196–198 (1979)
8. Gentry, J.W., Commuri, S.R., Burns, A.C., Dickinson, J.R.: The Second Component To Experiential Learning: A Look Back At How Absel Has Handled The Conceptual And Operational Definitions of Learning. Developments in Business Simulation and Experiential Learning 25 (1998)

Part II
Frontiers in Gaming Simulation for Design and Experimentation

A Negotiation Game to Support Inter-organizational Business Case Development

Silja Eckartz[1] and Christiaan Katsma[2]

[1] TNO, Business Information Services, The Netherlands
Silja.eckartz@tno.nl
[2] University of Twente, The Netherlands
c.p.katsma@utwente.nl

Abstract. Nowadays, an increasing number of organizations in the supply chain are involved in business collaborations. The success of such collaborations is, among others, highly dependent on joint investment in IT system implementations. In this paper we will discuss how business cases can be used to determine the costs and benefits of such investments for each actor. Using design science as a research paradigm we develop a serious game, called SID4IOP, that helps partners in inter-organizational settings to come to an equal distribution of the costs and benefits of an investment. We will show how the introduction of anonymity, a bidding mechanism and structured information disclosure can help project partners to reach agreement on the distribution of the costs.

Keywords: Business Case Development, Serious Gaming, Coordination, Negotiation, Supply Chain Network.

1   Introduction

More and more organizations in the modern supply chain are involved in business collaborations with partners in business networks. The success of these business collaborations is, among others, highly dependent on the interoperability of the participating organizations. To increase this type of enterprise interoperability between organizations certain investments in IT systems are needed. However, the coordination and negotiation between the different partners is often quite challenging. Most organizations are willing to share general information with other business partners to improve interoperability, but sharing more sensitive business layer information like how value is shared is more difficult. One of the main challenges in such networks of businesses is to determine where in the network the benefits of an investment will be realized. Following, developing a shared business case (BC) that includes an optimal distribution of the investment costs proves to be difficult and often involves a complex negotiation process. A method is needed that supports the sharing of business layer information to come to a joint BC.

In this paper we will introduce a serious game, called SID4IOP (Structured Information Disclosure for Inter Organizational Projects) that helps partners in a

S.A. Meijer and R. Smeds (Eds.): ISAGA 2013, LNCS 8264, pp. 113–120, 2014.

network to share information to equally distribute the costs and benefits in the network, by providing negotiation support. The game approaches the situation where three or more actors in a supply chain network investigate the option to implement an Information System (IS) to achieve their goals. As part of the project the actors need to collaborate and develop a joint BC for the investment.

SID4IOP helps project participants to arrive at a fair cost distribution by supporting the negotiation process. During the negotiation process actors are making bids for their cost share. The method uses input from each individual BC to arrive at a shared quantitative BC. During the negotiation process more and more information is structurally disclosed to the participants.

Earlier research shows that the following factors have an influence on the willingness of actors to share information and cooperate to come to a joint BC: consensus of goals (Daneva and Wieringa, 2006), cultural and semantic similarities and the willingness of the actor to share information (Bolton et al., 2008, Schein, 2004). Trust and hidden profiles are two additional factors that are found to influence the decision-making process in inter-organizational projects (Eckartz et al., 2012). Our game is developed for dynamic business networks where the partners do not have long-term business relations with each other and thus trust is limited.

A method to structure the process is necessary, whenever there are no fixed rules or procedures to deal with the opposing preferences of multiple actors (Thompson, 1990) This is the situation when a shared BC is developed in an inter-organizational network. The existing literature identifies four main ways of dealing with opposing preferences: negotiation, mediation, struggle and arbitration (Carnevale & Pruitt, 1992). Negotiation and mediation have been deemed the most successful as they are less costly and friendlier than struggle. They further make it easier to find an acceptable solution for all actors and will be used in our solution. Empirical research has shown that group decision support systems (GDSS) fit well for highly complex problems with a lack of structure (DeSanctis, 2008), like it is the case for business case development (BCD) in inter-organizational projects. GDSS can improve decision quality and time efficiency in negotiation processes. GDSS are less suitable for group meetings that involve "one-to-many" communications. In this research we develop a serious game that provides negotiation support when developing the BC for IS implementation projects.

2   Research Method

We follow a design science paradigm in this research. This paper describes the solution design process following method engineering (Keith, 2010). Based on our literature analysis we started designing the SID4IOP game. Informal discussions with experts from industry as well as academia, iteratively improved the game until it finally reached its current format. During the design process we continuously collected feedback from experts in their field. The final validation of the SID4IOP was planned as an experiment, and we performed several pilot experiments during the design process to improve the game before the actual experiments were deployed.

We performed two types of pilot experiments: a) Two pilots with students to iteratively assess the functionality, efficacy and playability (Aldrich, 2009). During these experiments all bugs were repaired; b) Three pilots with academics that have low to medium experience with IS investment decision making. During these three pilots we iteratively improved our game and guidelines that we used to explain the purpose and steps of the experiment process.

One important step in design science is the solution validation. In order to test our serious game on its practical applicability we deployed it during four experiments with experts. We will discuss the validation process and present the findings in Section 4. But before we will discuss the design process, the game -and simulation logic and the presentation of SID4IOP, in section 3.

3   Introduction of SID4IOP

In this section of the paper we will introduce the outcome of our design research, SID4IOP. The serious game is designed to deliver the following contributions:

- Provide stakeholders in a complex and unstructured problem context with a structure that supports their decision making process.
- Help stakeholders in inter-organizational projects to come to an agreement on a shared BC, focusing on agreeing on a fair distribution of the investment costs.
- Hide the identity of the participating stakeholders to each other and keep their sensitive BC data confidential. Thus, no harm is done to stakeholders that need to cooperate in future projects or that are partially competitors.

3.1   Method Concepts behind SID4IOP

In this section we describe the concepts behind SID4IOP and the mechanisms that explain their impact and importance.

BC Data Input. One of the crucial elements of SID4IOP is the data that it is based on. All stakeholders involved in the project are required to prepare an individual BC for the project. This individual BC should include an analysis of the impact of the project specifying the expected costs and benefits of the investment. This information can be provided as input by the host of the serious gaming session.

Anonymous Information Exchange and Chatting. SID4IOP is built in such a way that each stakeholder owns parts of the total information. The anonymous chatting possibility of the method encourages the actors to communicate with each other and pool their unique knowledge to determine the best distribution of the costs. However, each individual stakeholder can decide to keep some information private during the entire negotiation process. The anonymous chatting facility gives the stakeholders the opportunity to discuss the motivations for their bid/cost distribution without revealing their identity.

Facilitator. The game makes use of a facilitator (either human or a smart system) to support the decision and negotiation process. He or she ensures that the game is filled with BC data as input for the cost distribution process. The facilitator is able to access the information of all stakeholders and thus has an overview of all financial information available. Having such an overview allows the facilitator to support the decision and negotiation process more effectively. By brokering the information the facilitator is in the ideal position to control the information disclosing process described below as part of the process formalization (Valley et al. 1995)

Base Factors for Cost Distribution. Before the start of the negotiation process several base factors can be entered into the game. These base factors will be used to calculate the cost share of each actor. These numbers will be disclosed later on in the process. Two commonly used base factors are expected profit of the investment and usage of the system.

Process Formalization. The SID4IOP formalizes the negotiation process by (i) introducing an online bidding process and (ii) providing a structure for controlling the disclosure of information about other stakeholders. The structure provided by SID4IOP is expected to help the participants to focus on the actual discussion during the decision making process and do not get distracted by random talk and the repetition of already know facts. SID4IOP suggests the following schema (Table 1) for the disclosure of information during the bidding process. The facilitator decides on certain base factors, e.g. Factor A and B. He also determines the point in time (Round x+y) when individual information is disclosed during the serious game in order to progress from the free bidding stage. During the structured information disclosure the facilitator can decide to either (i) increase the process duration by disclosing the individual information in three separate rounds; or (ii) shorten the process by disclosing all base factor information in one round. The same is true for the disclosure of information about the base factors of the other actors.

Table 1. Pattern for information disclosure

	Round x	Round x+y	Round ...	Round x+n
No information is shared = free bidding	X			
Individual financial information is shared		Factor A	Factor B	
Financial information about all actors is shared				Factor A...

3.2   Techniques and Tools behind SID4IOP

We build the serious game based on the free, web-based office suit "Google Docs" which allows for real-time collaboration with multiple stakeholders.

In order to support the BCD process, we develop two types of documents ((i) a master data sheet, which is only available to the facilitator of the negotiation process, and (ii) one specific dashboard per stakeholder showing, among others, individual information, like the individual BC. The master data sheet is linked to all stakeholder specific sheets. The facilitator can send and retrieve data through the tool to/ from the participants. He has the total overview of all financial game story data and bidding transactional data and can intervene accordingly. The participants get access to a simple chat web-interface (via gmail) that allows them to chat with one or several other actors during the course of the negotiation. The chat can be logged and saved for later analysis. Next to that each player gets a dashboard consisting out of the following six screens:

Process steps. An overview sheet where all steps of the negotiation process are shortly described.

Role Description. A sheet, which for each stakeholder containa a role description of his or her individual role in the serious game. It also includes a short role description of all other actors (business units), including sales and profit numbers.

Bid Form. A sheet where an overview of the individual bids is shown.

Financial Information/ Input. A sheet, which contains financial information such as the BC for each stakeholder. The data includes key figures, the profitability of the stakeholder, the costs and benefits expected from the investment and some additional information about e.g. changes in the number of employees.

Feedback Form. A sheet, which provides the participants with feedback on their bids (e.g. if the total amount of costs already got divided or not). After each round an overview of the bids of all other actors is shown. Most importantly, this is the sheet where the extra information, that participants can take into account for their next bid, is shown from a certain point onwards.

Worksheet. A final sheet (unprotected), named "worksheet" is provided to the participants to offer them some space where they can make their own calculations.

3.3   SID4IOP – Deployment Process

SID4IOP is deployed during the project preparation phase to support the BCD for an IS investment in an inter-organizational setting. More particular in the phase when the different BCs are consolidated and project participants try to find agreement on a payment structure. We divide the BCD process and thus also our serious game into three phases: start-up, negotiation and closing.

Start-up Phase. The *facilitator* makes sure that all *stakeholders* have access to the game. Each player gets access to a dashboard. Each stakeholder (internally) determines his own BC for the project and enters that data into the system using the input screen described above. The BC should contain financial information about the current and expected situation. The stakeholders are further encouraged to enter information about their expected benefits into the system.

Negotiation Phase. As soon as all information is entered into the system, the actual negotiation phase is beginning. The negotiation process is structured through bidding rounds and supported by our tool. Our experiments showed that a maximum of seven bidding rounds results in an efficient bidding process. Each round should last at least 5 minutes, but if the project team has more time available, this time span can easily be extended to allow stakeholders to make calculations, chat with each other and come to a profound decision about the height of their bid. Once all actors entered the amount that they are willing to contribute into the system, the system calculates the total and compares it with the total costs to be distributed. The stakeholders receive feedback about the difference to the total and the bids of the others via the system. During the entire negotiation process stakeholders are encouraged to make use of the anonymous chat program provided by the tool. Our method proposes to structurally make information about the individual financial situation available: First to the individual stakeholders, later to all stakeholders. Once the sum of all bids is equal or larger than the costs to be distributed, the bidding process is stopped. In the case that the sum is larger, a new cost distribution will be calculated based on the last proportion of the bids. This final cost distribution will be shown to the stakeholders via the system for approval.

Closing Phase. Once the entire costs of the investment are distributed among the stakeholders and all participants agree upon this distribution, the negotiation process is closed. Now, the fraction of the costs taken over by each stakeholder is entered into the individual BC of that stakeholder. Further, the shared BC is finalized and the game ends.

4   Validation

We conducted four experiments, with five experts each, to validate the deployment of our SID4IOP game. We especially analyzed the impact of anonymity, the process of structured information disclosure and influence of the possibility to see the bids of the other actors on the BCD process and outcome. During the experiment we used a shared service center case to deploy the serious game. We observed the bidding and chat behavior of the experiment participants and conducted multiple surveys before and after the experiment. In the ex- Ante survey we investigated the experiences and maturity of the participants. Summarizing our population includes a majority of senior business consultants with medium to high amount of experience with business cases.

Analyzing the process during the game play we found that both the benchmarks and the information that was made structurally available influenced the bidding behavior and helped participants to find a reasonable bid. This was reported by the majority of the participants during the evaluation after the game. We also see that the four instances of game play each have their own dynamic and we cannot conclude a kind of generic pattern between these four experiments. The bids, timing and benchmarks differ and during the gameplay it is the coincidental interplay between the different actors that mostly influences the course in the game. This is exemplified by our analysis of the chat logs. In one experiment there was an emphasized discussion between two actors and the others only followed their discussion and based their actions on this. In the other experiments one actor initiated a group chat and a more group dialogue evolved. But the content of the chat logs reveals a generic structure in the sense that we discern three main subjects the participants like to discuss and share; i) bid information, ii) social pressure, iii) sharing information.

Finally analyzing the evaluation of the game itself and its effectiveness we used a survey and panel discussion. The results of the ex Post survey show 70% were satisfied with the negotiation process as it was supported by the negotiation game. 50% of the participants were satisfied with the outcome of the game. 53% judge the process played in the serious game as being close to the real life BCD negotiation process. 82% of the experiment participants would use the serious game in a real life project situation.

The participants reported that the anonymous environment gave them an environment in which they felt safe to share parts of their sensitive information. The anonymous chat functionality produced a group dynamic in which information was shared and discussed and gradually social pressure was deployed to get to a more fair distribution of costs. Seeing the bids of the others was crucial to have a reference point and was further an important basis for discussion during the negotiation process. In our opinion there are two major observations: First, we observe that the outcome of the bidding process improved when more negotiation rounds were used, thus more information was structurally made available during the course of the game. This observation was shared by the participants. Secondly, we also see this effect causes the cost increase for sharing this information.

The experts note that the serious game would be very useful for large organizations, where not everybody has insights into the costs and benefits of the others, and often decisions are currently made based on rules of thumb.

5   Conclusion

This paper presents the design and validation of SID4IOP, a serious game that supports the structured, incremental disclosure of information during the BCD process. The focus of SID4IOP is especially on the last part of the BCD process, where costs and benefits need to be distributed among all participating actors in a way that is favorable to all actors and that is agreed as fair amongst all of them. Our various experiments during the design process show that the method can be very useful when different actors in a network need to agree on the entire BC. It also can be used parallel to existing analysis -and design methods that often are used to specify parts of the BC, e.g quantitative ROI or NPV techniques. The game simulation improves the negotiation process by providing a structure to this process, by allowing for anonymous information exchange and by introducing a bidding system. Especially these two elements distinguish the method from current BCD techniques. Our results show that our experienced testing participants evaluate our game as useful and effective. The gameplay and learning elements that are included in the game are recognized by the participants. Especially the negotiation mechanism and anonymous information exchange is valued as effective.

Our experiments and the panel discussions afterwards also show that the game as such can be used as a serious game to learn and gain experiences in a negotiation settings, but it can also be supplied with extensive real data and it then becomes a negotiation platform.

Projects with multiple stakeholders that discuss typical business case aspects can benefit from SID4IOP as it enables them to discuss it in a safe environment in which the key stakeholders decide for themselves what information they want to share, but also are facilitated via a structured bidding and negotiation process. We conclude that SID4IOP is usable for real life projects and currently we have been developing a dedicated web 2.0 based platform based upon the results of this study to increase quality of the gameplay and become independent from the Googledocs platform.

References

1. Aldrich, C.: The Complete Guide to Simulations and Serious Games: How the Most Valuable Content Will Be Created in the Age Beyond Gutenberg to Google. Pfeiffer (2009)
2. Bolton, G., Loebbecke, C., Ockenfels, A.: Does competition promote trust and trustworthiness in online trading? An experimental study. Journal of Management Information Systems 25, 145–170 (2008)
3. Carnevale, P., Pruitt, D.: Negotiation and mediation. Annual Review of Psychology 43(1), 531–582 (1992)
4. Chen, D., Doumeingts, G.: European initiatives to develop interoperability of enterprise applications, basic concepts, framework and roadmap. Annual Reviews in Control 27(2), 153–162 (2003)
5. Daneva, M., Wieringa, R.J.: A Requirements Engineering Framework for Cross-organizational ERP systems. Requirements Engineering 11, 194–204 (2006)
6. DeSanctis, G., Poole, M.S., Zigurs, I.: The Minnesota GDSS Research Project: Group Support Systems, Group Processes, and Outcomes. Journal of the Association for Information Systems 9(10), 551–608 (2008)
7. Douma, A.M., Hillegersberg van, J., Schuur, P.C.: Design and evaluation of a simulation game to introduce a Multi-Agent system for barge handling in a seaport. Decision Support Systems 53(3), 465–472 (2012) ISSN 0167-9236
8. Eckartz, S., Katsma, C., Daneva, M.: Exploring the BC Development Process in Inter-Organizational Enterprise System Implementations. Information Resources Management Journal (IRMJ) 25(2), 85–102 (2012)
9. Eckartz, S.M., Katsma, C.P., Oude Maatman, R.: A Design proposal for a Benefits Management Method for Enterprise System Implementations. In: Proceedings of the 45th Hawaii International Conference on System Sciences (HICSS 2012). IEEE Computer Society, Maui (2012)
10. Keith, C.: Agile Game Development with Scrum. Addison-Wesley Professional (2010)
11. Schein, E.H.: Organizational culture and leadership. John Wiley and Sons (2004)
12. Thompson, L.: Negotiation behavior and outcomes: Empirical evidence and theoretical issues. Psychological Bulletin 108(3), 515–532 (1990)
13. Valley, K.L., et al.: Agents as information brokers: The effects of information disclosure on negotiated outcomes. Organizational Behavior and Human Decision Processes 51(2), 220–236 (1992)

Gaming Simulation Design for Individual and Team Situation Awareness

Julia C. Lo[1] and Sebastiaan A. Meijer[2,1]

[1] Delft University of Technology, Faculty of Technology, Policy and Management,
Delft, The Netherlands
j.c.lo@tudelft.nl
[2] KTH Royal Institute of Technology, Division of Traffic and Logistics,
Stockholm, Sweden
smeijer@kth.se

Abstract. Situation awareness is a key concept in understanding operator behaviour. Shortly, it can be described as knowing what is going on. For the past
decades, human-in-the-loop simulators have been the traditional type of gaming
simulations for studying or training situation awareness. The overall characteristic of gaming simulations is that they are a simulation of a system using gaming methods in which humans take part. Depending on a range of design
choices, these gaming simulations take upon different visualizations and approaches to simulate aspects of the real world. Thus, a fundamental question is:
what are the minimal requirements of a game to ensure natural levels of (team)
situation awareness? This paper aims to capture and define the boundaries and
limitations of gaming simulation design, in which the situation awareness of individuals and teams can be simulated and measured.

Keywords: Individual situation awareness, team situation awareness, gaming
simulation design, validity.

1 Introduction

In the 1990s, the development and research on situation awareness made huge advances in the applied cognitive psychology and human factors field [1]. A simplified
description of situation awareness (SA) is knowing what is happening around oneself
in a complex environment, in order to take an optimal decision. Nowadays, situation
awareness (SA) is an accepted concept of cognition in complex, socio-technical and
dynamic environments [2], as a predictor for good decision-making and indirectly of
performance [3]. Loss of SA has been closely linked to performance failures, which
resulted in accidents, e.g. driving accidents, operational errors in air traffic control [4]
and loss of performance. As operators often need to collaborate, situation awareness
can be extended beyond the individual to a team or group level. Although the concept
has been originally of interest to aviation psychologists, it has been increasingly investigated across different domains, e.g. medicine, military, robotics, driving [5][6].
Due to the technological advancements in computer game development, virtual

S.A. Meijer and R. Smeds (Eds.): ISAGA 2013, LNCS 8264, pp. 121–128, 2014.

environments are more frequently used instead of the more expensive and traditional physical full-scope human-in-the-loop simulators for investigations on situation awareness. However, in a field where psychologists developed a body of theory on how to measure SA in the as-if-real physical simulators, this change of technology requires a bridge between game designers, psychologists and computer scientists. This bridge is relatively new and underexplored in the literature, due to different disciplinary approaches and emphases.

A range of gaming simulations - or in short 'games' - have been developed for the Dutch railway infrastructure organization ProRail, to test new process innovations with (parts of) the railway operational chain. The Railway Gaming Suite consist of different types of games, ranging from low-tech multi-actor board games to high-tech virtual human-in-the-loop-like simulators [7]. The purpose of these games is usually twofold; to use games as a platform for policy development, such as the introduction of new traffic control concepts, and secondly as a research tool to test hypotheses on human behaviour within the railway system. As situation awareness is a cognitive indicator for good decision-making, it is not possible to ensure reliable and moreover, safe decisions in an operational environment without a good SA.

Given the importance for SA and the use of the Railway Gaming Suite, it is crucial to design a gaming simulation environment in which an accurate and 'natural' establishment of situation awareness is expected. Thus, a fundamental question that needs to be addressed before actual SA measurements can take place is: what are the minimal requirements of a game to ensure natural levels of (team) situation awareness? Or in other words, what are the design limitations of a gaming simulation to construct similar SA levels that operators normally establish in their work environment? This is especially relevant when alternative modes of a system are simulated in which a reality is created that shows a large discrepancy with the existing operating environment.

The current paper firstly provides a description of gaming simulation design and validity aspects, followed by an elaborate description of the situation awareness concept. Subsequently, the game design framework and cognitive components of situation awareness are connected, resulting in a number of premises.

2   The Design and Validity of Gaming Simulations

Gaming simulations are in this paper defined as a simulation of a system using gaming methods in which humans take part, in accordance with Duke and Geurts' definition [8]. Gaming simulations mainly have three purposes for which they are used: as a research tool for hypothesis testing, as a policy making tool and as an educational or training tool [7][9]. Different game design frameworks or guidelines exist for the development of these games that each provide a valuable approach, depending on the type and objective of the game [10].

For the current approach, the meta-framework from Meijer [11] is used to assess different game characteristics as it applies to all types of gaming simulations and which is built upon the framework of Klabbers [12]. The meta-framework describes two types of sciences that can be conducted with gaming simulations; analytical science and design science. Games with an emphasis on testing hypotheses relate to the analytical approach, whereas an aim to facilitate change (e.g. in understanding, skills, behaviour) is an aspect of policy and education focused games and relates to the design science. The following game (design) components can be derived from the framework:

- Roles: the personification of an individual within the game
- Rules: the specific and general do's and don'ts for the different roles
- Objectives: the goal(s) of an individual or multiple roles
- Constraints: the range of possible actions in the game
- Additionally to the game design elements, parameter settings need to be defined
- Load: difficulty of the roles, rules, objectives and constraints
- Situation: external variables that might influence the session, e.g. location, selection of participants

Testing hypotheses with gaming simulation is particularly bound to meet certain validity and reliability requirements. Peters, Vissers and Heijne [9] specified the importance of four different validity criteria that were originally identified by Raser:

- Psychological reality: the degree that participants perceive the gaming environment as realistic
- Structural validity: the degree to which the structure of the gaming simulation is comparable to the reference system, e.g. actors, information
- Process validity: the degree to which the processes in the gaming simulations are comparable to the reference system, e.g. interactions between actors
- Predictive validity: the degree of accuracy of the outcomes of the game

3   Individual and Team Situation Awareness

Despite the large acceptance of, and research on, situation awareness across domains, the field is marked with numerous definitions of SA [13]. The discrepancy in definitions can be largely subscribed to two different schools of psychology; information processing and ecological psychology [6]. Whereas the information-processing stream of research relate situation awareness to memory, inference and knowledge, the ecological school of thought emphasize the direct perception as affordances of objects and events. One of the most accepted definitions of situation awareness is that of Endsley [14], who defines SA as the perception (level 1 SA), understanding (level 2 SA) and projection (level 3 SA) of elements in future states (see Figure 1), whereas the ability to project future status of elements in a situation is the highest level of SA that can be achieved. Most of the studies on situation awareness have been using this three-level model when defining and measuring situation awareness on an individual level. However, beyond the individual as a unit of analysis, the ecological perspective receives more attention as well.

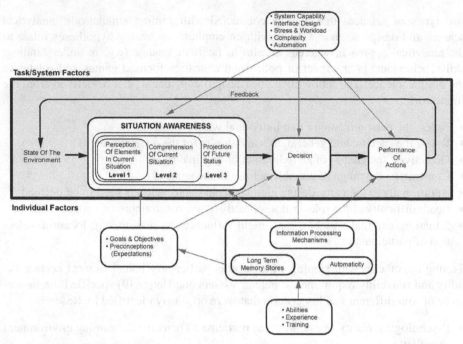

Fig. 1. Information-processing perspective of situation awareness (Source: Endsley, 1995, p. 35)

Distributed cognition and interactive team cognition (ITC) theory are both more holistic theories that recognize teams as unit of analysis [15] or the system level as a unit of analysis [16] for cognition. The ITC theory is approached from an ecological psychological perspective and argues that team interaction and processes are key variables for investigation as they are inextricably tied to their context. The distributed cognition theory applies concepts of the information-processing perspective, in which individuals and artefacts are part of the cognitive system. For the current matching of situation awareness elements and components in game design all theoretical approaches will be taken into consideration. However, a main focus will be on the information-processing perspective from Endsley [3] as this theory has been developed furthest.

4   Simulating and Measuring Situation Awareness in Gaming Simulations

The three-level model of Endsley (see Figure 1) argues that situation awareness is a state that is reached by obtaining one of the three levels. SA is steered by a number of individual factors, such as goals and objectives, expectations, experience and knowledge structures (mental models), and task or system factors such as system capability, interface design, stress and workload, complexity and automation. [14][17].

In the remaining part of the section, a number of premises are outlined that indicate which game environment conditions are necessary to simulate and measure valid SA levels of operators. Cognitive components for SA are discussed and connected with the different validity types for gaming simulations and game design components.

4.1   Premise 1: Gaming Simulations for Measuring SA Need High Structural and Process Validity

For a high structural and process validity, the structure and process of the gaming simulation should be comparable to its reference system. In essence, these two validity types focus on the similarity of the gaming simulation with the real environment, whereas the psychological reality relates to the accuracy and subsequent acceptance of the level of similarity.

The acceptance level of similarity between the simulated and reference system is affected by the knowledge, information and cues that are incorporated in the design of the game. A prerequisite of a good situation awareness is that participants need to have a well-developed (shared) mental model of the task and team elements (of other team/group members) in a certain system [18][19]. Mental models are knowledge structures, that can be distinguished in declarative, procedural and strategic types of knowledge. The amount of experience of an individual influences the maturity of the mental model; more experience leads to a more developed mental model. In ideal circumstances, the mental model of the simulated environment is equal to the reference system. This implies levels of similarity regarding roles, rules, objectives and constraints of participants in the gaming simulation compared to their reference system. To derive the knowledge of the participants, a cognitive task analysis can be used. The goal-directed task analysis (GDTA) is a method to derive 1. the goals of a certain role, 2. related decisions and 3. related knowledge (information) that is needed to make the decision [19]. GDTA is specifically designed to uncover elements that are needed to obtain a high SA. Through this method, information that is used by individuals for decision-making can be identified and included in the game design. Also the inclusion of cues, which is more pertinent from the ecological psychological perspective, should be included, although they are more difficult to identify.

4.2   Premise 2: Gaming Simulations for Measuring SA Need High Psychological Reality

A high level of structural and process validity are imperative to obtain a high level of psychological reality. Without a certain degree of similarity between the game and real environment, it is impossible to create a sense of realism in the simulated environment. As the level of psychological reality focuses on the accuracy of the two environments, physical representations of task and system factors, such as system capability, interface design, stress and workload, complexity and automation, play a crucial role. Here, the main difference between human-in-the-loop simulators and more abstract forms of gaming simulations again becomes apparent, as interface design, complexity and automation are largely depending on the technical capabilities of the gaming simulation design. However, the more abstract physical representation may be compensated when the mental model of the task and team elements are sufficiently matched with the structure and process design of the game, and participants are able to retrieve all necessary information and cues from their environment adequately through communication and their information tools, under similar stress, workload and automation conditions. This is in line with the distributed cognition approach.

Additionally, individual skills and positive attitudes towards the tools used in the gaming simulation is necessary to facilitate psychological fidelity. When participants have difficulties in managing certain (alternative) tools or environmental representations in the game, the focus may be shifted towards the development of their knowledge (i.e. mental model) and skills. Finally, an overall indicator for psychological reality might be immersion in the gaming simulation, which can be measured through a number of objective and subjective measurement techniques.

4.3   Premise 3: Gaming Simulations for Measuring SA Need High Predictive Validity and Measurements of SA May Provide a High Predictive Validity

As situation awareness is an indicator for decision-making, its measurement is often used in studies for the exploration of operator's cognition in current systems and for the design of systems [19]. This implies that gaming simulations for situation awareness need to have a high predictive validity. However, research on the predictive validity of gaming simulation are under assessed. Dorman [20] argues that the use of theoretical notions, such as indexical (degree of the causal relation between rules of the game and the source) and symbolic (resembling mechanisms of the reference system in a game) simulation can support the reduction of the game system to basic elements, with minimal consequences for the game play and implications for the predictive outcomes of the gaming simulation.

Insights into levels of SA might be valuable, as SA has the predictive power to function as an indirect indicator for behaviour and performance. Thus, this indicates that SA may be an indicator as well for the predictive validity of a game.

4.4   Premise 4: Emergence of Team Processes in an Open and Voluntary Way is Necessary to Measure Team SA

For situation awareness in (virtual, co-located or distributed) teams, common goals, interdependence and specific roles of team or group members are key characteristics [19][21]. Following the information-processing approach of SA, the development of SA in teams is influenced by a number of factors: shared SA requirements, mechanisms, devices and processes. Basically, shared SA requirements refer to the three SA levels with regards to other team members, shared SA mechanisms to their shared mental models (SMM), shared SA devices to the communication and (shared) information systems, and shared SA processes refer to a range of team processes. The first three factors need to be identified to support a high psychological reality, structural and process validity of the gaming simulation as discussed earlier, in which it is assumed that the fourth factor, shared SA processes or team processes, such as communication and coordination [15] are to emerge. An example of a gaming simulation type that relate to these elements are pervasive games, which have a characteristic of interlacing games with everyday life and have room for social variability [22].

Another indicator to determine the maturity level of (virtual) teams is to look into the group development process of forming, norming, performing and conflict resolution [21]. Novice teams focus during the initial two stages especially on social interaction, goal setting, role selection and norms, which can be connected to the development of their shared mental models. For a high team SA it is necessary that a certain SMM level is already developed, which can be identified in the gaming simulation through these group development processes.

5   Discussion and Conclusion

More abstract forms of gaming simulations are a low-cost and time-saving alternative to simulate an environment for operators other than human-in-the-loop alike simulators. The current paper addressed validity issues on simulating and measuring (team) situation awareness in a gaming environment by connecting cognitive components of situation awareness with game design and validity types. An emphasis has been on the information-processing approach for SA. Through these game design requirements, it is aimed to establish comparable levels of situation awareness as in a work environment. This does not only have implications for measurements of (team) situation awareness, but also for the validity of a gaming simulation session, in which SA may be an indicator for the under investigated and difficult measurable predictive validity. Further studies need to be conducted to validate these premises.

Acknowledgments. This research was funded through the Railway Gaming Suite program, a collaboration between ProRail and Delft University of Technology.

References

1. Wickens, C.D.: Situation Awareness: Review of Mica Endsley's 1995 Articles on Situation Awareness Theory and Measurement. Human Factors 50(3), 397–403 (2008)
2. Durso, F.T., Crutchfield, J.M., Batsakes, P.J.: Cognition in a Dynamic Environment. In: Smith, M.J., Salvendy, G., Harris, D., Koubek, R.J. (eds.) Usability Evaluation and Interface Design: Cognitive Engineering, Intelligent Agents and Virtual Reality (2001)
3. Endsley, M.R.: Towards a Theory of Situation Awareness in Dynamic Systems. Human Factors 37(1), 32–64 (1995)
4. Durso, F.T., Sethumadhavan, A.: Situation Awareness: Understanding Dynamic Environments. Human Factors 50, 442–448 (2008)
5. Salmon, P.M., Stanton, N.A., Young, K.L.: Situation Awareness On The Road: Review, Theoretical and Methodological Issues, and Future Directions. Theoretical Issues in Ergonomics Science, 1-21 (2011)

6. Tenney, Y.J., Pew, R.W.: Situation Awareness Catches On: What? So What? Now What? In: Williges, R.C. (ed.) Reviews of Human Factors and Ergonomics. Human Factors and Ergonomics Society, Santa Monica (2006)
7. Meijer, S.A.: The Power Of Sponges – High-Tech Versus Low-Tech Gaming Simulation For The Dutch Railways. In: Proceedings of CESUN (2012)
8. Duke, R.D., Geurts, J.L.A.: Policy Games for Strategic Management. Dutch University Press, Amsterdam (2004)
9. Peters, V., Vissers, G., Heijne, G.: The Validity of Games. Simulation & Gaming 29(1), 20–30 (1998)
10. Bekebrede, G.: Experiencing Complexity: A Gaming Approach for Understanding Infrastructure Systems. Next Generation Infrastructures Foundation, Delft (2010)
11. Meijer, S.A.: The Organisation of Transactions: Studying Supply Networks Using Gaming Simulation. Academic Publishers, Wageningen (2009)
12. Klabbers, J.H.G.: Guest Editorial. Artifact Assessment Vs. Theory Testing. Simulation & Gaming 37(2), 148–154 (2006)
13. Salmon, P.M., Stanton, N.A., Walker, G.H., Baber, C., Jenkins, D.P., McMaster, R., Young, M.S.: What Really Is Going On? Review Of Situation Awareness Models For Individuals And Teams. Theoretical Issues in Ergonomics Science 9(4), 297–323 (2008)
14. Endsley, M.R.: Design And Evaluation For Situation Awareness Enhancement. In: Proceedings of the Human Factors Society 32nd Annual Meeting (1988)
15. Cooke, N.J., Gorman, J.C., Myers, C.W., Duran, J.L.: Interactive Team Cognition. Cognitive Science, 1-31 (2012)
16. Artman, H., Garbis, C.: Situation Awareness as Distributed Cognition. In: Proceedings of ECCE (1998)
17. Endsley, M.R.: Theoretical Underpinnings of Situation Awareness: A Critical Review. In: Endsley, M.R., Garland, D.J. (eds.) Situation Awareness Analysis and Measurement, Lawrence Erlbaum Associates, Mahwah (2000)
18. Salas, E., Stout, R.J., Cannon-Bowers, J.A.: The Role of Shared Mental Models in Developing Shared Situational Awareness. In: Gilson, R.D., Garland, D.J., Koonce, J.M. (eds.) Proceedings of a CAHFA Conference Situation Awareness in Complex Systems (1994)
19. Endsley, M.R., Bolté, B., Jones, D.G.: Designing for Situation Awareness. Taylor & Francis Group, New York (2003)
20. Dormans, J.: Beyond Iconic Simulation. Simulation & Gaming 42(5), 610–631 (2011)
21. Johnson, S.D., Suriya, C., Won Yoon, S., Berrett, J.V., La Fleur, J.: Team Development and Group Processes of Virtual Learning Teams. Computers & Education 39, 379–393 (2002)
22. Montola, M.: Exploring The Edge of The Magic Circle: Defining Pervasive Games. In: Proceedings of Digital Experience: Design, Aesthetics, Practice (2005)

A Game for Requirements Formulation for a Distributed Gaming and Simulation Environment

Emdzad Sehic[1], Alexander Verbraeck[2], and Sebastiaan A. Meijer[2,3]

[1] ProRail, The Netherlands
[2] Faculty of Technology, Policy and Management,
Delft University of Technology, The Netherlands
[3] Department of Transport Sceience, KTH Royal Institute of Technology, Sweden

Abstract. ProRail is the owner of a number of high fidelity train traffic simulators for designing and managing the physical rail infrastructure. Gaming simulation is used to support the analysis and redesign of rail management and control processes. The games should use the existing train traffic simulators as much as possible to reduce costs and keep the existing knowledge base and acceptance. Because of their high fidelity level, these simulators lack the more abstract level that is necessary for interaction with humans in a gaming setting. Therefore they need to be adjusted. As there are several simulators to be used and multiple disciplines involved, this is not a trivial task. On the basis of the played Early Decision at Disruptions Game it is examined what requirements need to be fulfilled to make ProRail simulators suitable for use in gaming, in order to maximize profits of the coupling between simulators and games. This paper describes the process followed and provides a refined set of requirements for coupling of simulators for use in management and control games in rail (physical) infrastructures.

1 Introduction

The development process for coupling of simulators started begin 2012 in a cooperation project called Railway Gaming Suite (RGS). The project followed the Distributed Simulation Engineering and Execution Process (DSEEP)[1]. DSEEP is a recommended practice that defines the processes and procedures to follow to develop and execute distributed simulations.

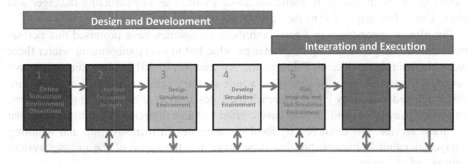

Fig. 1. DSEEP seven step model [1]

S.A. Meijer and R. Smeds (Eds.): ISAGA 2013, LNCS 8264, pp. 129–139, 2014.
© Springer International Publishing Switzerland 2014

The DSEEP process includes seven steps (Figure 1) that are followed in the current project. In Step Two, amongst others, we determine the requirements for such an environment. This happens on the basis of predetermined scenarios and a conceptual model of the simulation environment. A group-wise formulation of Use Case diagrams for determination of the requirements has been used to involve all stakeholders in the process. Added value of the Use Cases is that they act as a bridge between technical and business stakeholders. But Use Cases also have their disadvantages. Use Case diagrams lack well-defined semantics, which may lead to differences in interpretation by stakeholders [2], and that is precisely what we experienced. Each department has its own interpretation of the requirements and fidelity levels of the simulation environment. Now the question is how to overcome these differences and to get one shared view. The current paper describes the experiences of using a game as an experiment on a specific example problem to get a common view on the Use Cases. Through the regular business lines of ProRail, a request came to answer a specific business question through gaming simulation. This question was the perfect Use Case of the end situation that is envisioned by the project team.

The paper first describes the reasons for coupling gaming and simulation for the Dutch Railway System. Then it reviews the use of gaming as a method for requirements elicitation, after which follows the description of the game used. Then it describes the requirements found, followed by conclusions.

2   Dutch Railway System

ProRail is the Dutch railway infrastructure manager that is responsible for the lay-out, maintenance and safety of the Dutch railway system, where 1 million train journeys are made every day and where 115.000 tons of goods are being transported daily over 7000 kilometers of railway. The Dutch railway system is one of the most intensively used railway systems in the world.[3]

The Netherlands suffered a lot of snow, glazed frost and low temperatures during winter in the last couple of years. These, for the Netherlands, unusual weather conditions caused a lot of trouble for the railways. There have been a number of 'blackout days' during which only a few or no trains at all were driving. As a result, politicians raised many questions about the functioning of the railway system and railway companies in the Netherlands, in particular about ProRail as infrastructure manager and about Dutch Railways (NS) as the largest train operator [4] [5] [6].

For already three years in a row, both these companies have promised that performance would improve during the winter months, but in every subsequent winter there were blackout days, like on February the 3rd and 4th in 2012, when during a heavy snowfall the train service in almost the whole country came to a stop. Travelers were hours delayed and many could not reach their destination at all. Due to this incident, Dutch Railways (NS) and ProRail have carried out an evaluation [7]. It turned out that the train service was disturbed by local disturbances in infrastructure and resulting delayed personnel changes, but that these were not the cause of the railway system getting out of control.

It turned out that the root causes lie in:

1. The way of management and adjustments of the daily rail service is directed especially at the resolving of local problems by Regional Transport Control (RBC) and
   Train traffic control centers (TTCC). This regularly causes problems somewhere
   else by which a chain of consecutive problems and adjustment measures occur.
2. Decision-making takes place at different locations by people who have different information, which results in a slow process.
3. The recently introduced complex operational (winter) measures undermine the routine work processes.

The deviation from usual working method appears to have a counter-effective effect
in a stressful situation. It can be therefore be concluded that the railway sector needs
to work on a fundamental improvement of the operational management and adjustment in all aspects of robust railway operations, instead of solving specific situations.
This is a process that NS and ProRail have started.

The cooperation in the railway sector did not keep pace with the increased complexity and sensitivity of the railway system. The lack of cooperation has historic
grounds as in the nineties of the last century, as series of structural changes have been
determined the present-day organization of the railway sector. Guideline 91/440/EEG
[8] has been the starting point for rearrangement of the sector. This EC guideline stimulated the competition in the rail sector as well as the efficiency of transport by rail.
The most important element of the guideline was splitting the traditional national rail
companies into transporters and an infrastructure manager. With the splitting, a complex situation has been created with conflicts of interest that have led to ProRail and
NS being more interested in their own product than giving attention to the whole
railway chain.

Where earlier there was one company with employees who got to know all aspects
of the train service during their careers, now new people on both sides were hired who
only would get experience with a part of the product. These new hires have little
knowledge/insight about how their own decisions influence the entire network.

Lately, triggered by the winter problems, ProRail and NS have become more aware
that they have to work with each other and also with other railway companies to improve railway system operations. The improvement of cooperation is mainly needed
at the operational level in managing the train service according to the time table.

An environment where all involved players from the operation could train or could
test all new measures without influencing the real work, before they become implemented, does not exist yet at this moment within the Dutch rail system, but is heavily
needed to help with the system level innovation.

3   Gaming for Requirements Elicitation

A basic question in Requirements Engineering is how to find out what user really
need. IEEE has defined the Requirements as [9]: 1. a condition or capability needed
by a user to solve a problem or achieve an objective. 2. a condition or capability that

must be met or possessed by a system, system component, product, or service to satisfy an agreement, standard, specification, or other formally imposed documents *3. a documented representation of a condition or capability as in (1) or (2).* Requirements Engineering can be decomposed into the activities of requirements *elicitation, specification*, and *validation*.

Requirements Elicitation can use any of the following techniques: Brainstorming, Document Analysis, Questionnaires, Focus Groups, Interviews, Prototyping, Requirements Workshops and Reverse Engineering to proactively identify and document customer and end-user needs. Eliciting requirements for complex systems is a difficult and expensive process, and consequently a key issue in software and systems engineering. Christel and Kang [10] grouped the problems of Requirements Elicitation into three categories:

- problems of scope;
- problems of understanding; and
  problems of volatility, i.e., the changing nature of requirements.

The theoretical contribution of this paper is in the introduction of gaming simulation as an novel approach for Requirements Elicitation. Simulation and gaming scholar Dick Duke argued in his 1974 text that 'gaming is the future's language', underlining the value of jointly creating or experiencing a system that does not exist yet. Since then, thousands of gaming simulation have been made for many different areas and purposes of use like research, education, training, and link many areas of enquiry and professional practice.

Requirements are information. If we want to find out about requirements we must consider how it is produced and used, and not merely how it is represented. Much of the information needed for requirements is embedded in the social worlds of users and managers. It is informal and depends on context for its interpretation. The end user does not really know what is needed or wanted and has to experience problems to identify such needs.

Games are social systems. While playing a game, people apply knowledge and skills to triumph over difficulties set by fellow players or by socio-economic circumstances. They shape organizations and act within the boundaries of organizations, guided by the rules.[11]. Through gaming we have identified user requirements by experiencing shortcomings while playing daily collaborative business routines in a risk free environment.

In gaming literature, the use of gaming simulation for learning is dominant, where the use for research games and games for design is smaller and upcoming. Specifically for requirements elicitation, Zapata and Awad-Aubad used a game as a way to simulate software development conditions in a competitive environment similar to real life [12]. Beatty used games to enhance RE training as a first step to apply games for requirements elicitation in applied situations [13].

Zarvic et al[14] applied games as an approach for collecting end user requirements in the context of work funded through COIN (COllaboration and INteroperability for networked Enterprises) Framework Research Programme).

4   Railway Gaming Suite Backbone

After a successful introduction of gaming simulation within ProRail in 2009 by Delft University of Technology (TUD) [15][16][17] it became clear to ProRail management what the added value of gaming could be for decision making in the company itself. In 2010, TUD and the Innovation department of ProRail started a collective project: Railway Gaming Suite.

With completion of this project ProRail will have a Gaming Suite that connects to the existing train simulators of ProRail. Today, there are several simulators within the organisation to design, analyse and evaluate the infrastructure, safety and scheduling:

- FRISO, a simulator that uses a microscopic infrastructure model and handles areas like corridors and nodes,
- TMS, an traffic optimization simulator that is able to determine conflicts, to reschedule the train movements and to calculate advisory speeds to increase punctuality and safety and to reduce energy consumption,
- PRL Game, a simulated man-machine interface for train dispatchers,
- BITS, a microscopic, dynamic, stochastic simulator to test signaling safety applications before being installed in the field.

The above-mentioned simulators and tools are used by different departments of ProRail and are developed for different purposes, usually for a small part of the railway process. To simulate processes in the bigger picture, it is necessary to connect these simulators with each other, and to link them with gaming.

The Railway Gaming Suite project team choose High-Level Architecture (HLA) to build a backbone for the simulation and gaming experiments [18]. HLA is an architecture that enables several simulation systems to work together. This is called interoperability, a term that covers more than just sending and receiving data. The systems need to work together in such a way that they can achieve an overarching goal by exchanging services [19]. The DSEEP process is the accompanying process through which an HLA environment can be designed. HLA is an open international standard, developed by the Simulation Interoperability Standards Organization (SISO) and published by IEEE. HLA is a standards document that describes the components of HLA and what interfaces and properties they must have.

5   Early Decision by Disruption Game

The game session played at the beginning of 2013 was designed to compare two different models of handling a disruption. The first method is the current way of handling a disruption, and the second was a new model designed by a project team. Corman defines disruption as: "the modification of some infrastructure characteristics, such as the temporary unavailability of one or more block sections, which causes alterations in the train travel times and routes" [20].

From our experience with earlier played simulations within ProRail we paid a lot of attention to the immersion of the players, a real-time model and the presentation of data. Because we are only at the beginning of the process of developing a simulation surrounding and we cannot use the existing simulators yet we had to use low tech resources for the game session.

Table 1. Core description of Early Decision at Disruptions Game

Core aspect	Description
Purpose	To compare two different models of handling a disturbance in the train service
Roles	Local train traffic controller, Decentralized network controller, Network Controller, Driver rescheduling , Rolling Stock rescheduling, RBC monitor , LBC en MRI
# of players	10 in role, 5 in support roles, 7 in support presentation data, 10 observers, 1 game leader
Own/real/fictitious role	Own role
Scenarios	2 Scenarios (present day handling of a disturbance and the new procedure)
Intervention range	Facilitators could start, stop and pause the scenarios.
Simulated world	Detailed infrastructure between Amsterdam and Den Helder, detailed current timetabling
Time model	Continuous
# of sessions	1 full day session
Type of data generated	Quantitative and qualitative

The players were divided over 4 rooms like in real-world situation. Two Train Traffic Control Centers (TTCC Amsterdam end TTCC Alkmaar), Regional Transport Centre (RBC) and the national Operational Control Centre Rail (OCCR).

The train traffic controllers had detailed schedule of the own working area. Each train traffic controller had its own control area in the front of him presented on a canvas. The trains were visualized with clothes-pegs and moved over the canvas by one of the Support roles. – called automatic route setting (ARI). The train controller had the possibility to leave the execution of the timetable to ARI or to move the trains over the canvas by himself according to the timetable that was available on paper. The changes in the time table were shown on a screen. The train controller also had a survey of delays of all trains in their area which was fed by the support roles in both TTCCs. The train controllers had a their disposal a telephone with the numbers of all other players.

One decentralized network controller (DVL) was present in the game, who had several screens at his disposal. One screen showed information about calamities (Information System Train Control - ISVL). On the other screen he could make changes in the timetable, which were visible to all other players via screens in all other rooms. Furthermore he had at his disposal a screen that showed the position and delays of the trains. The information which DVL had was also visible and changeable in the other rooms, OCCR and RBC.

The players in the RBC room were equipped with a rolling stock list. Each clothes peg (train) had its own rolling stock number that resembled the train number in the timetable. A number of support roles were also present like train driver, dispatchers and back office. These roles were necessary to imitate reality in the scenarios.

Before the game session, meetings were held with the players in which they got an explanation about the purpose of the project and about the new model. The day itself was divided in two parts: morning and afternoon session. The morning session contained the current model of handling a disruption. After gaming the first scenario we evaluated this. In the afternoon the new model of handling a disruption was again explained and after gaming the second scenario this was evaluated after which a comparision and the day itself were debriefed.

During the game session an observer was present at all players. The Employee Travel Information (MRI) were exceptions, the played no active role but they could observe what the new model could mean in their work. Before and after each session the players filled in a questionnaire.

6   The Requirements

Apart from the direct business question, the aim of the game session was to refine the existing requirements for simulation environment. DSEEP defines the requirement as: A statement identifying an unambiguous and testable characteristic, constraint, process or product of an intended simulation environment. We observed the requirements for future environment in the following way:

- Question lists
- Observation lists
- Analyzing recorded video
- Evaluation with players after each played scenario

All the players filled in a questionnaire before and after the played scenario. These questionnaires were meant to assess the validity of the game according to the criteria for validity identified by Raser (1969). Below an example (Table 2) of how we categorized and used the data from the questionnaires.

Table 2. Validity of played game

	Scenario 1			Scenario 2		
	#	M	SD	#	M	SD
Psychological reality						
Realism (1-5)	12	2.7	1.23	11	2.0	.89
Immersion (1-5)	12	3.3	.79	11	2.9	1.14
Attitude towards the game (1-5)	12	3.4	.67	11	3.4	.92
Process & structural validity						
To be aware of the obtained aims (1-5)	12	2.8	.45	11	2.7	.47
Satisfied with the decision (1-5)	11	2.9	.30	11	2.8	.60
Needed information (1-5)	12	2.0	.00	11	1.8	.60
Clearity of the game structure (1-5)	12	3.8	.85	11	3.5	.85
Difficulty of the game (1-5)	12	2.4	1.44	11	2.1	1.51

We also observed the communication lines during the game with video recordings and observation lists.

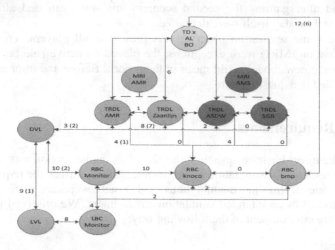

a (b)
a= frequency contact (total)
b= frequency of conversation (total)

Fig. 2. Communication lines scenario 1

The most important information we have obtained through evaluations at the end of each scenario and at the day evaluation.

Played game has helped us to refine the requirements for the simulation environment. Table below shows a number of beforehand put requirements, how these were represented in the game and what our observation was.

Requirement	Represented in the game	Observation of requirement	Requirement addition or refinement
The RGS shall simulate train movements i.e. the trains shall be moved over infrastructure under the following conditions: - trains follow the switch positions - trains react on aspect of a signal (stopping in front of red signal or driving when the signal has another aspect than red), - trains respect speed restriction signals	Simulation of train movements has been done by moving the pegs (trains) over the board by the ARI facilitators	Bottle-neck in the game. The train controllers thought this was not realistic enough.	The RGS shall display the rail section reservation and route blocking in the same way (same interface) as in reality.

The RGS shall represent the current state of the simulated infrastructure	Infra drawings were printed on vinyl. Each train controller had his own infra area in front of him.	Because there were a large number of ARI facilitators around and not a realistic reproduction of the train movements the train controllers had some difficulty with following the game.	The RGS shall be able to visualize the current state of infrastructure on a as small as possible (rail section) level.
The RGS shall have the possibility to simulate the timetable of trains based on day or basic hour pattern.	A list printed on paper in sequence of time per area.	As soon as a delay occurred it was hard for the ARI facilitators to follow the time schedule. Manual simulation and visualization is no feasible method for this requirement with detailed real-time traffic control.	The simulation of the time table should be automated.
The RGS shall be able to simulate train delays.	The caused delays were manually noted.	The delays made during the game were not realistically represented in the game.	The RGS shall be automatically track the train delays at all positions in the infrastructure.
The RGS has to have the possibility to change the time table of the trains, to set up new trains and to remove trains from the time table.	The DVL had the possibility to enter a text message. Changing real timetable was not possible	A lot of players were dependent during the game session on the information (actions) of the DVL.	The changes of the time table through DVL shall be automatically pushed to other players.
In the RGS surrounding the minimum simulation speed should not be behind the speed of the clock.	The game was set up as a real-time game.	The speed of getting information was often behind the time of the clock.	The information shall get to the players on time and synchronic.
The data have to be sufficient registered to reproduce or reconstruct the original session.	By filling in the observation lists and recording the session on video.	The amount of data during the session was so large that it was not possible to record it all.	Data collection mechanisms shall be registered in RGS for all roles.

7   Conclusion

With this played game we have tried to come a step closer to the future RGS environment. Lots of M&S projects are being executed for large companies where time and (and money) does not count. Technical complexity, project management and intern organization difficulties and especially incomplete or absent requirements make this projects lasts years. Requirements grow old in course of the length of the project. This is not desirable for an organization as ProRail.

Playing a game to refine the requirements is a different way to use the games. The gaming approach is very useful for bringing together many people from different areas within a short time in a lab-controlled business environment. Requirements elicitation with different stakeholders also mean elicitation of different requirements. Analysis of the game shows us that this way can help us with the developing of desired simulation environment. Future investigations and evaluations of made environment will show if this method can give better results.

Acknowledgment. This research has been funded by ProRail and the Next Generation Infrastructure Foundation (NGI).The authors would like to thank Gert Jan Stolk and the Gaming Street of TU Delft for their contribution to the production of the software and Julia Lo for her help with processing the results of the gaming sessions.

References

1. IEEE Computer Society, IEEE Recommended Practice for Distributed Simulation Engineering and Execution Process (DSEEP). IEEE Computer Society, New York (2011)
2. Soares, M.S.: Architecture- Driven Integration of Modeling Languages for the Design of Software - Intensive Systems. Technische Universiteit Delft (2010)
3. Ramaekers, P., De Wit, T., Pouwel, M.: Hoe druk is het nu werkelijk op het Nederlandse spoor? Den Haag, Heerlen (2009)
4. Commissie Kuiken, Rapport van Parlementair onderzoek onderhoud en innovatie spoor, Den Haag (2012)
5. Schultz van Haegen, M.H.: Functioneren spoor, Den Haag (2011)
6. Schultz van Haegen, M.H.: Antwoorden op feitelijke vragen inzake functioneren spoor, Den Haag (2011)
7. NederlandseSpoorwegen, ProRail, Ministerie van Infrastructuur en Milieu, Programma winterweer op het spoor (2012)
8. EEG Richtlijn van de Raad betreffende de ontwikkeling van de spoorwegen in de Gemeenschap 50, 1–32 (1991)
9. IEEE Computer Society, International Standard ISO / IEC / IEEE, Systems and software engineering — Vocabulary (2010)
10. Christel, M.G., Kang, K.C.: Issues in Requirements Elicitation (1992)
11. Klabbers, J.H.G.: The gaming landscape: A taxonomy for classifying games and simulations. In: Digital Games Research Conference (2003)
12. Zapata, C.M.J., Awad-Aubad, G.: Requirements Game: Teaching Software Project Management. Clei Electronic Journal 10(1) (June 2007)

13. Beatty, J., Alexander, M.: Games-Based Requirements Engineering Training: An Initial Experience Report. In: 2008 16th IEEE International Requirements Engineering Conference, pp. 211–216 (September 2008)
14. Zarvić, N., Duin, H., Seifert, M., Thoben, K., Bierwolf, R.: Collecting End User Requirements Playfully. In: 15th International Conference on Concurrent Enterprising: Collaborative Innovation: Emerging Technologies, Environments and Communities (2009)
15. Meijer, S.A., Mayer, I.S., Van Luipen, J., Weitenberg, N.: Gaming Rail Cargo Management: Exploring and Validating Alternative Modes of Organization. Simulation & Gaming 43, 85–101 (2011), doi:10.1177/1046878110382161
16. Meijer, S.A., Van der Kracht, P., Van Luipen, J.J.W., Schaafsma, A.A.M.: Studying a control concept for high-frequency train transport. In: 2009 Second International Conference on Infrastructure Systems and Services: Developing 21st Century Infrastructure Networks (INFRA), pp. 1–6 (2009), doi:10.1109/INFRA.2009.5397864
17. Kortmann, R., Sehic, E.: The Railway Bridge Game – usability, usefulness, and potential usage for railways management. ISAGA, Spokane (2010)
18. Kortmann, R., Meijer, S., Seck, M., et al.: RGS Work Package 1: Systems Architecture, pp. 1–64 (2011)
19. Moller, B.: The HLA Tutorial (2012)
20. Corman, F.: Real-time Railway Traffic Management: dispatching in complex, large and busy railway networks. Technische Universiteit Delft (2010)

Co-creating Networked Educational Innovations via Process Simulations

Riitta Smeds, Svante Suominen, and Päivi Pöyry-Lassila

Aalto University School of Science,
Department of Industrial Engineering and Management, SimLab
{riitta.smeds,paivi.poyry-lassila}@aalto.fi,
svante.suominen@gmail.com

Abstract. Three facilitated, discussion-based process simulation workshops were arranged to enable the actors of an emerging school network to co-develop their educational processes. The workshops applied specific visual boundary objects in subsequent phases. The workshop data and the follow-up interviews show that the workshops supported a stepwise double co-creation of novel ideas for educational innovations, and of the necessary ties for their successful implementation. More analysis of the longitudinal data is still needed to refine and test this hypothesis.

1   Introduction

Our societies are getting more and more interconnected and networked, in their environments, in their economies, and in their social interactions. Interconnected processes increase vulnerability, but they also create opportunities for innovations that increase sustainability and well-being.

Sustainable process innovations call for a participative, human-centered co-creation approach. In organizational change, employee participation yields better process and system innovations (Mumford 1981); in software development, end-user involvement ensures acceptance into use (Kristensen et al. 2006); in service innovation, the producers and consumers of the service should together design the service process (Vargo & Lusch, 2008). And, for networked innovations, all actors of the network, including the customers, should participate (Smeds & Pöyry-Lassila, 2011).

In the core of co-creation is sharing and creating knowledge in social interaction. The members of a knowledge creating community bring together their knowledge and expertise, and co-create new knowledge and designs through co-developing shared artifacts, so called boundary objects (Paavola & Hakkarainen 2005). In the co-creative discussions, the actors also construct the necessary new ties for their inter-organizational collaboration (Hardy et al. 2005).

This paper analyses the dynamic co-creation of educational innovations in simulation discussions that are facilitated by researchers applying boundary objects.

S.A. Meijer and R. Smeds (Eds.): ISAGA 2013, LNCS 8264, pp. 140–147, 2014.

2   Boundary Objects and Discussion for Knowledge Co-creation

Boundary objects help to transfer and transform knowledge between people over knowledge boundaries (Star 1898; Carlile 2002). Boundary objects play a double role in knowledge co-creation: 1) they serve as catalysts of communication that help to share knowledge across the boundaries of individual thinking, and 2) they are the very objects that are collaboratively elaborated and created (Paavola & Hakkarainen 2005).

Visual process maps can catalyze a group of people to envision their future, to understand the upcoming changes, and make the change more concrete for all stakeholders (Fenton 2007). Visual representations can also be used as the objects of collaborative development (Smeds et al. 2006; Ewenstein & Whyte, 2009).

Scenarios can be used as boundary objects, to collaboratively envision future solutions (Carroll 2000; Smeds & Pöyry-Lassila 2011; Salmi et al. 2012). Scenarios are narratives about people and their activities. They describe the context, the actors with their goals and objectives, and their actions when pursuing their objectives. Scenarios are incomplete, and can thus be collaboratively elaborated.

Collaborative innovation is in essence a process of knowledge co-creation over boundaries. This collaborative effort requires joint discussion. According to Hardy et al. (2005), effective inter-organizational collaboration requires two types of conversations that construct the necessary ties for a "collective identity" (Hardy et al. 2005, 63-65):

1. Conversations in which **joint issues** are constructed. These conversations produce **generalized ties** that connect participants to **shared issues and vision** that have relevance for their home organizations and legitimize the collaboration.
2. Conversations that refer to **specific issues**, persons, places and objects, and help the participants to position themselves as connected in the collaboration in identifiable ways. These conversations produce **particularized ties** that relate participants directly to each other, and help them to determine what **roles and responsibilities** they take in the collaborative process.

Hardy studies real-life inter-organizational negotiations, and speaks of conversation. We study situated simulation workshops, and use the term discussion instead. Our aim is to study, **how the necessary ties for process innovation are co-created in the simulation workshops that apply boundary objects.**

3   The Case Research

The research deals with the three year development process (2007-2010) of a public school network of five comprehensive schools - the so-called Kuninkaantie schools – in the City of Helsinki, Finland. The schools employed together over 100 teachers and five principals, and taught around 1800 students. The larger network contained other schools, the Department of Education and its Media Center, other municipal branches of the City of Helsinki, NGOs, companies, local clubs and associations, third sector actors and other interested stakeholders, and the parents and families of the students.

The overarching development goal of the school network was to provide the community with regionally consistent comprehensive education on the grades K-10 (ages 6 to 16). The development process started in 2007, driven by active developer teachers that initiated five pilot projects on new inter-grade and inter-subject teaching methods and processes.

The development process was supported via three discussion-based SimLab™ process simulation projects (e.g. Smeds et. al 2006; Smeds & Pöyry-Lassila 2011). For each simulation, the researchers conducted thematic interviews of those people that were active in the networked case process. Based on the interviews, the researchers prepared visual boundary objects such as text citations, process maps, scenario process models, and network models. In the workshops, the boundary objects were projected on a 10 meter video screen, and the actors discussed and co-developed their collaboration processes using these boundary objects, facilitated by the researchers. Each simulation project produced a lot of data: interviews, observational data, notes, and audio and video recordings of the workshops. – In 2012, follow-up interviews of the principals and teachers were conducted, to analyze the transfer of knowledge from the simulations to real life in the schools, and to find out their impact on the implementation of the educational innovations.

The first simulation workshop (2007) focused on the visioning of the collaboration objective of the Kuninkaantie schools, and related the five pilot projects to this overall vision. Among the workshop participants were 30 teachers and the principals from the schools, and four representatives from the Department of Education of the City of Helsinki.

The second simulation workshop (2008) concentrated on the merger of two of the network schools: the elementary school (grades K-6) and the upper school (grades 7-9). Almost 70 participants attended the workshop: the teachers and principals from the merging schools, and several representatives from the Department of Education of the City of Helsinki. Only the principals had been interviewed before the simulation - the teachers had not yet participated in any development projects or simulations.

The third simulation workshop (2009) had two separate topics: 1) the public-private network of the school and its value creation potential and 2) testing and further planning of a future project-based learning environment. The simulation community consisted of actors from many organizations of the potential educational network, thus bringing into the co-creation workshop a rich variety of knowledge and experience. The participants consisted of 15 teachers / principals, four students, seven company people, two officials from the Department of Education and Media Center of the City of Helsinki, and one from the Ministry of Education.

From the discussion data of the workshops, we analysed the emergence of joint and specific issues, and the collaborative formulation of generic and particularized ties, when specific boundary objects (BO) were used in facilitation.

4   Results from the Process Simulation Workshops

The emergence of issues in the facilitated, boundary-object-mediated discussions, and the subsequent co-creation of relational ties, is given in Tables 1-3.

Table 1. Simulation 1: Visioning regionally consistent comprehensive education

PHASE 1	*BO: visualized thematic interview citations concerning the new vision*
Facilitated discussion	**Joint educational issues:** future curriculum, characteristics of a good learning environment, project-based pedagogy, goals of comprehensive education.
	Joint regional issues: what does regional collaboration require from the schools; how can a regional and professional identity be established to enable collaboration; safer learning environment for the students, implementation of project-based learning in the region.
Result	**Generalized ties emerged:** A shared vision of the future way of educating students in the regional school network was co-created
PHASE 2	*BO: a visual scenario process model describing a student's fictive school week 5 years from now, instantiating the ideas of the vision*
Facilitated discussion with Future Recall Method	**Joint issues:** participants related their schools to the Kuninkaantie collaboration
	Specific issues: flexible working time arrangements in the future, so that the teachers would have time to develop their work; re-organization of the collaboration between class and subject matter teachers; how technology and administration would support the schools better than earlier.
	Identification of requirements and constraints concerning the future vision: requirements concerning the city administration, and the teachers' vocational organization. – No discussion about the participants own tasks or roles.
Results	**Generalized ties emerged:** the participants began to talk about themselves as "the Kuninkaantie teachers" or "the Kuninkaantie schools", not as representatives of their home schools.
	Towards particularized ties: the vision was concretized towards requirements for the participants in face of the future collaboration
PHASE 3	PARALLEL GROUP ASSIGNMENTS: develop concrete actions for the five pilot projects, and develop further the project plans, focusing on how to best serve the students.
Discussion	**Specific issues:** reflecting and relating the participants' work roles to the overall development process. E.g. the teachers of special education realized that they have an important role in the innovation process, since their students already move between the network schools, and special education also brings together representatives and organizations from several municipal branches.
Results	**Particularized ties emerged:** Awareness of the benefits that the teachers can gain from regional collaboration, and also about the challenges connected with the teachers' new roles. The development teachers started to realize their specific roles and responsibilities in the change.
	From particularized ties towards generalized ties: Realization of the significance of collaboration between subject and class teachers, and of concrete possibilities to realize the collaboration. The teachers started to talk of themselves as "teachers of comprehensive education". They expressed the need to do things together, but had varying opinions about next steps.

Table 2. Simulation 2: Merger of two schools

PHASE 1	*BO: Visualized text citations from the published strategies and educational objectives of the two schools*
Facilitated discussion	**Joint issues:** the educational objectives and operational ideas of the future merged school. The students' sound self-esteem and its importance as an educational goal, the tolerance of diversity in schools, motivating the students to study and learn, the success of the students and its significance as educational goal, sustainable development and environmental issues, collaboration with families.
Results	**Generalized ties emerged:** The discussion clearly connected the participants to general, commonly valued issues.
PHASE 2	*BO: visual process model of the merger, prepared by the researchers based on a modeling session with the principals*
Facilitated discussion	**Joint issues, connecting with specific issues:** talk-through of the process model, with the roles, central events and decision points, and the timeline of the change. Clarification of the merger process.
Results	**Generalized ties, and particularized ties** between the participants in the merger process started to build up in the discussion
PHASE 3	PARALLEL GROUP DISCUSSIONS on four themes concerning the merger: the management and organization of the school as a work community, the wellbeing of the student community, the communality and wellbeing of personnel, and the participation of the students in the new merged school.
Discussion	**Specific issues:** the participants' hopes and worries concerning the merging process, ideas for concrete actions, suggestions for change in the merger process
Results	**Particularized ties emerged, and linked back to generalized ties:** The participants started to see themselves as part of the new merged school, and developed concrete ideas to improve the merging process. They realized the need of joint responsibility for well-being at school. The well-being of students and the development-orientation of teachers were crystallized as two important shared objectives for the school. Familiarity of the teachers and prevention of bullying were seen as important factors for student well-being.

Table 3. Simulation 3, topic 1: Visioning the public-private school network

PHASE 1	*BO: visual models of two school networks: Kuninkaantie and Mesa school (USA)*
Facilitated discussion	**Shifting between joint and specific issues:** comparing and commenting the two network models and generating ideas related to the development of the Kuninkaantie network; identifying missing actors that should be included into the network, realizing the significance of some actors not thought of before, and defining development needs. Ideas about close collaboration with the firms in the region and with a local newspaper. New ways of involving parents in school life. Possibilities for utilizing the school's neighborhood for teaching and learning. No vision, nor generalized ties emerged.
Results	**Specific ideas** concerning the network emerged, but the participants did not discuss their own roles or responsibilities, or include any implementation issues; no particularized ties emerged.

Table 3. (*continued*)

PHASE 2	PARALLEL GROUP DISCUSSIONS of the network topic with given assignments.
Discussion	**Specific issues:** the role of the teachers in the public-private collaboration is often based on personal relationships, commitment to network collaboration grows, but time and resources are limited. New roles were defined that would be needed in the school network: subject-based and regional collaborators (usually a role of teachers), contact people from the schools, other collaborators, and some kind of superintendent or a "chief networking officer".
Results	**Particularized ties emerged** that defined the roles of the future teachers and related them to each other

Table 4. Simulation 3, topic 2: A future project based learning environment

PHASE 1	*BO: visualized scenario process model of using the Learning Environment, pre-planned by a group of teachers*
Facilitated discussion with Future Recall Method	**Specific issues, and joint issues:** e.g. evaluating the learning management tool in use, involving the students in planning the studies. Envisioning the use of novel learning technology and collaboration with a science center. Identifying problems and requirements to be taken into account in the development.
Results	**Generalized and particularized ties** started to emerge, moving from the abstracts visions towards concrete actions.
PHASE 2	PARALLEL GROUP DISCUSSIONS about the operational processes and practical objectives of the imagined project-based learning environment.
Discussion	**Specific issues, relating back to joint issues:** Concrete new roles and responsibilities that are required to use the new project-based learning environment, a new educational resource shared by many teachers, students and other users. Project room maintenance and ICT-support, space reservation rules, concrete means to share knowledge about the new environment to all Kuninkaantie teachers. "It is the task of all teachers to develop the regionally consistent comprehensive education, not just the teachers participating in the pilot projects and the simulations".
Results	**Particularized ties emerged**: Concrete ideas about the collaboration process with many network partners, e.g. the science center and companies, about the use of novel learning technology, and the roles and responsibilities of the users of the learning environment.

5   Transfer of the Results to the Schools

The first findings from the follow-up interviews tell that the particularized ties that emerged in the three simulations have actually transferred into real life school collaboration. The teachers and principals have been able to develop their collaboration based on the ties that were formed in the simulation projects.

> Principal 1: "There you can tell that collaboration has been realized. Some of the teachers now know each other rather well. This has been a big help, and has built the foundation for the merger [and for collaboration]."

The carefully facilitated simulations have formed the necessary ties for collaboration that other training does not provide:

> Teacher 1: "They [The Media Centre of Helsinki] are not organizing any special training for us Kuninkaantie teachers anymore. But when you know the faces [from the simulations] it is much easier in the training sessions to start [to collaborate]."

> Teacher 2: "It is quite difficult. There should be some outside party, who sells the [collaboration]. We just had a training session, where we were specifically put to the same table [with the teachers of another school]. It was a bit like "talk this through together". But we still were discussing the issue amongst the teachers of our own school, since we didn't know the others. [...]So if there had been someone I knew, we probably would have done it cross-school."

In the larger educational network, the teachers have initiated negotiations with ICT companies. However, the companies' sales people still acted like hardware providers, whilst the schools would like them to become co-developers of the schools' practices and processes. Ties have yet to be co-created between the company people and the teachers, for networked innovation to emerge.

The educational process ideas that were collaboratively developed in the simulations have to a great extent been implemented into innovations in the schools:

1. Project-based teaching, a cornerstone of inter-subject teaching, has been realized, although the course-based curriculum poses challenges.
2. The project-based learning environment that was co-developed in the third simulation was actually built into one of the schools.
3. The ICT-based learning and collaboration environment is widely used for sharing teaching materials and for communicating with parents.

The schools have also been able to develop a **co-creative culture**. The teachers use some methods from the simulation workshops in the development of their teaching, e.g. in a new development project on different learning styles. The principals are re-using internally the visual merger process model of the second simulation workshop, to support the participative management of a new school merger.

6   Discussion

The facilitated simulation workshops supported a stepwise co-creation of both the novel ideas for educational innovations and the necessary ties for their implementation. All workshops started with a facilitated discussion on joint issues related to the innovation, supported by rather abstract visual boundary objects. The participants started to co-create a shared vision, and generalized ties that connected them to the vision. Thereafter, the facilitators applied more concrete visual process models. This enabled the participants to collaboratively develop new process ideas, and to realize how they themselves would relate to the new process and to each other. These particularized ties between the participants were further co-developed in the parallel group discussions that concluded the workshops.

The follow-up study of our case network indicates a "double co-creation" effect of the simulation workshops: Facilitated simulation discussions that apply boundary objects in a systematic way, ensure the co-development of viable process ideas and of the necessary ties, which lead to successful implementation of the innovations in real life. More analysis of the data is still needed to test this hypothesis.

References

1. Carlile, P.R.: A Pragmatic View of Knowledge and Boundaries: Boundary Objects in New Product Development. Organization Science 13(4), 442–455 (2002)
2. Carroll, J.M.: Five reasons for scenario-based design. Interacting with Computers 13(2000), 43–60 (2000)
3. Ewenstein, B., Whyte, J.: Knowledge Practices in Design: The Role of Visual Representations as 'Epistemic Objects'. Organization Studies 30(7), 7–30 (2009)
4. Fenton, E.M.: Visualising Strategic Change: The Role and Impact of Process Maps as Boundary Objects in Reorganisation. European Management Journal 25(2), 104–117 (2007)
5. Hardy, C., Lawrence, T.B., Grant, D.: Discourse and Collaboration: The Role of Conversations and Collective Identity. Academy of Management Review 30(1), 58–77 (2005)
6. Huhta, E., Smeds, R.: Supporting the Management of educational service development in a school network through participative simulations. In: Schönsleben, P., Vodicka, M., Smeds, R., Riis, J. (eds.) Learning and Innovation in Value Added Networks. Proceedings of the 13th IFIP 5.7 Special Interest Group Workshop on Experimental Interactive Learning in Industrial Management, ETH Zurich, Switzerland, Druckpartner Rubelmann, Hemsbach, Germany, May 24-25, pp. 37–46 (2009)
7. Kristensen, M., Kyng, M., Palen, L.: Participatory Design in Emergency Medical Service: Designing for Future Practice. In: Proceedings of CHI 2006 Conference, Montréal, Québec, Canada, April 22-27, pp. 161–170 (2006)
8. Mumford, E.: Participative Systems Design: Structure and Method. Systems, Objectives, Solutions 1, 5–19 (1981)
9. Paavola, S., Hakkarainen, K.: The Knowledge Creation Metaphor – An Emergent Epistemological Approach to Learning. Science & Education 14, 535–557 (2005)
10. Salmi, A., Pöyry-Lassila, P., Kronqvist, J.: Supporting Empathical Boundary Spanning in Participatory Workshops with Scenarios and Personas. Special Issue of International Journal of Ambient Computing and Intelligence (IJACI) 4(4), 21–39 (2012)
11. Smeds, R., Jaatinen, M., Hirvensalo, A., Kilpiö, A.: SimLab process simulation method as a boundary object for inter-organizational innovation. In: Hussein, B., Smeds, R., Riis, J. (eds.) Multidisciplinary Research on Simulation Methods and Educational Games in Industrial Management. Proceedings of the 10th International Workshop on Experimental Interactive Learning in Industrial Management: NTNU Trondheim, NTNU Trondheim, Norway, June 11-13, pp. 187–195 (2006)
12. Smeds, R., Pöyry-Lassila, P.: Co-designing Value Networks in Process Simulations. In: Smed, R. (ed.) Co-designing Serious Games. Proceedings of the Special Interest Group on Experimental Interactive Learning in Industrial Management of the IFIP Working Group 5.7., in Collaboration with the EU Network of Excellence GaLA. Aalto University Publication Series, Science + Technology (October 2011)
13. Star, S.L.: The structure of ill-structured solutions: Boundary objects and heterogeneous distributed problem solving. In: Huhns, M., Gasser, L. (eds.) Readings in Distributed Artificial Intelligence. Morgan Kaufman, Menlo Park (1989)
14. Vargo, S., Lusch, R.: Service-dominant logic: continuing the evolution. Journal of the Academy of Marketing Science 36, 1–10 (2008)

A Grassroots Gaming Simulation:
The Case of "Crossroad"

Toshiko Kikkawa

Keio University

Abstract. The author introduces a game, "Crossroad", which was originally designed as a tabletop exercise to teach disaster preparedness (Kikkawa et al., 2004) and that has been used in an increasing number of fields. In this paper, the author describes the history of the expanding application of this game, focussing especially on the evolution of its rules and content as a result of input from ordinary people who have participated in the game. Through this process, it has become a kind of grassroots gaming simulation tool for the general public. Examination of the development of the game reveals that its simple rules and structure as a frame game have led to its increasing popularity. Indeed, the game is still evolving.

1   The Game of "Crossroad"

In this paper, the author introduces a game, "Crossroad", which was originally designed as a tabletop exercise to teach disaster preparedness and responsiveness. About 10 years after the Great Hanshin–Awaji earthquake in 1995, which had its epicentre beneath Kobe, extensive interviews were conducted with Kobe city employees who had participated in the response to the disaster. The game presents the results of these interviews on "episode cards" that describe dilemmas that people may face in disaster situations (see an example in Table.1).

The original game was played as follows. First, each group of five-to-seven players read each episode card, and each player then predicted the majority opinion by choosing a "YES" or a "NO'" card provided to them. Players received a blue zabuton (point) if they correctly predicted the majority opinion. When a player in a given group offered a prediction that differed from that offered by the rest of the group, s/he gained a gold zabuton (point). A zabuton is a Japanese cushion that signifies approval of an utterance. It is sometimes used in daily Japanese conversations as a symbol in response to an animated comment (e.g., "I give you a zabuton").

Discussion about the situation followed each round. At the end of the game, when all 10 episode cards have been read, the person with the most zabutons (points) won.

The original game, named "Crossroad: Kobe", was sold through a shop affiliated with Kyoto University. A short time later, another variation, "Crossroad for Citizens", was developed by the game designers (including the author) in response to a request by individuals who had participated in the original version to include more mundane episodes because the seriousness of the Kobe situations sometimes embarrassed them.

S.A. Meijer and R. Smeds (Eds.): ISAGA 2013, LNCS 8264, pp. 148–152, 2014.

Therefore, the second game was created and named for citizens who are interested in disasters but who want to discuss them in more casual ways. In 2009, a third version, "Crossroad: Safety Management for Volunteers", became available for purchase.

Since 2004, about 3000 copies of "Crossroad: Kobe" and "Crossroad for Citizens" have been sold through the shop affiliated with Kyoto University. That is, given that one game kit can be played by 20 players, 60,000 players now have access to some version of this game.

2   Variations of "Crossroad"

Many variations of this game have been created and played since its original publication (Kikkawa et al., 2009). In the early stage of its development, the variations focussed on various natural disasters (Yamori, 2008). Later versions did not restrict the themes to natural disasters. For example, situations involving food risks, infectious diseases, interpersonal conflicts, workplace dilemmas, social corporate responsibility (CSR), and so on, have been included as foci of play.

Every episode card follows the same format, which consists of three parts. The first part describes a certain role that is to be played when faced with a dilemma in a disaster situation. A short description of the situation follows. The third part consists of a description of both the YES and NO decisions. Because of the simplicity of both the episode cards and the game rules, people other than game designers can create original episode cards and play the game. Thus, personal experiences or lessons learned from such experiences can be described on cards and shared by many players. Examples of these variations are presented in Table.1. In this sense, the game has been developing at the grassroots level, a phenomenon that may have arisen from two common Japanese practices.

The first is the tradition of Haiku, a very short form of Japanese poetry with 17 morae consisting of three phases of five, seven, and five. Most Japanese are very familiar with the Haiku format, which probably facilitates understanding of how to create variations within the constraints of the structured format of "Crossroad". That is, episode cards contain three parts and can contain only a limited number of characters (i.e., approximately 100 Japanese characters) due to space constraints. Indeed, participants easily understand how to make their own "Crossroad" episodes in response to facilitators' saying, for example, "Making your own episode cards is like creating Haiku."

The second possible underpinning of the grassroots nature of the game may be the multitude of grassroots activities in Japan. These include Quality Circle activities in the workplace and self-help disaster preparedness organisations in communities. In both cases, decisions are usually made in a bottom-up manner, which the author interprets as reflective of a participatory culture and a relatively classless society in Japan. These characteristics may support the popularity of "Crossroad".

After the earthquake off the Pacific coast of Tohoku on March 11, 2011, various actual dilemmas were added to the game. One example is included in Table 1.

Table 1. "Crossroad: Kobe" and variations of "Crossroad"

Number	Situation	Decision(YES or NO)
Kobe1002	You are: A senior administrative officer and 24 hours have passed since an earthquake. City Hall is full of people who have been evacuated, but the hall is not an authorised evacuation centre. Do you force them to leave City Hall?	YES (force them out) / NO (do not force them out)
Food safety	You are: An official of the Ministry of Agriculture. The Japanese government is promoting the safety of genetically modified (GM) soybeans based on a scientific assessment of risk. You are asked by a journalist if you actually allow your daughter to eat GM food. Do you let her eat this food?	YES (let your daughter eat GM food) / NO (do not let her eat it)
Workplace	You are: Working part-time in a fast-food restaurant. A customer is eating bread that is not sold in the restaurant, which is prohibited. Do you ask him to stop eating the bread?	YES (ask him to stop eating) / NO (do not ask him to stop eating)
3.11 Earthquake	You are: A citizen who works as a volunteer at an evacuation centre. You are distributing food; 150 loaves remain, but their expiration date is today. Do you distribute them to whomever wants them?	YES (distribute them) / NO (do not distribute them

These variations enable players to share the experiences of those who originally described the episodes included in the game. Indeed, experiences from the 1995 earthquake have certainly been shared by those who have played the game. For example, a group of people in Kobe who were interviewees during the creation of the original "Crossroad: Kobe" use it at workshops and describe their experiences to people playing the game. Some people who were affected by the March 2011 disaster told the author that the lessons they had learned from playing "Crossroad: Kobe" before the disaster greatly helped them in the sense that the discussion during the game play suggested several strategies that were useful when they were faced with an actual disaster.

3   "Crossroad" as a Flexible Tool for Facilitation

As the rules of "Crossroad" are relatively simple, people also make changes to the original rules or use the game in workshops in combination with other material. Thus, "Crossroad" is a very flexible facilitation tool.

A typical rule change involves expressing one's own opinions instead of predicting the opinions of others. The original rule of predicting others' opinions offers the advantage of encouraging players to express their opinions without hesitation. That is, players are not required to express their own opinions during the game even if later, in the discussion session, they choose to do so. This contributes to reducing mental load involved in discussions of serious dilemmas, such as making triage decisions (i.e., setting priorities about which lives to save) in the face of disaster. In contrast, predicting others' opinions has the disadvantage of being cognitively difficult, especially for elderly individuals and young children, who sometimes find this rule to be confusing. For this reason, a rule asking players to frankly express their own opinions was introduced and is now frequently used.

Another type of change involves conducting the discussion session before the YES/NO decision is made. According to the original rule, the closed-ended question (i.e., YES or NO) precedes the open-ended question (e.g., "Why did you choose 'Yes'?" or "How did you come to that decision?", which is posed during the discussion session. Alternatively, open-ended questions such as "How do you interpret this situation?" or "How do you think this situation will develop?" could be posed before the YES/NO decision is made. In the next step, players choose a course of action (i.e., by answering YES or NO) to follow in each situation.

Other approaches to facilitating the game can also be adopted. Indeed, workshops frequently focus on creating episodes in addition to playing using existing scenarios. For example, one workshop held in Vietnam asked international players to share their experiences with the risks experienced by small-scale miners (Suzuki et al., 2010).

These variations on rules, the inclusion of new episodes, discussions of the experiences behind the episode cards, and facilitation tips are shared among facilitators and participants via the Internet (http://maechan.net/crossroad/shinbun.html, in Japanese only). Facilitators are also able to receive feedback from readers of articles appearing on the website. In this sense, the game does not end after play has concluded. Continuous information exchanges extend the dialogue between facilitators and participants.

Additionally, a grading system for "Crossroad" facilitators encourages people to use the game. Although this system is informal, many use it to improve their facilitation skills. Moreover, informal training sessions for facilitators are also available.

The author would like to add that there are some downsides to this kind of self-evolving game. For instance, the popularity of the game has made it difficult to maintain its quality. Imitations of "Crossroad" that lack the quality of the original game, have been made and used.

4   The Future: Continued Evolution

"Crossroad" continues to evolve and expand its applicability. In the author's opinion, its simple structure and rules as a frame game enable this flexibility. Indeed, it is possible that the game will be used in even more domains in the future. For example, in Japan, it has been gaining popularity in the field of education (i.e., in schools). Additionally, the Facilitators Association of Japan has started to use "Crossroad" as a facilitation tool, and professional facilitators could extend its application beyond its grassroots origins. The author hopes to continue reporting about both this new direction and other areas of future development.

References

1. Kikkawa, T., Yamori, K., Ajiro, T., Hayashi, H.: 'Crossroad: Kobe': A training tool for disaster preparedness and response. In: Kriz, W.C., Eberle, T. (eds.) Bridging the Gap: Transforming knowledge into Action Through Gaming and Simulation, pp. 245–253. SAGSAGA, Munich (2004)
2. Kikkawa, T., Yamori, K., Sugiura, J.: Crossroad and more...: Learning risk communication through gaming. Nakanishia Suppan, Kyoto (2009) (in Japanese)
3. Suzuki, S., Kikkawa, T., Murao, S.: Development of a participatory program for sorting out the risk problems: A case of small-scale miners. Japanese Journal of Risk Analysis 20(1), 41–48 (2010) (in Japanese with English abstract)
4. Yamori, K.: Narrative mode of thought in disaster damage reduction: A crossroad for narrative and gaming approaches. In: Sugiman, T., et al. (eds.) Meaning in Action, pp. 241–252. Springer, Tokyo (2008)

Games for Searching Technology Landscapes

Jop van den Hoogen[1] and Sebastiaan A. Meijer[2,1]

[1] Delft University of Technology, Faculty of Technology Policy and Management,
Delft, The Netherlands
[2] KTH Royal Institute of Technology, Division of Traffic and Logistics, Stockholm, Sweden
j.vandenhoogen@tudelft.nl, smeijer@kth.se

Abstract. The value of gaming simulation for the search process in innovation projects is currently unknown. This paper studies this value in the railway sector. Based on models of search, we build a typology of different search strategies. In a case study we focus on several innovation projects that have either used real-world case studies or gaming simulation as a test method. We found that the use of gaming simulation has two interesting influences. Firstly, they allow searchers to apply a lucky-shot search strategy by which they can recognize promising solutions further outside the local optimum. Game players help to determine the robustness of the solution by searching neighboring configurations during and after the gameplay. Secondly, we found hints that search breadth is limited to the extent that game players are able to recognize the simulated system. We portray both the opportunities and threats for gaming simulation in innovative projects.

Keywords: innovation, search, technology landscapes, gaming simulation, railways.

1 Introduction

In sociotechnical systems both social and technical elements function together to deliver the services the system is designed for. One tool that allows decision makers to search for improvement of sociotechnical systems is gaming simulation. Gaming simulation is based on an operating model of reality [1] to which gaming elements are added [2]: real life operators interact with a simulated system. For the purpose of optimizing a sociotechnical system, ProRail, the Dutch railway infrastructure manager, started using gaming simulation as a test method. Due to budgetary and spatial constraints, optimizing the railway network is more a case of fine-tuning micro elements such as railway switches, operational procedures and signaling than massively building tracks.

Through interviews and participatory observations we studied four innovation projects of which two were carried out using gaming simulation as a decision support tool and two used real-world case studies. Our research question was: How does gaming simulation influence the search strategy employed by decision makers in the context of innovation of railway infrastructures?

S.A. Meijer and R. Smeds (Eds.): ISAGA 2013, LNCS 8264, pp. 153–160, 2014.

2   Theoretical Framework

Innovation can be described as a trial-and-error problem solving activity [3]. Designers generate solutions and test these against requirements after which the results serve as input for another generate-test cycle [4]. To extend the model, Thomke [5] incorporated the notion of learning from tests to redirect the search for solutions in the next cycle and the model consists of four activities:

- Design: based on previous cycles conceive a better solution
- Build: develop models or build prototypes that can be tested
- Run: test the model or prototype in real or simulated use environment
- Analyze: analyze findings and use this for input of the next cycle

2.1   Design as a Search Activity

Similar to Fleming [6] we portray design as the search over a set of combinations of system elements. This set is called the design space [7] and contains all possible combinations of a system. For instance, if a car can be described with 10 elements, each element having 2 states, the design space would be 2^{10} = 1024 combinations. Thus, designers consider the current system and its configuration of elements and conceive of improvements by changing either one or multiple elements and testing this system in the real world or in a simulation

Within this perspective, the NK-model [8] has been extensively used to model search. The model portrays any system as containing N-elements with a finite set of values and random K-interrelations between these elements. The technology landscape reflects the fitness values of all possible configurations and its topography is determined by the complexity of the system. In systems with many interrelated elements or high values for K, the interaction effect of multiple elements causes multiple locally optimal hills to exist (see figure 1).

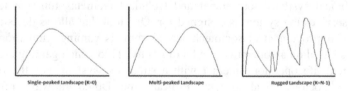

Single-peaked Landscape (K=0)   Multi-peaked Landscape   Rugged Landscape (K=N-1)

Fig. 1. Technology Landscapes for simple and complex systems

2.2   Typology of Search Strategies

In general, search consists of two dimensions: depth and breadth [9-10]. In terms of the NK-framework, depth would involve the amount of configurations under consideration before choosing the most optimal one, while breadth would involve the amount of changes in elements that can done simultaneously in a test. Whereas depth relates to the carefulness by which alternatives are considered, breadth relates to the newness of these alternatives. The dimensions allow us to characterize search using a 2x2 typology:

Table 1. Four search strategies

	High Search Depth	Low Search Depth
High Search Breadth	Exhaustive Search	Lucky shot search
Low Search Breadth	Greedy Search	Modular Search

Exhaustive search would involve studying all possible configurations in the search space and finding the optimal one. However, exhaustiveness is costly and time-consuming [11]. The marginal gains from additional search will decrease as the already found solution is relatively fit.

Greedy search involves evaluating all configurations that differ by one element and are hence neighbors of the current system. Thus, within the boundaries of myopia, all possible configurations are considered [7].

Modular search takes place when search responsibilities are distributed on an element basis. Searchers only alter their element if it increases the fitness of the element, independent of its effects on other elements. The lack of coordination makes this strategy less costly and time-consuming than more extensive search strategies [12].

Search can also involve looking for configurations far away from the current configuration, which we call *lucky shot search*. This search strategy is often related to the discovery of radically novel solutions and the overcoming of lock-ins in local, but suboptimal, optima. However, its lack of depth hinders the learning effect of search. For more complex systems hold that configurations might be dramatically better or worse than its neighboring configurations due to the ruggedness of the technology landscape [13] and for a searcher it is hard to determine what mechanism mainly determined the final fitness value [14]. Applying this strategy thus hinders feedback from test results to subsequent design efforts.

3   Searching for a Better Railway System

To support innovation, ProRail started using gaming simulation as a support tool under the Railway Gaming Suite program (RGS). The games played range from low-tech board games to high tech human-in-the-loop simulators in which a model of a railway system (time table, infrastructure, stations, and trains) is operated by real-life operators such as traffic controllers.

The program allowed us to interview innovation managers and make participatory observations. We use the design-build-run-analyze model of Thomke [5] to partition the findings on four projects and looked for activities that described the search strategy. See Meijer [2] for an overview of the gaming simulations employed at ProRail.

Table 2. Four projects compared

	COUNTDOWN	PASSENGERS	NAU	BIJLMER
Goal:	Decrease dwelling times at stations	Speed up boarding procedure	Make central node of network more robust	Find new control concept
Design	Design team found that delay in giving right-of-way and departure procedure caused dwelling times to be high and variable. Solution was to tell train drivers when to depart through a machine placed on the platform	Design team found that an uneven spread of waiting passengers was the main problem. Solution was to provide information about train length on the time table through colors corresponding with places on the platform.	High dependence between train services was main problem. Solution was to control traffic according to corridors, separating railway lines	Traffic control based on slots instead of fixed points in time table. Concept needed for coping with higher frequencies on main corridors.
Design restrictions	No interference with infrastructure, safety and IT-systems	No changes in infrastructure and railway stations	Not explicitly mentioned	Only focus on operational measures
Elements changed	Additional signal at platform	Timetable, Information on platform, Rolling stock composition	Work division, railway switches, operational rules	Time table, operational rules, communication
Build	Proof-of-concept built and tested on small-size station	Proof-of-concept built and tested on small-size station	Gaming simulation built in few weeks	Gaming simulation built in few weeks
Run	Test was carried out during other test involving an increase in frequency. Heightened managerial attention because of other test.	Test was carried out under ideal circumstances (good weather, little last minute time table changes)	During run, disruptions were to be handled by game players. Both large and small disruptions tested.	Players had problems with unrecognizable interface. During run, participant were able to pinpoint additional measures
Analyze	Dwelling times decreased, but no evidence for a relation with the measure. Uncertain what the influence was managerial attention during test on train driver behavior. Measure also proved to be influencing boarding behavior of passengers	Valuable but very low external validity due to many restrictive assumptions in the experiment. Test assumed static train composition and no last minute changes in platform assignment	Valuable, but additional rules for using switches needed as well as better cooperation between different layers of traffic and train control	Valuable, but additional measures in operational communication, infrastructure and stations needed.
Current status	New test planned for 2013 involving railway stations and level crossings to synchronize departure process	Newer solutions are sought that are less dependent on train composition	Solution implemented, renewed focus on cooperation between layers	Solution not implemented, waiting for higher order measures to be implemented first.

3.1   Design

Project managers in all studied projects were restricted in their search space. Certain elements perform lead functions [15]: these functions are optimized prior to the problem formulation for the project managers. Planning a railway system is hierarchical with infrastructure, safety and rolling stock elements being optimized before operational measures are considered [16]. In all four cases we see empirical evidence for this.

In project 1 we see that project managers simply accept this restriction and find a solution within this space. The signal box that was placed in front of the train did not interfere with any of the other elements such as IT and safety infrastructures. By doing so, the design team cancelled out potentially better solutions just to come to a proof-of-concept quickly. In project 2 we see that the solution is also sought in this confined search space but that based on this solution, additional demands are placed on other elements. Given infrastructural, timetable and rolling stock constraints they found a solution for which the proper working could only be guaranteed if rolling stock composition and timetables were static. Because in gaming simulation the simulated system was easily modified, elements not considered directly under the influence of the project manager entered the search space. For instance, in testing traffic control based on corridors instead of geographical areas around Utrecht, the possible removal of obsolete railway switches was discussed and the Bijlmer game was carried out using a new time table.

3.2 Build

In both projects that used real-world case studies, the additional elements in the search space delayed the process. Only when those elements were changed by other project managers the test could take place. In project 1, ProRail needed cooperation of Dutch Railways for interfering in the operation of train drivers. Furthermore, they had to wait for the high-frequency train transport test to take place. In project 2, the design team looked for a specific day the train operating company could guarantee a static rolling stock composition and chose a specific railway station at which last minute platform assignment changes were not to be expected. Building a gaming simulation takes less time because manipulation of elements in the simulated system did not depend on the actions of other departments.

3.3 Run

The run of a real-world case study is rigid. No changes could be made to elements during the experiment. During the run of a gaming simulation, elements that are part of the search space can be changed. For instance, the strictness of the separation between corridors was dynamically changed to test whether the separation would have to be made permanent and whether railway switches would become obsolete. By doing so, project managers were able to compare different configurations neighboring the configuration that was initially tested.

Search depth is further increased with gaming simulation because game players are able to pinpoint where additional measures are to be taken if the solution needs to be further improved. During and after the Bijlmer game, traffic controllers and machinists showed exactly where extra measures were needed if high-frequency train transport was to be realized using the new traffic control concept. Platform length and additional side-tracks were seen as critical [17]. Project managers neglected these measures since the responsibility for these was located elsewhere. During evaluations of gaming sessions, project managers acknowledged that this information exchange between operational personnel and higher echelon decision makers is rare but valuable. We saw that designers and operators of the system speak different languages from highly conceptual to operational. Gaming simulation promises to serve as an intermediate level of abstraction thus allowing communication [18]. Our findings seem to show how this communication can lead to greedier search.

Search breadth within gaming simulation seems to have limits. The Bijlmer game signaled that the simulated system needs to resemble to a large extent the system the operators are familiar with [17]. It points to two potential shortcomings. Firstly, as gaming simulation is a model of a real system, the more encompassing this reference system is, the more iconic certain elements of the simulated system will be. Especially the analogue versions of gaming simulation can only allow for a certain level of detail. The Bijlmer game, but also other gaming simulations, showed that this level of detail is critical for operators to understand the game. Secondly, studies on operator decision-making have shown how decisions are more based on if-then recipes than on a rational process [19]. Higher search breadths will cause if-then recipes to become invalid. These recipes are built through experience and these might only hold for this specific system. Radical innovations therefore might be difficult to test with gaming simulation.

3.4   Analyze

Since in a case study less manipulation of elements is possible, project managers found it hard to understand what in the end caused changes in system behavior. In project 1, managers saw a decline in the variety of dwelling times but were unsure if this effect was caused by their solution or by extra managerial attention. In project 2, they tested the solution under strict assumptions which were only met on a specific day. After the test it remained highly uncertain if their solution would be valuable under less stringent assumptions such as a changing rolling stock composition and more last-minute changes in platform arrival.

The fact that gaming simulation allows for search to take place even during the run increased the confidence of the project managers in their solution. Results showed what additional measures were needed for their solution. Furthermore, as they were able to observe the system holistically (the games were played either in one room or in several adjacent rooms), they were better able to see what processes were mediator variables between their solution and the behavior of the system.

3.5   Search Strategies

All projects started with a form of lucky shot search. They formulated a solution that differed from the current system in multiple elements and only this solution was tested. We note here that gaming simulation allows more elements to be changed without the interference of other departments and organizations, increasing the ability to test out more new systems. For real-world case studies this strategy remains in effect during the test. Little can be learned from the results and subsequent tests involve another lucky shot in a different direction. Gaming simulation allows for a greedy search to take place around the configuration that is tested in this lucky shot search strategy. Project managers are able to find out if in the vicinity of this solution more optimal solutions lie. Gaming simulation allows for a stronger feedback between test results and subsequent designs.

4   Conclusion

Although both real-world case studies and gaming simulation allow for larger search breadths, the organization of a real-world test that involves manipulation of multiple elements takes more time and effort than the manipulation of an element within a simulated system. On top of that, we see that the greedier search around this configuration during a gaming simulation increases the confidence of the project managers in the test results and enhances learning for subsequent designs. In both gaming simulations project managers learned what additional measures should be taken to make the solution more optimal.

However, using gaming simulation seems to have its limits. More radically new systems that differ on a large number of elements compared to the system operators are familiar with, are potentially difficult to test in a gaming environment.

Using a more conceptual and abstract lens, we were able to signal both the opportunities and threats of using gaming simulation to support innovation processes. However, by solely focusing on search as an activity we neglected organizational issues. Firstly, fitness of a system can be described in multiple dimensions and different stakeholders can describe a system differently. Optimizing a railway system is therefore a multi-dimensional and multi-actor problem. Future research should do justice to these qualities. Secondly, although a cornerstone of our argument we only slightly touched upon the search activity of game players. This needs to be further studied: are they really searching? What is the influence of experience and other traits and to what extent is this activity strategic? Thirdly, we pointed to the problem of testing radically new systems using operators. This problem, and its solution, is an interesting avenue for further investigation.

Acknowledgments.   We like to thank those involved in the Railway Gaming Suite for allowing us to delve deeper in the innovative activities of ProRail.

References

1. Ryan, T.: The Role of Simulation Gaming in Policy-making. Systems Research and Behavioral Science 17(4), 359–364 (2000)
2. Meijer, S.A.: Gaming Simulations for Railways: Lessons Learned from Modeling Six Games for the Dutch Infrastructure Management. In: Perpinya, X. (ed.) Infrastructure Design, Signaling and Security in Railway. IntechOpen, Croatia (2012)
3. Thomke, S.H., Von Hippel, E., Franke, R.: Modes of Experimentation: an Innovation Process -and Competitive- Variable. Research Policy 27(3), 315–332 (1998)
4. Simon, H.A.: The Science of the Artificial, 3rd edn. MIT Press, Cambridge (1969)
5. Thomke, S.H.: Managing Experimentation in the Design of New Products. Management Science 44(6), 743–762 (1998)
6. Fleming, L.: Recombinant Uncertainty in Technological Search. Management Science 47(1), 117–132 (2001)
7. Frenken, K.: Innovation, Evolution and Complexity Theory. Edward Elgar, Cheltenham (2006)

8. Kauffman, S.A.: The Origins of Order. In: Self-organization and Selection in Evolution. Oxford University Press, New York (1993)
9. Katila, R., Ahuja, G.: Something Old, Something New: a Longitudinal Study of Search Behavior and New Product Introduction. The Academy of Management Journal 45(6), 1183–1194 (2002)
10. Rosenkopf, L., Almeida, P.: Overcoming Local Search Through Alliances and Mobility. Management Science 49(6), 751–766 (2003)
11. Kauffman, S.A., Lobo, J., Macready, W.G.: Optimal Search on a Technology Landscape. Journal of Economic Behavior & Organization 43(2), 141–166 (2000)
12. Marengo, L., Dosi, G.: Division of Labor, Organizational Coordination and Market Mechanisms in Collective Problem-Solving. Journal of Economic Behavior and Organization 58(2), 303–326 (2005)
13. Erat, S., Kavadias, S.: Sequential Testing of Product Designs: Implications for Learning. Management Science 54(5), 956–968 (2008)
14. Loch, C.H., Terwiesch, C., Thomke, S.H.: Parallel and Sequential Testing of Design Alternatives. Management Science 45(5), 663–678 (2001)
15. Mihm, J., Loch, C.H., Huchzermeier, A.: Problem-Solving Oscillations in Complex Engineering Projects. Management Science 46(6), 733–750 (2003)
16. Goverde, R.: Punctuality of Railway Operations and Timetable Stability Analysis. Trail, Delft (2005)
17. Meijer, S.A., Van der Kracht, P., Van Luipen, J.J.W., Schaafsma, A.A.M.: Studying a Control Concept for High-frequency Train Transport. In: Infrastructure Systems and Services: Developing 21st Century Infrastructure Networks, pp. 1–6 (2009)
18. Duke, R.D., Geurts, J.L.A.: Policy Games for Strategic Management. Dutch University Press, Amsterdam
19. Klein, G., Orasanu, J., Calderwood, R., Zsambok, C.E.: Decision Making in Action: Models and Methods. Ablex, Norwood (1993)

A Design Science Approach to Youth Care through Online Simulation Gaming

Kees J.M. van Haaster

Utrecht University of Applied Sciences

Abstract. Design thinking, design methodology and design science gain much attention in the domain of gaming and simulation and their theories offer parallels to knowledge exchange in youth care services. Design science research covers context independent engineering and constructionist creativity in pursuit of general values and is built on the synthesis of what already exits and of what might be. Design thinking and design methodology address questions that show similarities to youth care problem solving and future scenario development. The core business of youth care workers is to support positive change and to develop beneficial opportunities for child-rearing. Effective knowledge exchange in networks is the key to successful intervention and simulation gaming might help to study its processes and outcomes, however, we need appropriate validation tools and methods. The author argues that the design and analytical sciences complement each other in research of network exchange. Analytical approaches might develop and test theories about knowledge acquisition and transfer, while design approaches could enhance the exchange of situational, interactional, and interventional expertise. This proposition is explored in a multiple case study in which an analysis tool has been used to structure and study knowledge exchange in youth care networks through simulation gaming.

1 Introduction

There are those who look at things the way they are, and ask why.
I dream of things that never were, and ask why not.
(Robert Kennedy)

With 'youth care' we mean professional support and intervention as to parenting in families and other child-rearing practices. Youth care is imbued with normative decisions about existing and future situations and behavior. In complex problem situations, value-driven decisions about intervention are mostly taken in multi-disciplinary networks of professionals and the quality of exchanges is vital to successful help. Youth care services in the Netherlands are in need of better ways of knowledge exchange (Heijnen, 2010; Van Yperen & Woudenberg, 2011). In research, policy and practices, there is a general consensus about the importance of harmonization, cooperation and coordination in chains and circles of youth care. And yet, we know little about exchange practices. To improve network exchange and professional proficiencies, we must study actions, interactions and performance in networks. The supposition is that online simulations can provide the means and methods for this. Online

S.A. Meijer and R. Smeds (Eds.): ISAGA 2013, LNCS 8264, pp. 161–172, 2014.
© Springer International Publishing Switzerland 2014

simulations are role-playing serious games on the internet, in which actors explore problems to co-create solutions or options for intervention. The results can be used to support positive change in the actual situations. They can also be studied to analyze how practitioners share knowledge, explore the unknown and co-construct meaning and strategies. There are some evident, practical advantages to online exchanges, such as time- and cost effectiveness, however, online simulations place high demands on design and analysis, as well as on its use and methods. We should find appropriate ways to analyze and validate the interactions and outcomes of game sessions and develop methods of transfer between game world and real world. We should bridge collaborative design-like approaches and analytical validation. Social intervention research can be linked to design science and to analytical science, and yet is difficult to formalize, as its problems and situations are highly dynamic and variable. It's academic background is pluriform and cannot be fully described with the scientific language of analytical research. Practices are characterized by uncertainty, ambiguity and values with a plurality of legitimating principles. Often extended participation of all stakeholders is necessary to attain durable results. Researchers make use of a multitude of theories, and we could range social work in the territory of post-normal science. Klabbers (2003, 2009) uses the term 'post-normal science', as opposed to the puzzle-solving strategies of analytical science, which is seen as not always appropriate to resolve societal and environmental issues. Klabbers connects the concept of post-normal science with the broader scope of the design sciences and in particular with objectives and processes of social change. Following the ideas of Herbert Simon (1969), he explains that design science deals with creating things, which do not yet exist, and with enhancing problem situations. Changing problem situations into preferred future states is essentially what social interventionists do. With references to Simon (1969), Klabbers (2009, p. 186 ff.) delineates the difference between design science and natural science as bearing, respectively, prescriptive and descriptive objectives. In his theory of gaming simulation, 'design-in-the-small' refers to prescriptive ways of the construction of games and 'design-in-the-large' is used for prescriptive, normative objectives of game evaluation in larger frameworks of change programs. Both levels require normative prescriptions of purposes and functions of the artifacts. Normativity is central to youth care and to simulation design for knowledge exchange in networks. Choosing the position of an observer to describe practices of youth care or to measure results in change programs, requires a framework of analytical science. Descriptive approaches serve to find, in retrospect, causal links between decisions of systems intervention and the differences between the initial state and the intermediate or final state of a problem situation (Klabbers, 2009, p. 140/2). Klabbers elaborates the views of March and Smith (1995) on design science to clarify some of the basic questions that game science is addressing since the 1950s. The analytical sciences, often considered as the golden standard of scientific research, encompass both the natural sciences and parts of the behavioral and social sciences that favor a positivist approach to their fields of study. For game science and for social intervention research that scope is too restrictive. March and Smith (1995, p. 254) state that the distinction between design and natural science must be based on the research purpose: "natural science aims at understanding and explaining phenomena;

design science aims at developing ways to achieve human goals." Klabbers (2009) adds that design science creates and assesses artifacts to serve human purposes to change situations, against criteria of value and usefulness or purpose. This research paradigm suits many intricate contemporary societal and global problems, of which values are in dispute and unclear. Societal issues often reveal multiple realities of various stakeholders, causing conflicting reality definitions. These conflicts can easily provoke complex and intertwined problems. Many of the most difficult youth care problems share these features and ask for understanding, experimentation and the adaptation of methods to local conditions. The fundamental uncertainty, which stems from the intrinsic indeterminism of complex parenting problem situations, demands new strategies of interthinking (Mercer, 2002), connectedness, situatedness, relationships and contextuality. In systems approaches, the essential properties of a situation arise from the interaction and relationships and they can only be understood in an holistic way. This contextual thinking differs from analytical thinking, though both ways of reasoning are complementary.

In this article, we take a closer look at design thinking and design abilities in youth care network exchange. Designerly ways of practice research are elaborated in a framework that has been applied to a multiple case study of youth care knowledge exchange through online simulation gaming.

2   Design Thinking and Design Abilities

Characteristics of both simulation gaming and youth care knowledge exchange resemble 'designerly ways of knowing' (Cross, 2007). This is a concept in the realm of design science research and refers to the articulation and understanding of design cognition and the idea that designers of all sorts use particular ways of knowing, thinking and action-interaction patterns for the construction of knowledge, actions, and products. In domains of design science, game theory and youth care intervention, actors and researchers are involved in design-like actions of reflection. Analyzing processes and outcomes of online knowledge exchange in networks can reveal aspects that shape collaborative reflection-in/on-action. With the results, we might develop generic knowledge, understanding and validation of interventions in youth care practices. In the last decade, many studies have been published about the idea of developing a 'design methodology of the social sciences' (Dorst, 2004, 2010; Van Aken, 2004, Van Aken, et al 2011). These studies show that there is not one comprehensive, rational design method, but rather a shared diversity of methodologies and techniques. It might be interesting to borrow some of the ideas of design thinking in the pursuit for better, well-timed and more effective ways of youth care help. Design thinking has to do with design abilities (Cross, 1990; Dorst, 2004) and its levels could be equally valid for youth care. By applying the merits and scopes of design thinking, we might identify and relate patterns of interaction and performance to the development of contextual know-how. By way of example, we compare some design aspects of simulation gaming with professional abilities and competences in youth care services:

1. Building models of practice problems is developing contextual know-how and preparing for action, change and development;
2. Modeling situational problems demands a trans-disciplinary attitude and multi-modal thinking and acting;
3. Modeling complex problem situations can lead to a better understanding of values and interests.

Related professional abilities of youth care knowledge exchange:

- *Having interest in complicated problems;*
- *Appreciating systems thinking;*
- *Esteeming the co-evolution of problems and solutions;*
- *Displaying eagerness to draw learning from any discipline or expertise;*
- *Possessing a sense for imaginative and constructive solutions*
- *Valuing multimodal communication and multimedia expression;*

4. Multi-actor role-play allows perspective change and imagination;
5. Change of perspective might lead to appreciation of plurality of interests;
6. Simulation is practicing knowledge-in-action in a realistic way;
7. Simulations facilitate risk assessment and experimentation;
8. Simulations offer experiential and transactional learning.

Related professional competences in networks of youth care:

- *Having professional ambition and being flexible;*
- *Using capabilities of reframing problems into challenges;*
- *Showing awareness of backgrounds and the bigger picture;*
- *Paying respect to social and cultural contexts ;*
- *Taking account of differences in morals, ethics, standards and habits;*
- *Dealing with incomplete information and with uncertainty;*
- *Practicing good cooperation, active participation and taking initiative;*
- *Producing unexpected, novel solutions.*

Drost (2003) states that design problems have a threefold nature: problems and solutions are partly determined, underdetermined and undetermined. This can be compared with youth care knowledge exchange, as the contextual dynamics in complex situations can be extremely messy, fuzzy and unpredictable, with open-ended information, uncertainties and unknown aspects of present and future situations. Thinking like a designer might help to avoid preconceived hypotheses and might stimulate curiosity and learning in iterations of collaborative thinking, in order to find unique solutions to unique problems. Problems and interventions are partly determined. Each situation of youth care contains lots of details to investigate. Part of the information (facts and figures) is beyond doubt and certain circumstances (safety measures) are beyond dispute. The major part of the information, however, is underdetermined. A great deal of the situational information has to be 'excavated' and asks for further investigation. Another part of difficult youth care issues contains undetermined information. Some sides of the problem and of the intervention will remain doubtful, undecided, unknown or obscure. The interpretation is left to professional discretion, in dialogue with clients. In youth care much is left undetermined and cannot be turned into solid accounts. It often is impossible to see straight lines between professional intervention and the actual situational changes. Reflection-in/on-action is of major significance to dialectical processes of youth care intervention and contains many of the same cognitive elements as described in design theories (Dorst, 2010; Van Aken, et al, 2011). Aspects of learning and construction, like imaginative reasoning, conceptualizing, modeling and interpreting, are at the core of youth care. Design thinking requires the ability to see different sides of problems and brings out prediction, intuition, creativity and visualization. A fruitful mode to activate these capacities is through interaction with clients, network actors and fellow-professionals. It is not exceptional in multi-problem and multi-actor situations that social workers have to adapt themselves to shifting, multi-level objectives or to changing rules of engagement. Co-creation might help to overcome personal limits of knowledge, know-how and experience and to adapt to new facts and information. The modus operandi in most youth care practices is doubt. Design abilities help to respond to uncertainty. Knowledge exchange, inspired by design thinking, requires a learning intention and a willingness to explore 'what-if' and 'why-not' questions that can lead to new horizons.

3   Designerly Ways of Practice Research

Despite the fact that youth care practice is more concerned with how things might evolve and change, much social research is dominated by the paradigm of analytical science, thus aiming to describe and explain situations, facts and phenomena and causal relationships. The aim of design-oriented research is the development of theories that help to find solutions for practical problems that add value to situations. Design science is purposeful, prescriptive, value-driven and aims at change in unique contexts and from the perspective of usability. Analysis is a retrospective activity in which the researcher, from the observer's position, comments on process and outcome, aiming at knowledge accumulation and truth finding (Kriz & Hense, 2006; Klabbers, 2009). Design science is concerned with pragmatic values (does it work?), in contrast to the explanatory values (is it true?) of analytical science. We can look at the world, as consisting of physical objects that are in causal relationship, and we can consider the world as a context of intentional actors. (Dorst, 2010). This ambiguity can be projected on the artifacts of gaming simulation. It is pointless to define artifacts only in their physical state, because as such, there would be no place for their normative functions. Reversely, artifacts cannot be fully described in intentional conceptualizations, because their functionalities can only be realized in physical structures that serve them best (Kroes and Meijers, 2002). This is an interesting point of view, as youth care service depends on the prescription of functional characteristics that bear normative judgments for practical action. Artifacts of simulation gaming are contingent on normative judgments (they perform their functions well or badly) and are designed structures that aim at normative choices of intentionality. We must be attentive to the risk of becoming too adherent to behavioristic attempts to fix complex and unpredictable problems with logical frameworks of practice-based evidence. It should be acknowledged that there is not enough proof that the application of scientific methods always leads to success in practices of youth care intervention. The focus of analytical science is mainly on 'tame' problems, whereas 'wicked', untamed problems are more compliant to 'designerly ways' of practical research. Simon (1969) says: *'The natural sciences are concerned with how things are ..., design on the other hand is concerned with how things ought to be.'*. Both paradigms are concerned with future development, however, design science is constructive (shaping new structures), whereas analytical science is explanatory (identifying existing phenomena). Analytical science is generated through replicable results, whereas design science is not primarily directed towards repeatable outcomes. Designerly approaches to practice research evoke open-minded explorations of situations, problems, strategies, and challenge to invent, to think the unthinkable, to question, to stimulate curiosity and active participation. Youth care is about constructing positive change, and yet, this cannot be done without scrutinizing the past and without examining facts, conditions and perspectives. The future is constructed partly on experiences and knowledge from the past and partly on developing prospects of how situations could be.

Hevner (2007) positions design science between the relevancy of context and the rigor of knowledge, thus drawing three design cycles (figure 1)

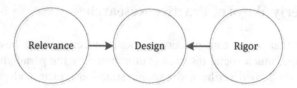

Problem situation   Construct and model   Knowledge base

Fig. 1. Hevner's three design cycles, 2007

The central design cycle signifies the loop of research activities for the construction and evaluation of artifacts, processes and results. Design gets input from the relevance cycle of contextual facts, interpretations and perspectives, and must be based on the rigor cycle of knowledge, evidence and experience for its scientific foundation. The design research cycle iterates between building and evaluating on the basis of pragmatic relevancy from any practice situation, and theorizing and justifying of constructs, models, methods and instantiations, based on scientific consistency. Hevner's view on design corresponds with the design research framework of March & Smith (1995). They relate design activities to output. To link design activities for youth care knowledge exchange to the relevancy of usability and to the rigor of its knowledge base, we added four categories of analysis to the model: knowledge, behavior, performance and intervention (table 1). Design research activities imply building, evaluating, theorizing and justifying, and outputs are derived from constructs, models, methods and instantiations. In *constructs* we define problems and solutions (Schön, 1983). *Models* represent constructs of problem situations or desired future states

(Simon, 1996). *Methods* depict processes and help to explore problems and solution spaces. *Instantiations* demonstrate how constructs, models and methods work together to achieve change (Hevner, e.a., 2004). The design research categories of analysis can be applied to *knowledge*, which is accumulated in simulation games, to *behavior* in actions and interactions, to individual and group *performance* and to *intervention*, including the transfer and effectuation in real situations. The framework concerns design science and analytical science, however, you might say that *build* and *evaluate* relate easily to design, whereas *theorize* and *justify* are primarily associated with analysis (table 1). The model corresponds with findings in earlier studies that show that it is possible to interrelate design science and analytical science (Van Aken, 2004; Mallon & Webb, 2006; Kriz & Hense, 2006; Klabbers, 2006, 2009). It helps to connect domains of academic research and practice based research by focusing on usability and testing theories (Kriz & Hense, 2006).

Table 1. A design research framework (adapted from March & Smith, 1995)

		Design research activities			
		Build	Evaluate	Theorize	Justify
	Construct				
Design research outputs	Model				
	Method				
	Instantiation				
		Knowledge	Behavior	Performance	Intervention
		Design research categories of analysis			

Design approaches may help to develop artifact construction in simulation gaming, though we need empirical evidence and theoretical validation. Analyzing game session results helps to achieve theoretical and justifying consistency. This can be a pragmatic way to understand the behavior of components in complex systems and to experience how changes in one part reverberate into other parts, and to learn how to handle dynamics within systems. Such components in youth care knowledge exchange can be situational cognition, actor participation and reflection on intervention. Collaborative ways of identifying and analyzing problems can generate systems response and active support for future behavior of the actors. These qualitative effects might be achieved by designerly ways of practice research. Funtowicz and Ravetz

(1993) state that not 'truth', as pursued in analytical sciences, but 'quality', as contextual property of scientific information, is a relevant guiding principle in design science research. Quality is connected to contextual values, which are essential input to open dialogues in extended peer communities of everyone affected by the problem situation and with a common concern to reach solutions. As Hortulanus states (2011), in social work practice, different perspectives and ambivalences often lead to conflicting argumentations. We need instruments to address these pluralities of perception. If we design simulation games as shared knowledge workplaces of extended peer communities, the actors would not only be producers of their own enlarged situational cognition, they could also gain responsibility for the co-construction and sustainable co-evolution of future scenarios. In order to achieve durable results in complex multi-actor and multi-problem situations, we must integrate scientific knowledge, technical and contextual expertise and know-how and combine this with local behavior, standards and moralities, thus legitimating local interests, values and future desires of the people involved. Reflective dialogues, as debriefing and learning activity, can serve as what Munda (2004) calls: *social multi-criteria decision making*, in which transparency is the main ingredient, in order to be as clear as possible about the structuring of the problem, the definitions used, the values and interests considered and the ethical positions taken. Social multi-criteria decision making can suit the interdisciplinary character of complex problem situations and can support scientific ways of seeking consistency between assumptions used and results obtained. Social multi-criteria evaluation implies adherence to co-acceptance of responsibility in extended communities and involves ethical judgments and moral positioning (see also Hoijtink & Van Doorn, 2011).

4   Analyzing Knowledge Exchange in Online Simulation Games

March & Smith (1995) argue that design science must not only determine what works, however also why artificial phenomena are successful. Scientists can contribute to both activities of creation and of analytical study by linking multidisciplinary design to a demarcated and specified domain of theory, thus developing an appropriate vocabulary from a cross-over of theories. This is what is envisaged in a case study, in which we compared game theory with youth care theory, in order to design simulation games for professional knowledge exchange[1]. A large body of data resulted from the sessions, in which 55 youth care professionals played the actors in a multi-problem and multi-actor situation from practice. One of the research questions was how to structure the outcome for analysis in order to improve our understanding of the exchange process and to make recommendations for its effectiveness. The overall interest of the study is *to investigate what the significance is of using online simulation games for the improvement of professional exchange in view of better and durable help in child-rearing*. Applying Mark & Smith's framework (table 1), the project spanned three stages of research activities:

---

[1] The model contained four variants and was played in 11 sessions in the *Cyberdam* application (games.cyberdam.nl). Every single player was engaged in one session only.

1. *Build*. The representation of the problem to be studied, the game design and artifact creation;
2. *Evaluate*. The assessment of situational knowledge production, exchange processes and role performance in sessions, and the quality check with the actors about the transfer of outcomes and effects to work practice;
3. *Theorize* and *Justify*. Analyzing and validating outcomes of the research project and the drawing up of hypotheses for further research and validation.

As to building the game, we followed a path of interviewing practice experts for the co-construction of artifacts. Several youth care organizations were involved in preparatory and trial test-simulations to develop concepts and to determine content criteria. The participants were involved in each of the 4 design research outputs of the research framework, though their involvement was more significant in the first and fourth stage:

1. The *construct* of the problem situation;
2. The *model* of the game;
3. The *method* that guides the task accomplishment;
4. The *instantiation* of the game and its evaluations.

The output of the game contains future scenarios, strategy agreements and normative frameworks for intervention. The outcome shows that online simulation gaming helps to explore situations, find new interventions and strategies and supports professional proficiency. In addition, the participants stated that online simulation gaming might help to improve chain-cooperation in youth care networks and to enhance efficacy of team meetings. They think that the tool can be used to improve network collaboration form a cost-effective perspective. Participating in anonymous role-play had reported effects on individual performance and learning-on-the-job. Following the above, we acknowledged that theorizing and justifying ask for a meticulous assessment of rival explanations of findings, including validity threats of the researcher's bias or possible systematic errors (Yin, 2009). Therefore, we compared the subjective experiences with objective inventories of what actually happened in the simulation sessions. The full track-record of all sessions provided a lot of data, but analyzing appeared to be difficult without a structuring logic. The first analysis made clear that the role-players interacted in free sequences of *informing*, *reflecting* and *decision making*. It was hard to see patterns that would explain the interdependencies between interactional behavior and the production of practical knowledge.

Applying sensitizing concepts of knowledge exchange in youth care networks, we built an analysis tool to structure session interaction and results (fig.2).

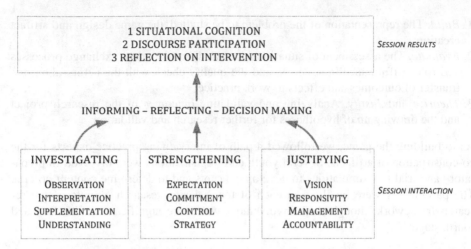

1 SITUATIONAL COGNITION
2 DISCOURSE PARTICIPATION   *SESSION RESULTS*
3 REFLECTION ON INTERVENTION

INFORMING – REFLECTING – DECISION MAKING

INVESTIGATING	STRENGTHENING	JUSTIFYING
OBSERVATION	EXPECTATION	VISION
INTERPRETATION	COMMITMENT	RESPONSIVITY
SUPPLEMENTATION	CONTROL	MANAGEMENT
UNDERSTANDING	STRATEGY	ACCOUNTABILITY

SESSION INTERACTION

Fig. 2. Analysis tool for youth care knowledge exchange through simulation gaming

The analysis tool provides a system to define code categories for structuring mass data from simulation sessions and serves to apply methods of inter-rater reliability. The 1st field of knowledge is about the situation (*situational cognition*), the 2nd concerns the actors (*discourse participation*), and the 3rd covers the accountability (*reflection on interventions*). The three fields of action are: *investigating* the problem situation and broadening options and solutions; *strengthening* the network abilities and relationships; and *justifying* choices of interventions. Each of these three fields of action has been articulated in sub-categories, as indicated. Structuring the session results with this analysis tool helped to analyze the coherency and consistency of exchange activities in the sessions and knowledge production in this particular case. The comparative, proportional ratio of fields of knowledge and action delivered clues and reference points for analysis and for the comparison of players' experiences with factual game data, both on session- and case-level. The tool supports theorizing and justifying in replication and verification research (*design-in-the-large*), and in assessing the model (*design-in-the-small*).

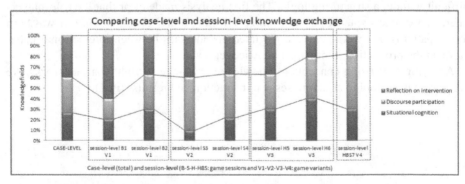

Fig. 3. Comparing case level and session level knowledge exchange

Figure 3 offers a view of the results, as a diagram of the accumulated practical knowledge on case level (total) and on session level. In addition to comparing knowledge production, we get an impression of the differences in session performance in all action fields and their respective categories. With the help of the analysis tool, we could produce diagrams and overviews on all different levels of knowledge production and session interaction. By way of example, figure 4 displays the variances of session performance in action field 'justifying choices of interventions' and its subsequent categories. Likewise, each of the other action fields and categories leads to a different graph and sheds light on that particular concept, revealing unique details about performance and productivity.

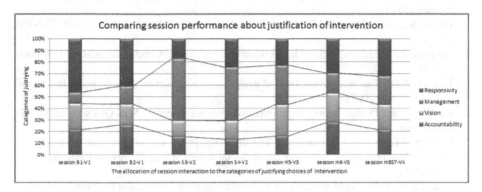

Fig. 4. Comparing session performance about justifying choices of intervention

Comparing these results and discussing possible backgrounds and relations between outcome, design choices and players' behavior, is vital to learning cycles in youth care networks. The model proved to be useful for the confrontation of players' experiences and factual information about the interaction and knowledge production in sessions, though additional external validation research is necessary.

5   Conclusion

Design-like approaches of online simulation gaming for knowledge exchange in youth care networks contribute to game design theory and youth care theory and applying design abilities to youth care knowledge exchange in online simulation gaming supports deep reflection-in/on-action. Session outputs must be related to research activities and research analysis, in order to investigate the usability of the model and to analyze the effects in view of durable and well-timed interventions. The in-game behavior and the elicitation of case-related knowledge must be studied under the rigor of explanatory ways of theorizing and justifying. This calls for well-defined and grounded rules of replication and verification, in which design approaches alternate with hypothesis testing. In the cross-over of design thinking and simulation gaming in value-driven domains like youth care, we can improve evaluation tools and methods in order to develop and test tentative propositions in consecutive design research activities.

References

1. van Aken, J.E.: Management research based on the paradigm of the design sciences. Journl of Man. Studies 41(2), 219–246 (2004)
2. van Aken, J.E., Andriessen, D., et al.: Handboek ontwerpgericht wetenschappelijk onderzoek, Boom, Den Haag (2011)
3. Cross, N.: The nature and nurture of design ability. Design Studies 11(3), 127–140 (1990)
4. Cross, N.: Designerly ways of knowing. Birkhäuser, Basel (2007)
5. Dorst, K.: Investigating the Nature of Design Thinking. In: Future Ground: DRS Conference, Melbourne (2004)
6. Dorst, K.: The nature of Design thinking. In: Proceedings of the 8th DTR Symposium, Sydney (2010)
7. Funtowicz, S.O., Ravetz, J.R.: Science for the post-normal age. Futures 25(7), 739–755 (1993)
8. Heijnen, P.: Jeugdzorg dichterbij. Werkgroep Toekomstverkenning Jeugdzorg, Den Haag (2010)
9. Hevner, A.R.: The three cycle view of design science research. Scandinavian Jrn. of Inf. Syst. 19(2), 87 (2007)
10. Hevner, et al.: Design science in information systems research. MIS Quarterly 28(1), 75–105 (2004)
11. Hoijtink, M., Doorn, L.V.: Bestuurlijke turbulentie in het sociaal werk: de uitdaging van meervoudige coalitievorming. Journal of Social Intervention: Theory and Practice 20(3), 5–23 (2011)
12. Hortulanus, R.P.: Ambivalenties in het sociale domein. Humanistics University Press, Utrecht (2011)
13. Klabbers, J.H.G.: Gaming and simulation: Principles of a science of design. Simulation and Gaming 34(4), 569–591 (2003)
14. Klabbers, J.H.G.: Artifact assessment versus theory testing. Simulation and Gaming 37(2), 148–154 (2006)
15. Klabbers, J.H.G.: The magic circle: principles of gaming & simulation. Rotterdam, Sense (2009)
16. Kriz, W.C., Hense, J.U.: Theory-oriented evaluation for the design of and research in gaming and simulation. Simulation & Gaming 37(2), 268–283 (2006)
17. Kroes, P., Meijers, A.: The Dual Nature of Technical Artifacts. Techné: Research in Philosophy and Technology (2002)
18. Mallon, B., Webb, B.: Applying a phenomenological approach to games analysis: A case study. Simulation and Gaming 37(2), 209–225 (2006)
19. March, S.T., Smith, G.F.: Design and natural science research on information technology. DSS 15(4), 251–266 (1995)
20. Munda, G.: Social multi-criteria evaluation. European Journal of Operational Research 158(3), 662–677 (2004)
21. Mercer, N.: The art of interthinking. Teaching Thinking 7, 8–11 (2002)
22. Schön, D.: The Reflective Practitioner. Basic Books, New York (1983)
23. Simon, H.A.: The sciences of the artificial. MIT Press, Boston (1969 & 1996)
24. Yperen, T.V., van Woudenberg, A.: Werk in uitvoering. Bouwen aan het nieuwe jeugdstelsel. NJi, Utrecht (2011)
25. Yin, R.K.: Case study research: Design and methods. Sage Publications, Inc. (2009)

Analyzing the Social Dynamics of Non-Player Characters

Magnus Johansson, Björn Strååt, Henrik Warpefelt, and Harko Verhagen

Dept. of Computer and Systems Sciences, Stockholm University,
Forum 100, S-16440 Kista, Sweden
{magnus,bjor-str,hw,verhagen}@dsv.su.se

Abstract. Much of the current research into artificial intelligence (AI) for computer games has been focused on simple actions performed by the characters in games (such as moving between points or shooting at a target, and other simple strategic actions), or on the overarching structure of the game story. However, we claim that these two separate approaches need to be bridged in order to fully realize the potential of enjoyment in computer games. As such, we have explored the middle ground between the individual action and the story – the type of behavior that occurs in a "scene" within the game. To this end we have established a new model for that can be used to discover in what ways a non-player character acts in ways that break the player's feeling of immersion in the world.

1 Introduction

Games provide challenges and immersive experiences to the player. In both areas non player characters (NPCs, the characters in games that are "played" by the computer rather than by a human player) play a role. Apart from the visual impression it is NPC behavior that is key. Game AI is the branch of game research and development focused on creating fitting NPC behavior. Unfortunately, just as in AI in general, game AI is based on what (Russell and Norvig 2009) calls "rational agency" rather than "agents that act humanly". Thus, most work on game AI is focused on solving the problem of ,e.g., route finding and planning in the most efficient way, making the most common path finding algorithm (A*) the main AI challenge in computer games AI. In this article we will not further expand on path finding algorithms since this problem can be considered largely solved in most current games (Juul 2003). Instead, we like to address the behavioral properties of Non Player Characters (NPCs) and the social awareness of and amongst NPCs aiming for humanlike behavior in NPCs. In essence, we will describe an area that is largely unexplored and thus holds a large potential for improving player enjoyment of games.

One central aspect of games is that they need to be challenging and lead to some outcome that is valued by the player in order to be interesting (Juul 2003). Challenges deal primarily with obstacles associated with reaching predefined goals in a game. Challenge or, to use another word, struggle gives games meaning, and has different aspects as shown by (Costykian 2002):

S.A. Meijer and R. Smeds (Eds.): ISAGA 2013, LNCS 8264, pp. 173–187, 2014.

"Part of the struggle lies in the opposition posed by monsters and NPCs; part of it in exploration of the world and the story; part of it in traps or puzzles posed in the game's physical world, or in social difficulties posed in the game's social realm" (Costykian 2002, p.15)

All these aspects of struggle are also associated with possible rewards in order to create a meaningful experience for the players (Salen and Zimmerman 2004), where exploring the world, unlocking parts of the narrative when defeating monster/NPCs, or solving puzzles are all part of creating a balanced challenge for the player.

The concept of immersion has been used to describe the sensations of being absorbed by a game as "[d]eep but effortless involvement, reduced concern for self and sense of time" (Sweetser et al 2012, p.2) and further describe the concept of "player enjoyment" (ibid.) which coincides with the "flow"-concept (Csikszentmihalyi 1990). Immersion has also been studied in an interview study of players by Brown and Cairns (2004), indicating that there are different degrees of involvement or immersion for players, ranging from engagement, engrossment, and finally total immersion. The relation between flow and immersion is mentioned in e.g., (Salen and Zimmerman 2004; Sweetser et al. 2012). Immersion is also related to the challenge of gaming and the flow-concept, where a balance in the difficulty of the challenge is needed in order to make the player enjoy the game. When immersion is established it also makes players more prone to overcome difficulties in the game (Cheng 2005).

In Ermi and Mäyrä (2007) a very useful distinction between three different types of immersion is presented:

- *Sensory-based immersion* – This type of immersion is related to the audiovisual execution of games and the experience enabled through for instance a three dimensional game world.
- *Challenge-based immersion* – The second type of immersion is based on achieving a satisfying balance between challenges and abilities, related to motor skills, mental skills such as strategic or logical thinking, and even problem solving.
- *Imaginative immersion* – The third type of immersion is directed at capturing the imaginative aspects of being immersed in characters and story elements or the game, and also being immersed in the world.

The three types of immersion have much in common with Costykian's aspects of game struggle presented above and also point out some of the aspects of games game developers try to refine. In games such as L.A Noire or Façade the emotional aspects of NPCs are part of creating the illusion of smart adversaries, contributing to imaginative immersion. In Skyrim , The Witcher 2: Assassin of Kings and Assassin's Creed 3 both the sensory and imaginative immersion are stimulated. Lastly in RAGE and Starcraft 2 the opponents of the game, the NPCs, are strategically competent leading to a more interesting challenge for the player and therefore are part of the challenge-based immersion.

Of these types of immersion it is perhaps challenge-based immersion that most directly influences immersion and flow in games where skills and tactics are more pronounced.

2   Analyzing NPC Behavior

Previous research into the area of NPC behavior has, as seen above, primarily been focused on the description of the atomic actions taken by NPCs – such as moving to a specific position or firing on a given enemy. The actions taken by these NPCs usually affect a rather limited scope of time. In essence, they deal with acting in "the now" and have at best a tenuous connection to the overarching story of the game.

On the opposite end of the spectrum, there has been some research into how characters (and by extension, NPCs) fit into the story of the game. One example of this is the work of Lankoski (2004) that explores how characters must act within the context of the fictive world that they inhabit. Much like in a play or movie, each character must be described in such a way that the player can relate to and feel some sort of empathy for it. According to Lankoski, this is done by describing the character's form (sex, race, gender, age) as well as describing the inner working and behavior of the character, such as mannerisms, temperament, and attitudes. Furthermore the character must be contextualized in the game world – in short it must be described from the aspects of social ranking, occupation, and affiliations.

However, the space between these two extremes is at the moment poorly described. Some inroads have been made by Lankoski and Björk (2007), Johansson and Verhagen (2011), and Warpefelt and Strååt (2013) but these studies are as yet limited to describing in what ways the NPCs violate the player's sense of immersion in different situations. Given that we have a fairly firm grasp of how NPCs should act in reaction to a certain stimulus (the now) and how NPCs should act in context to the ongoing narrative (the story), the continued exploration of the middle ground between these types of behavior become more important.

Analyzing NPCs from the story perspective would focus on the overarching narrative of the game and the characters place therein while the scene approach instead would focus on the character in an occurring situation. While it is impossible to completely disengage a situation from the ongoing narrative not all NPCs in a game will be relevant in the grand scheme of things. These could for example be the type of NPCs whose purpose in life, as described by Bartle (2003), is to be "killed for loot". While these characters may not matter much, they must still exhibit behavior that is consistent and believable for their role. However, in order to be able to describe these types of behavior we need tools that let us do so.

2.1   Measuring Tools for the Believability of NPCs

Johansson and Verhagen (2011) proposed a first step towards an evaluation method for NPCs, based on the original "social fractionation matrix" by Carley and Newell (1994). Carley and Newell's matrix was developed in an attempt at visualizing what they called a Model Social Agent (MSA) using several sociological theories of human behavior, where the MSA is a close approximation of a human being. The study by Johansson and Verhagen showed that by mapping existing NPCs to the matrix would indicate a lack of social awareness between NPCs, as well as indicate the structural and static representation of NPCs in games. A continuation of this study described by

Warpefelt and Strååt (2013) found that using all combinations of traits from the fractionation matrix NPCs did not display that many possible behaviors.

A similar evaluation has also been performed by Lankoski and Björk (2007) using design patterns to qualitatively describe the believability of an NPC. Unfortunately, Lankoski and Björk's study has the drawback that the design pattern approach is rather fluid and may lack transferability between cases. The approach of fine-grained qualitative evaluation using loosely defined design patterns is also rather time consuming. This drawback was addressed by Warpefelt and Strååt, who as mentioned above utilized a modified version of the Carley and Newell fractionation matrix to locate specific areas where the NPC's behavior may be considered immersion breaking while maintaining some level of transferability and comparability between games.

However, Warpefelt and Strååt (2013) also found that their matrix's expansive nature (with 80 different values) made it somewhat unwieldy to use and that some of the values in their matrix could be removed without impacting the analytical capability of the model. Warpefelt and Strååt also found that not all values in the Carley and Newell fractionation matrix were applicable for NPCs analyzed from a black box perspective since they deal with the internal workings of an agent rather than externally visible actions. Lastly, they found that the matrix was unable to account for some aspects of NPC behavior, such as NPC pathfinding and navigation.

3   Constructing the Game Agent Matrix

In order to remedy the shortcoming mentioned in (Warpefelt and Strååt 2013) we propose a matrix adapted for NPCs (game agent matrix) that remedies the two main issues of its predecessors; the large number of values, and the inability to account for pathfinding issues. We do not need the comparison between Carley and Newell's Model Social Agent (MSA) (1994) and different types of NPCs. In Russell and Norvig (2009), AI is introduced starting from an agent perspective. Research in AI is by the authors classified into 4 different flavors: Systems that think like humans, systems that act like humans, systems that think rationally, and systems that act rationally. Whereas we aim at systems that (to some extent) act as humans (AI in the sense as proposed by Alan Turing), (Russell and Norvig 2009) focuses on rational agents. In the Carley and Newell matrix (Carley and Newell 1994), the different rows indicate different views on how to model systems that think as humans; while the columns discuss which environments the systems act in. In (Russell and Norvig 2009) different types of environments are discussed as well. However, since they start from a rational individualistic perspective, most of the characteristics of the environment are directly related to a task. The only exception is the presence of other agents, i.e. acting entities that are modeled as such. For our model we want to combine the following agent types from (Russell and Norvig 2009): simple reflex agents (i.e., having no model of the changes of the world), and model-based reflex agents (i.e., agents that have a model of the world on which it projects possible changes as a result of its own actions and an evolutionary force which may involve other agent's actions). We wish to add a category of agents to address the multiagent aspect in a more meaningful sense, namely agents that have a model of the world containing other intentionally acting entities with which it can together change the world. As such, we've replaced the original agent types in Carley and Newell's matrix with three types of agents:

- Acting agents (simple reflex agents). The *acting* agent does not change its behavior according to changes in the context since it is static and executes the actions it is created to perform. Therefore the acting agent is unaware of other agents that appear in the columns: "multiple agents" situation, the "social structural" situations, situations marked by "social goals" and "cultural historical".
- Reacting agents (model-based reflex agents). The *reacting* agent differs slightly from the acting agent in that it perceives changes in its environment and can react accordingly. When the reacting agent is socially aware, social knowledge and models of others is seen as a prerequisite.
- Interacting agents. The *interacting* agent has a continuation of actions that can have various levels of dynamics, depending on the information that is available in the agent's environment. It also reacts dynamically in contrast to the reacting agent and the acting agent that does so in a less dynamic and changing way.

	Single Agent	Multiple Agents	Social Structural	Social Goals	Cultural Historical
Act	Goal directed Route following Uses language Uses tools	N/A	N/A	N/A	N/A
React	Adaption Acquires information Crisis response Interruptability Lack of awareness Models of self Rapid emotional response Navigation	Learns from others Models of others	Class difference Mob action Social ranking	Disillusionment	Advertising Institutions Roles
Interact	N/A	Face to face Group making Social interaction Turn taking	Coercion	Clan Wars Cooperation Group conflict Patriotism Power struggles Team player	Etiquette Norm maintenance Sanctions

Fig. 1. The game agent matrix

Our Game Agent Matrix (see figure 1) also uses the columns from the adapted Carley and Newell fractionation matrix used by Warpefelt and Stråât (2013), however the "Real Interaction" column from (Warpefelt 2013; Carley and Newell 1994) is since all interaction with agents our new model is aimed at identifying is in real-time. The relevant values have been subsumed into other columns.

With the structure in place the cells in the Game Agent Matrix were populated using data produced for (Warpefelt and Stråât 2013). In order to populate our matrix we examined all values from Warpefelt and Stråât's updated fractionation matrix that were found to have significantly impacted1 immersion.

It should be noted that not all rows and columns result in meaningful combinations. For example, a purely acting agent will not be aware of other agents, and as such no values exist for the intersection of Act/Multiple agents. Similarly, there are no meaningful behaviors that can be categorized as Interact/Single agent since agents cannot interact without there being more than one agent. The finished matrix can be seen in figure 1 and the definitions of the values found in it can be found in appendix 1.

4   Evaluating Games Using the Game Agent Matrix

Like Warpefelt and Stråât (2013), we have taken the aforementioned black-box perspective, and will be reusing some of the video data from that study. These observations were made by playing the games "as a player would". Warpefelt and Stråât described this as both playing the crafted story line, but also roaming around the game world in order to discover behaviors not directly related to the story line.

In this explorative study, which is aimed at evaluating our new Game Agent Matrix as a tool for NPC believability evaluation, we studied three games; L.A. Noire, Skyrim and RAGE. These games each primarily utilize a different type of immersion, where L.A. Noire tries to immerse the player using motion captured actors and facial expressions (sensory based immersion), while Skyrim uses it's Radiant AI system to create a dynamic and adapting world, ergo imaginative immersion. Finally, RAGE features enemies who adapt to the player's combat tactics in order to provide more realistic enemies, thus providing challenge-based immersion.

These games were compared against our Game Agent Matrix, where each value in the matrix was graded as increasing, maintaining or reducing the player's sense of immersion. This analysis will be broken down by agent type. For each relevant combination agent type and social situation (figure 1), we'll present a summarized version of our findings. The values for the different categories in the game agent matrix can be found in appendix 1.

---

[1] Warpefelt and Stråât's study consisted of two iterations. In this case, "significant" means that the value occurred more than once in one study, and at least once in the other.

4.1   Acting Agents

Acting agents are, due to their non-processing of the outside world, limited to the Single Agent social situation.

Single Agent
In this cell, all values were almost exclusively found to be portrayed in a manner that was beneficial for the player's sense of immersion. The only exception we found was that a single fugitive in Skyrim exclaimed "We're routed! Fall back!" when he was clearly alone, thus violating the Uses language value.

This result isn't all that surprising. The values in the Act/Single agent intersection are fairly basic behaviors that almost all NPCs in a modern game will exhibit. Route following is one of the products of many years of A* research, and is rarely a problem anymore. Furthermore, making an NPC seem goal directed is trivial as it simply has to act in rather direct ways without exhibiting doubt. A similar situation exists for the use of language or tools – these can simply be "pantomimed" by playing sound clips originating from the NPCs and by putting tools (such as weapons or cameras) in their hands.

4.2   Reacting Agents

The reacting agents encompass all of the possible social situations, with half of the values residing in the Single Agent social situation. Whereas acting agents portrayed a very convincing picture, the same is unfortunately not true for reacting agents. Many of the values describing reacting agents in different social situations indicated that the NPC behavior was immersion breaking.

Single Agent
In Single agent situations, the games showed overall negative values – the only value that was rated as only positive was Rapid emotional response. Overall, only Adaption, Crisis response, Rapid emotional response and Navigation showed non-trivial (i.e. occurring more than once) positive values. The positive reinforcement in regards to adaption often showed itself as enemies adapting in combat. For example, an archer in Skyrim may pull out a dagger if the player attacks them in melee and a soldier in RAGE will duck down into cover if he is hit. Displays of Crisis responses are similar; NPCs in RAGE will run away if the player gets too much of an upper hand and enemies low on health in Skyrim will beg for their life if badly wounded. Positive reinforcement of the Rapid emotional response value was displayed when another entity performed something that may elicit an emotional outburst, for example when the player hit almost hit a pedestrian while driving in L.A. Noire. Lastly, Navigation was usually reinforced by NPCs moving in a convincing way, such as a police officer navigating around the player and a lot of furniture while at a crime scene in L.A. Noire. However, the reinforcement provided by navigation was usually rather small.

As for values that were rated as negatively impacting immersion, the foremost of these was Lack of Awareness. Like Warpefelt and Strååt describe in their article, this is exhibited as an NPC being either too aware or completely unaware of events occurring around it. In L.A. Noire enemy thugs would be instantly aware of where the player is if he relocated without them seeing him moving (sneaking behind a wall, for example). In Skyrim, town guards would immediately know when the player broke the law without anyone calling for a guard. They would attack the player without trying to straighten out what actually happened. In RAGE, the Lack of Awareness trait is somewhat tightly tied to Adaption, since enemies would often fail to dodge grenades thrown by players. This lack of Adaption further ties into Crisis Response and Interruptability. In another example from Skyrim, the player encounters a hunter in the forest. A nearby crab attacks the hunter as he begins talking to the player. Instead of terminating the conversation and defending himself from the crab, he finishes the conversation with the player and promptly drops dead once the conversation ends. This also shows a distinct lack of Models of self, since the hunter is obviously unaware of the bodily harm being inflicted on him.

Multiple Agents
In multiple agent situations, reactive agents only displayed behavior related to Models of others. This was primarily displayed as negative, but was positive in some cases. A negative example is the hunter and crab example from Skyrim seen in the previous section, where the hunter is obviously unaware of the crab and its actions. In RAGE, the NPCs exhibited behavior that was considered to reinforce immersion. Once the player shot enough of their number with a sniper rifle, the group decided to flee. This shows that they are aware of other NPCs and what happened to them.

Model of others is in essence a somewhat complicated value. On one hand it enables the NPCs to act according to what other agents are doing and where they are, but on the other hand it seems that tracking a lot of NPCs may be difficult. Furthermore, we found no examples of Learns from others. This should not be taken as surprising as the sample size for this study is rather small, and that it was not a commonly occurring value in Warpefelt and Strååt's study.

Social Structural
In a social structural situation we found that reactive agents displayed class differences and social ranking in an immersion-reinforcing way. These two were often displayed at the same time, since class is often tied into social ranking, for example when NPCs interacted with a local king ("jarl") in Skyrim.

Social Goals
Unfortunately we were unable to find Disillusionment in any of the games. As with Learns from others (see the Multiple Agents above) this may be because of a limited data set.

Cultural Historical
Behavior related to cultural historical situations were found in the games, albeit rarely. Reacting agents primarily exhibited behavior that reinforced the sense that there are roles and institutions in the world, for example by acting like there are police officers and a police force in L.A. Noire or by referring to, and acting as, governing bodies in RAGE or Skyrim. We also found that NPCs would perform Advertising in Skyrim, where merchants would hawk their wares (as it were) in the town square.

It should, however, be acknowledged that the behaviors here are often either acted out in a very static manner (for example advertising), or induced by the scenario, i.e. the existence of a king or a police force. In essence, this is where our model begins to touch on Lankoski's design rules (Lankoski 2004).

4.3   Interacting Agents

Interactive agents encompass all the social situations except for single agents, since it would be impossible for an interactive agent to interact with itself. The values here, to the extent that they were found, were generally positive. However, the rate of occurrence was rather low.

Multiple Agents

In this social situation the agents most often reinforced immersion by performing actions related to the Face to face and Social interaction values. Agents would turn towards each other when speaking, and generally interact in a realistic way. This was very evident in L.A. Noire's interview scenes.

As for negative impact on immersion, NPCs in Skyrim would sometimes not "understand" when it was inappropriate to speak at the same time, for example telling the player something while he was involved in a conversation with another NPC. This has a negative impact in immersion in relation to the Turn taking value.

We did not find any immersion-affecting behavior related to Group Making.

Social Structural

We were unfortunately unable to find any evidence of Coercion being performed in any of the games. Once again, this may be because of the limited data set.

Social Goals

In the social goals situation we found that the NPCs exhibited behavior related to Cooperation, Group conflict and Team player. In all cases the behavior served to reinforce the player's feeling of immersion. However, these behaviors were shown only rarely. The most common of the three was Group conflict, in which NPCs in all games worked together to fight an opposing faction. This was primarily shown in combat scenarios. The same can be said for Cooperation, where the NPCs would utilize cooperate in order to defeat their enemies. Team player behavior was exhibited when one of the NPCs "took one for the team", for example covering the retreat of their fellows.

It should be noted that the groups above were often pre-defined by the story line, and as such not an evidence of the NPCs dynamically forming groups. Furthermore, while NPCs could be said to show cooperation by building towns, this was not a product of NPC behavior as much as it was of the story of the game. As such it falls inside the domain of Lankoski's work.

Cultural Historical

In the cultural historical situations we found that behaviors related to all values were exhibited by interactive agents. As with many of the behaviors for interactive agents, they appeared only rarely. The most commonly enforced value was Sanctions, which was usually performed by NPCs who tried to uphold the law. For example, if the player drives badly in L.A. Noire his partner will call him a maniac. Similarly, guards in Skyrim will attack the player if he commits a crime. We also found that the NPCs in Skyrim will act according to Etiquette, for example using honorifics when addressing the king.

As for negative reinforcement, we found that the NPCs in L.A. Noire didn't interfere with the player when he was following a woman down the street. While this would have had impact on the game mechanics, the situation becomes slightly ridiculous when no one reacts when the player jumps over fences into private yards and kicks trashcans across a parking lot.

Once again, these values were not commonly occurring, and when they were they were more a product of the story than the behavior itself. The possible exception here would be sanctions, which is actually exhibited as dynamic behavior.

5   Conclusions

In this article we have used a refined tool for measuring the believability of NPCs and also where NPCs might jeopardize or break immersion in games. The data set was limited and only consisted of videos from 3 games, with approximately 2 hours of videos from actual game play for each of the games. Even though the initial data set for analysis was limited it rendered both negative and positive examples of immersion breaking and enhancing effects in the games studied.

5.1   Conclusions Regarding Method

The method used in this paper is in its early stages of development and even though useful for detecting and describing specific both negative and positive traits of NPC complexity, some alterations and tune-ups remain to be addressed. In its current the state the method is useful for finding issues with NPCs, but some of the values in the matrix are just too similar and the "nuances" of these definitions too fine-grained to be illustrative for most games. In addition one effect of Lack of awareness is that it, although a highly illustrative name for a value in the matrix, is prone to create confusion when assigned a negative value, due to the fact that the NPC failed to exhibit realistic Lack of awareness – which creates a double negative of sorts. The use of this value should more intuitive if it was called Awareness. This does not affect the descriptive power of the model since the method allows values to be assigned both negative and positive values. As such it is still possible to describe a Lack of awareness, but without the mental gymnastics of a double negative.

The two values that we added based on the conclusions presented in (Warpefelt and Strååt 2013), Route following and Navigation, proved to be quite useful. In essence, it lets us capture problems that are unique to the medium of agents in virtual worlds and lets us quickly identify if there are fundamental problems with the behavior of NPCs. It should be noted that the distinction between Route following and

Navigation isn't always clear, but also that it is important to distinguish between the NPC completely failing to follow a route through the world, and the NPC being unable to account for unexpected obstacles.

5.2   Conclusions Regarding NPCs and Games AI

As the results indicated there are levels of complexity that most standard NPCs are capable of displaying to a satisfying level, and mostly deal with the single agent acting in the world. Where the expectations on the actions performed by the NPC increasingly becomes more complex, much of these actions are performed in ways that disrupt gameplay, and also at times result in hilarious situations. One such example is the levelheaded hunter in Skyrim that politely engages in conversation while slowly being chewed to an agonizing (and rather unnecessary) death by a large crab. There are however other problems than Lack of awareness, no existing Model of self and Interruptability that even though responsible for some of the most illustrative examples in the data set, are only a subset of immersion breaking examples. Perhaps one of the most important aspects in the data set was behavior exhibited by NPCs that for some reason was not motivated by the narrative, indicating not only a Lack of awareness but also a lack of understanding for the context, in ways that are directly addressed in Lankoski's design rules (Lankoski 2004). In essence, the NPCs we encountered in our study were very well-developed when it came to the values in the intersection of Act/Single agent, but when one starts trying to make behavior outside this single box into account the believability of the behavior quickly deteriorates. In the intersections of React/Single agent and React/Multiple agent, the behavior is spotty at best and fails to uphold the immersion about as often as it manages to do so. If we move beyond this, and also include the Interact agent type and the Social Structural situations, we find that the behavior will either not be exhibited at all, or if present will almost always fail to uphold immersion. Values related to the Cultural Historical are likewise rarely exhibited, and when they are it is almost always within the context of a scripted sequence.

One of the most illustrating aspects of NPCs that was found during the data collection was that there is indeed an intention to create an illusion of smart, believable NPCs, but most of the interaction that goes beyond single agent acting in the world, when done successfully be part of a scripted sequence, such as a "playable cut scene". The NPCs of Skyrim, from a black box perspective seem to be much more complex in their behavioral repertoire compared to the NPCs in the rest of the data set, but they still lack models of self in combination with models of others.

As can be seen in the examples above, these problems mainly affect Skyrim. We believe that this is related to Skyrim being populated by slightly more advanced agents and the use of the Radiant AI system. In essence, Bethesda attempted to implement more dynamic NPC behavior with the advanced AI in Skyrim, and it sometimes turned out to cause problems. This reminds us of the results of (Johansson et al. 2012), where the developers said that the effort put into game AI isn't always visible. This is contrasted to RAGE and L.A. Noire where the dynamic behavior is fairly uncomplicated, and the more advanced behavior is handled by handcrafted scripted sessions.

Our intention here is to point out that NPCs in games are designed to seem believable, flawed and interesting, but the strategy for displaying these traits heavily relies on the designers temporarily taking control of the NPCs, suppressing their "natural" behavior in order to support the illusion of the NPCs being capable of showing emotions, models of others, Interruptability and Models of self. When these traits are implemented in the actual behavior repertoire of NPCs, it comes at the cost of control over the interaction between NPCs.

6   Future Work

Future work will be directed at collecting more data and analyzing more games in order to find out to what extent the slightly more demanding behaviors of NPCs are overall lacking and break immersion or if this is related to the limited scope of this article. Furthermore some values seem to appear in connection to each other, for example Adaption and Interruptability, and exploring the connection between these values and the situations in which they occur, could prove beneficial in order to further improve the model.

References

1. Bartle, R.: Designing virtual worlds. New Riders Pub., Indianapolis (2003)
2. Brown, E., Cairns, P.: A Grounded Investigation of Game Immersion. In: CHI 2004, April 24-29, pp. 1–58113. ACM, Vienna (2004); 1-58113-703-6/04/0004
3. Carley, K.M., Newell, A.: The nature of the social agent. Journal of Mathematical Sociology 19(4), 221–262 (1994)
4. Cheng, K.: Behaviour, Realism and Immersion in Games. In: CHI 2005, Portland, Oregon, USA, April 2-7 (2005), http://www-users.cs.york.ac.uk/~pcairns/papers/Cheng.pdf
5. Csikszentmihalyi, M.: Flow: The Psychology of Optimal Experience. Harper Perennial, New York (1990)
6. Costykian, G.: I have no words, I must design: towards a critical vocabulary for games. In: Mäyrä, F. (ed.) Proceedings of Computer Games and Digital Cultures Conference. Tampere University Press, Tampere (2002)
7. Ermi, L., Mäyrä, F.: Fundamental Components of the Gameplay Experience. In: Castell, S., Jenson, J. (eds.) Worlds in Play: International Perspectives on Digital Games Research. Peter Lang Publishing (2007)
8. Hartley, T.P., Mehdi, Q.H.: In-game tactic adaptation for interactive computer games. In: 16th International Conference on Computer Games (CGAMES), pp. 41–49 (2011), doi:10.1109/CGAMES.2011.6000358
9. Johansson, M., Verhagen, H.: "Where is My Mind"- The Evolution of NPCs in Online Worlds. In: ICAART, vol. 2, pp. 359–364 (2011)
10. Johansson, M., Eladhari, M., Verhagen, H.: Complexity at the cost of control in game design? In: CGAT 2012, Bali, Indonesia (2012)
11. Juul, J.: The Game, the Player, the World: Looking for a Heart of Gameness. In: Copier, M., Raessens, J. (eds.) Level Up: Digital Games Research Conference Proceedings, pp. 30–45. Utrecht University, Utrecht (2003)

12. Lankoski, P.: Character design fundamentals for role-playing games. In: Montola, M., Stenros, J. (eds.) Beyond Role and Play - Tools, Toys, and Theory for Harnessing the Imagination, pp. 139–148 (2004)
13. Lankoski, P., Björk, S.: Gameplay design patterns for believable non-player characters. In: Situated Play: Proceedings of the 2007 Digital Games Research Association Conference, pp. 416–423 (2007)
14. Russell, S., Norvig, P.: Artificial Intelligence: A Modern Approach, 3rd edn. Prentice Hall (2009)
15. Salen, K., Zimmerman, E.: Rules of Play – Game Design Fundamentals. MIT Press (2004)
16. Sweetser, P., Johnson, D., Wyeth, P., Ozdowska, A.: GameFlow heuristics for designing and evaluating real-time strategy games. In: Proceedings of the 8th Australasian Conference on Interactive Entertainment: Playing the System (2012)
17. Warpefelt, H., Stråååt, B.: Breaking immersion by creating social unbelievabilty. In: Verhagen, H., Noriega, P., Balke, T., De Vos, M. (eds.) AISB 2013 Convention. Social Coordination: Principles, Artefacts and Theories (SOCIAL.PATH). The Society for the Study of Artificial Intelligence and the Simulation of Behaviour (2013)

GAMES

1. Bethesda Game Studios. *Skyrim* (PC). Bethesda Softworks. Release date November 11th 2011
2. Blizzard Entertainment. *Starcraft 2: Wings of Liberty* (PC). Blizzard Entertainment. Release date July 27th 2010
3. CD Projekt red. *The Witcher 2: Assassins of Kings* (PC). Namco Bandai Games. Release date May 17th 2011
4. id Software. *RAGE* (PC). Bethesda Softworks. Release date October 4th 2011
5. Mateas, M and Stern, A. *Façade* (PC). Digital distribution. Release date July 5th 2005
6. Team Bondi, Rockstar Leeds, Rockstar Games. *L.A. Noire* (PC). Rockstar Games. Release date November 8th 2011
7. Ubisoft Montreal. *Assassins Creed 3* (PC) Ubisoft. Release date November 23rd 2012

7   Appendix 1: Value Definitions for the Game Agent Matrix

The table below lists the definitions we have used to analyze the behavior of NPCs. These are behaviors that the NPCs should exhibit, i.e. for the Goal directed value the NPC should seem to be striving towards a goal, either long or short term. The table is sorted from top to bottom and left to right according to the values in the matrix.

Value	Definition
Goal directed	Strives towards a goal in the long or short term
Route following	Able to transport itself across open ground between two points in the world
Uses language	Use of spoken or written language
Uses tools	Use of implements in order to seemingly achieve some sort of goal, for example a sword or a hammer.
Adaption	Able to adapt to changing social circumstances in the world at the given time.
Acquires information	Observes the world and seemingly gathers information on which to act.
Crisis response	Reacts rapidly to a crisis, for example if it is being attacked or if there's a fire.
Interruptability	Able to stop doing what it is currently doing when another task takes priority
Lack of awareness	Unaware of something it its immediate vicinity.
Models of self	Knowledge of its own existence as an entity, physical or mental
Rapid emotional response	Emotional response to actions taken by others in the world, for example the killing of innocents

Value	Definition
Navigation	Able to dynamically adjust its route through the world in order to account of for unexpected obstacles.
Learns from others	Learning from the actions of others, both by example and by direct teaching.
Models of others	Awareness of the existence of other agents, where they are and what they are doing.
Face to face	Turns towards the entity it is addressing.
Group making	Dynamic creation of smaller groups
Social interaction	Dynamic and meaningful interaction on a social level.
Turn taking	Awareness of whose turn it is, avoids speaking over each other unless socially prompted to do so.
Class difference	Acts on a difference in social ranking and class.
Mob action	Dynamic formation of larger groups with very low cohesion.
Social ranking	Acts on a difference in social ranking, affecting things like credibility and who has the most social power.
Coercion	Forced actions.
Disillusionment	Loss of belief in ideals.
Clan wars	Competition between groupings in the same area.

Cooperation	Ability to dynamically cooperate with other entities in order to achieve goals.		Institutions	Roles and organizations with large amounts of formal or informal power and a historical connection, for example kings or universities.
Group conflict	Conflict between groupings with different values and interests.			
Patriotism	Strong dedication to parent group, for example the place of residence or clan.		Roles	Roles within society, for example police officers and farmers.
Power struggles	Struggle for power between entities and groupings.		Etiquette	Observance of social rules and conventions.
Team player	Concept of being part of a team, and acting for the best of the team at the cost to itself.		Norm maintenance	Maintenance of norms and rules within society.
Advertising	Advertises products and services.		Sanctions	Application of sanctions towards entities and groupings that break the rules, law or norms of society.

Part III
Frontiers in Gaming Simulation for Transportation and Logistics

Modeling Network Controller Decisions Based Upon Situation Awareness through Agent-Based Negotiation

Reyhan Aydoğan[1], Julia C. Lo[2], Sebastiaan A. Meijer[2,3], and Catholijn M. Jonker[1]

[1] Delft University of Technology, Faculty of Electrical Engineering, Mathematics,
and Computer Science, Delft, The Netherlands
{r.aydogan,c.m.jonker}@tudelft.nl
[2] Delft University of Technology, Faculty of Technology,
Policy and Management, Delft, The Netherlands
j.c.lo@tudelft.nl
[3] KTH Royal Institute of Technology, Division of Traffic and Logistics,
Stockholm, Sweden
smeijer@kth.se

Abstract. The Dutch railway traffic control is in an urgent need for innovation and therefore turns to gaming simulation as a platform to test and train future configurations of the system. The presence of relevant participants is necessary to keep the fidelity of the gaming simulation high. Network controllers are often needed in such games, but are expensive, scarce, and often have limited action, thus making their involvement less than desirable. To overcome this, the current paper introduces the use of intelligent software agents to replace some roles. The cognitive construct of situation awareness is required to model the evaluation of an offer in a negotiation setting, in which a situation awareness model (SAM) is introduced for evaluating offers in complex and dynamic systems.

Keywords: Railway Transportation, Network Control and Management, Negotiation, Situation Awareness.

1   Introduction

The Dutch railway system is one of the most heavy utilized railway infrastructures in the world [1] comprising over 7000 kilometers of track to transport over 100.000 tons cargo and 1.2 million passengers per day [2]. Management of such systems is highly complex since it requires to take into account both social and technical aspects. Those aspects involve issues related to the infrastructure, such as track conditions and operational issues related to the trains and traffic control. Handling the aforementioned issues becomes even more challenging as they are influenced by a variety of factors such as environmental and technical factors [3]. For instance, some problems may occur on the tracks under hard weather conditions; consequently, it may cause (primary) delays. Due to interdependencies between the trains, delays affect other trains' schedules (secondary delays), which is especially a crucial issue in the highly interconnected and dense train traffic.

S.A. Meijer and R. Smeds (Eds.): ISAGA 2013, LNCS 8264, pp. 191–200, 2014.

When focusing on the social aspects of the railway system, in particular train traffic control, the complexity in such situations might also evolve when a group decision making process occurs, e.g. national and regional controllers often need to collaborate with each other when failures, incidents and/or emergencies in the train traffic network occur. In such cases, the interest of individuals from different divisions and in separated locations may conflict, since they perceive the problem from different perspectives – different information, knowledge and understanding of processes ('mental models') – of the railway domain. A decision might be favorable for one individual but unacceptable for the others. To reach a joint agreement they may negotiate on their decisions. Finding a mutually agreed decision would be time consuming under some circumstances. Especially in train traffic control, it is crucial to make fast decisions before conflicts in the system escalate [4]. A concept that has been often used for operational decision-making is 'situation awareness'. In simple terms, situation awareness is about knowing what is going on. A high level of situation awareness would be a predictor of a good decision. In a negotiation setting, a high level of situation awareness can be seen as a predictor of generating an offer.

The Dutch railway network infrastructure organization uses different decision support tools (e.g. case studies, computer simulations and gaming simulations) to improve decision-making mechanisms in terms of speed and quality. Gaming simulations are used by the Dutch railway infrastructure organization to understand the underlying problems, to explore alternative models of the organization, to experience exceptional situations, and to improve the decision making process, e.g. [5]. It is expected that the amount of gaming simulation sessions will increase from 5 to 50 per year. Since gaming simulations require the presence of individuals from different divisions, alignment of participation presence is not only problematic, but also costly in terms of time and resources. Employing intelligent software agents to act on behalf of human participants might save the latter two.

This paper presents an approach in which intelligent software agents negotiate as virtual represents of stakeholders in the operational traffic control process in gaming simulations. A key contribution is the way in which the situation awareness of human participants is modeled in the agent-based system for a negotiation setting. Section 2 provides a background on situation awareness and the Dutch railway traffic control system. Section 3 presents a model of situation awareness used for the evaluation of offers in a negotiation setting, followed by Section 4, which elaborates on the negotiation model. Finally, theoretical and practical implications are given, as well as remarks and recommendations for future work.

2   Background

2.1   Situation Awareness

A common concept of cognition used in complex and demanding activities, is that of situation awareness. In transport related research it is a common concept in studying driver and pilot behavior [6]. Situation awareness is argued to be an epiphenomenon of cognition [7] and forms critical input for decision-making [8]. One of the most widely used definitions of situation awareness is: "the perception of the elements in the environment within a volume of time and space, the comprehension of their meaning, and the projection of their status in the near future", p.97 [9]. Situation awareness is constructed through mental models or schemas, which can be seen as representations of a domain (e.g. traffic control) in terms of knowledge and processes [10]. This theoretical definition takes upon an information processing approach within the psychological domain, whereas long-term memory structures, such as mental models and schemas are significant parts of obtaining high situation awareness [11].

Situation awareness and mental models have been studied in a variety of research fields. For example, Jonker et al. [12] investigated shared mental models to increase the performance of teams using agents. Hoogendoorn et al. [13] focused on modeling situation awareness through mental models. McCarley et al. [14] presented a situation awareness model based on visual attention and memory decay. This model showed more alignment with plausible cognitive processes than other computational models in a review by Rousseau et al. [15]. However, the model mainly focuses on the role of attention and working memory to achieve situation awareness. So and Sonenberg [16] proposed a computational model of situation awareness in which the main focus was to evaluate and enhance the capability to predict foreseeable situations and act to these situations in a proactive manner. Their computational model of situation awareness is based on rule-based knowledge and forward chaining reasoning. Studies using models of situation awareness in train traffic control and/or the railway domain are fairly limited. There are some studies focusing on a situation model of the train driver's performance [17], and a model of the train driver's information processing [18]. In this paper, a situation awareness model of train network controllers is studied. Section 3 presents the situation awareness model, which will be used for evaluating offers in a negotiation setting.

2.2 Railway Traffic Control Operations

The operations of train traffic control can be divided into three traffic control roles, namely as train traffic controller, regional network controller and national network controller. Thirteen regional control centers in the Netherlands focus on an assigned area of the train traffic network. The coverage of the regional control center depends on the size of the stations and complexity of the railway conditions. The train traffic controller (TTC) is responsible for ready and correct availability of safe, distributed infrastructure capacity in a sub-region of a regional control center. In ideal conditions, the TTC solely needs to monitor the status and progress of the timetable. Allocation software (in Dutch ARI) automatically runs the predefined train allocation plan. The regional network controller (RNC) (also called a de-central network controller [4]) overlooks the status of the train activities in all sub-regions and coordinates between the train traffic controllers. As trains travel between multiple sub-regions, the RNC is responsible for the optimization and management of the train traffic at a regional control center. Similarly, but on a national level, the national network controller (NNC) (also called central network controller [4]) coordinates the activities between regional network controllers in case of failures, incidents and emergencies in the railway network and focuses on trains that need to cross the borders of multiple regional control centers. Additionally, the NNC interacts with the train service providers on the availability of personnel and timetable alterations for cross-regional and international passenger trains and on timetable alterations of freight trains.

As mentioned before, this paper focuses on the negotiation that may occur between the regional network controller and the national network controller.

3   Modeling Situation Awareness in Negotiations

As situation awareness is an important cognitive indicator for decision-making, this construct has similar theoretical implications for the decision making process in a negotiation setting. This section focuses on how situation awareness is used in a negotiation setting and accordingly introduces a situation awareness model for dynamic evaluation of the offers during a negotiation.

3.1   Situation Awareness Model (SAM)

In order to have the software agent for the NNC act coherently and to able to generate and respond to different proposals, the needs/preferences of the NNC on possible actions in certain situations need to be understood. Since the experts' preferences on actions in traffic network control can change with respect to time, situation and environmental factors, a dynamic and elaborate evaluation of offers is required. Furthermore, expected consequences of the possible actions play a key role in train traffic and network controllers' decision making.

This paper proposes a situation awareness model in terms of possible actions for a given situation and ranking of those actions, based on the desirability of the projected expected consequences. Consequently, dynamic evaluation of offers can be made according to the preferences induced from situation awareness model. The proposed model of situation awareness is based on the theoretical approach proposed by McGuiness and Foy [19], which extends Endsley's three-level situation awareness

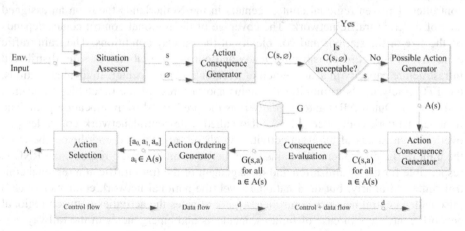

Fig. 1. Situation Awareness Model (SAM)

definition by adding a fourth level. According to this approach, SA consists of four levels: 1. the perception of the elements in current situation, 2. the comprehension of these elements in the current situation, 3. the projection of these elements in future states and 4. the evaluation of a subset of available projected actions. In this paper, the evaluation of the projected future states in a given situation is achieved by ranking the projected future states. In the model, the ability to evaluate the outcomes includes the attitudes, motivation and goals of an operator to yield the final level of situation awareness, prior to decision-making. Figure 1 shows the four-level SA consisting of the following modules:

- *Situation Assessor (SAss)* takes the environmental inputs (e.g. a malfunction of a signal), and outputs the current situation **s** where **S** is a set of all possible situations and **s** is a variable over **S**. For example, the situation "switch 1021 broke down between Schiphol and the junction to Amsterdam Lelylaan and Amsterdam Zuid" may represent the current situation. An environmental input can be anything that may cause a change of the current situation. For instance, "an accident in Amsterdam Central" will change the current situation. The current module refers to the first two SA levels (perception and comprehension).

- *Possible Action Generator (PAG)* considers the current situation, **s** and generates all applicable actions in that situation, **A(s)** where $A(s) = \{a \in A \mid app (a, s)\}$. Here, **A** is a set of all possible actions; **a** is a variable over **A** and **app(a, s)** denotes that action **a** is applicable in situation **s**. For example, rerouting a train between Amsterdam Central and Leiden Central station might be a possible action to be taken in order to deal with the current situation. PAG includes the comprehension of the situation, which relates to the second SA level (comprehension).

- *Action Consequence Generator (ACG)* generates expected consequences (future projected states) of each applicable action in the current situation **s**. For all **a** $\in$ **A(s)**, it outputs $C(s, a) = \{c \in C \mid pcons (s, a, c)\}$ where **C** is the set of all possible consequences, where a consequence is described by a subset of S $(C = \wp(S))$. Let **c** be a variable over **C**, and let **pcons (s, a, c)** denote that **c** is a possible consequence of action **a** in situation **s**. The module ACG focuses on the third situation awareness level (projection).

- *Consequence Evaluator (CE)* evaluates all possible consequences generated by ACG, **C(s, a)** and outputs which goals in **G** are satisfied by them. For all **a** $\in$ **A(s)** it outputs $G (s, a) = \{ c \in C(s, a), g \in G \mid satisfies (c, g)\}$ where **G** is a set of goals and **satisfies(c, g)** denotes that consequence **c** satisfies goal **g**. The *Consequence Evaluator* relates to the fourth situation awareness level (evaluation).

- *Action Order Generator (AOG)* orders all applicable actions in the current situation, **A(s)** with respect to how well they satisfy the goals in **G** (from most preferred action to least preferred one) and returns an ordered sequence of actions **O(s)**, where $O(s)_i$ refers to the ith element of the list, $i \in$ **N**, counting from 0. The first element of the list is the most preferred, and the last element is the least preferred applicable action and for all **i** and **j**, where $i < j$, $O(s)_i$ is preferred over $O(s)_j$. There are several ways to order the applicable actions. In our model, the actions are ordered according to either the goal-based *lexicographic* criterion or the goal-based *cardinality* criterion defined in [20]. When goals in **G** have priorities such as **g** is more important than **g'** where **g, g' ∈ G**, the lexicographic criterion is taken into account. That is, the preference on actions is determined by the satisfied goals with the highest priority. For example, if the expected consequence of action **a** satisfies goal **g** whose priority is higher than the priority of **g'** that is satisfied by the expected consequence of action **a'**, then the actions are ordered as [**a, a'**] where **a** is preferred over **a'**. When more than one goal is satisfied by taking an action **a**, the goal whose priority is the highest in comparison is considered. In case that the lexicographic criterion assigns all goals the same priority, then the ordering of actions is done by adopting the cardinality criterion, where the number of goals satisfied by each consequence is taken into account. If the number of goals satisfied by taking action **a** is greater than the number of goals satisfied by action **a'**, then **a** is preferred over **a'**. *AOG* is related to the fourth situation awareness level (evaluation).

SAM starts by interpreting the current situation through environmental inputs (SAss module). For optimization purposes, it checks whether taking no action is acceptable. To do this, SAM projects the expected consequences of not acting in the current situation and checks acceptability using a knowledge base. For example, a future in which trains are delayed by more than five minutes is not acceptable. In case doing nothing is not acceptable, SAM searches all possible admissible actions in the current situation (PAG module) and projects their expected consequences (ACG module). Afterwards, it evaluates the consequences with respect to which goals they satisfy (CE module) and accordingly orders the actions based on the satisfaction of goals (AOG module). The ordered actions will be used in decision making process by the negotiating agent.

3.2   Operationalization of SAM for a Specific Situation

Building the situation awareness model described above requires significant operational data for each specific region and railway traffic network. The following procedure has been developed and used to acquire the data:

- Use the automatic logging data that is obligatory for most rail traffic controllers to collect the environmental input, situation assessments and transformations, possible alternative actions, expected consequences of actions, and the decisions made by the controller;
- Analyze and select the collected data;
- Perform a Goal-Directed Task Analysis (GDTA). This technique is a variation of a cognitive task analysis (see e.g. [11]) and is specifically designed to uncover the operators' dynamic information needs (i.e. situation awareness requirements) by identifying the operators' major goals, sub goals, related decisions and necessary information for the decision;
- Align the set of goals **G** from the Goal-Directed Task Analysis (GDTA) to the SAM model;
- Interview (some) human actors to collect lacking in-depth information about alternative actions, expected consequences, priorities over goals, relations between goals and consequences, and preferences over actions in relation to expected consequences and goals.

3.3   Test Case Results

To test the feasibility of implementing a SAM for a specific situation, the aforementioned information was acquired for a test case on the busy Amsterdam-Utrecht-Amersfoort triangle. For a clear understanding, the example is simplified to one situation for one particular area of the infrastructure. To do so, a manual version of retrieving information was undergone with the assistance of one of the National Network Controllers working in The Netherlands. Only the related part of SAM for the current situation denoted by s is described as follows in Figure 2.

The applicable actions are ordered with respect to how many goals are satisfied by the expected consequences since it is assumed that all goals have the same priority for this scenario. The expected consequence of action a_2 satisfies five goals where those of a_1 and a_3 satisfy four and two goals respectively. The most preferred action is a_2. The ordered list is identical to the applicable action list ordered by the human NNC according to his preferences.

- s: the current situation after taking actions such as rerouting and turning to deal with the problem of the congested train traffic at Schiphol station during morning peak hours
- A(s) is the set of alternative applicable actions, {a_1, a_2, a_3} where
  - a_1 is to cancel a train series at Utrecht Central
  - a_2 is to cancel a train series at Amersfoort
  - a_3 is to cancel a train series at Maarssen
- C is the set of possible consequences, {c_1, c_2, c_3, ...} where
  - c_1: the track space of the cancelled train is occupied, limiting the infrastructure capacity of the station where the action has been taken.
  - c_2: similar loss of infrastructure capacity of a station as with c_1. However, the infrastructure capacity on a more critical area (Utrecht Central) is relieved with an extension for a longer term.
  - c_3: similar loss of infrastructure capacity on a station as with c_1. However, the infrastructure capacity on a more critical area (Utrecht Central) is relieved, but canceling train series at Maarssen is not allowed anymore.
- G = {g_1, g_2, ...} is the set of goals used to rank the actions. For this example, all goals have equal priorities. Specific goals are
  - g_1 = relieve the disrupted area (satisfied by c_1, c_2, c_3)
  - g_2 = minimize secondary delays (satisfied by c_1, c_2, c_3)
  - g_3 = include buffers in infrastructure capacity (satisfied by c_1, c_2)
  - g_4 = keep the infrastructure capacity of stations high (satisfied by c_1, c_2)
  - g_5 = reduce the infrastructure capacity load of major corridors (satisfied by c_2)

Action Consequence Generator:
  - $C(s_3, a_1) = c_1$; $C(s_3, a_2) = c_2$; $C(s_3, a_3) = c_3$

Consequence Evaluator:
  - $G(s_3, a_1) = \{g_1, g_2, g_3, g_4\}$; $G(s_3, a_2) = \{g_1, g_2, g_3, g_4, g_5\}$; $G(s_3, a_3) = \{g_1, g_2\}$

Action Order Generator:
  - Ordered action list = [a_2, a_1, a_3]

Fig. 2. An illustration of a test case

4   Negotiating Software Agents in Gaming Simulations

The focus in this paper is on the multiparty negotiation in which the software agent representing NNC denoted as A_{NNC} negotiates with a number of human RNC actors on which action needs to be taken. The number of RNC human actors may vary according to the situation.

The proposed negotiation protocol is inspired from the single text negotiation protocol [21], where the mediator agent generates offers and asks the negotiating parties for their approval or disapproval of the offers. The negotiation outcome is determined through the votes of the parties during the negotiation. In that protocol, the mediator's role is to help the negotiating agents reach a consensus. To do this, the mediator generates the offers based on the negotiating agents' responses, regardless of its preferences. That is, it generates the first offer randomly, and for further offers it modifies the most recently accepted offer by all agents, by exchanging one value with another value randomly in the offer.

5   Conclusion and Discussion

This paper introduces a human-agent negotiation approach in which a software agent negotiates with multiple RNC human agents on behalf of the NNC on the actions to be taken in a certain situation, during gaming simulations on operational innovation in railway traffic control. The dynamic evaluation of actions to be offered by the NNC is modeled through a situation awareness model (SAM). The model is a straightforward approach to deal with the complicated decision-making process. Ordering applicable actions in certain situations involves a reasoning task on consequences and goals. Furthermore, this approach enables the software agent to understand the preferences of the human NNC and to explain why one action is preferred over another.

Using the input of a human NNC, a particular situation was constructed in the situation awareness model. This shows that collecting the data required is feasible and yields meaningful results. In future studies, the accuracy of the model has to be evaluated with more situations that also involve more alternative actions. After construction of the model for a particular situation, the ordering of actions gained from the model can be compared to the real ordering of actions of multiple human NNCs. In the case of an inconsistency, the underlying reasons may help to understand the relation between consequences and goals, update the goal hierarchy if necessary, and find possible hidden factors that affect the preferences. Furthermore, in the current approach, direct transfer is used from actions to consequences based upon interviews with the NNC. Over time, the consequences of actions in gaming simulations can be observed and a probabilistic model can be built by associating probabilities to the consequences.

Another extension to the current approach is to apply the model of situation awareness for the RNCs in addition to the NNC, when one or more RNC human agents are not be available in gaming simulations. Moreover, shared situation awareness can be used in order to improve the negotiation outcome.

Finally, next steps are to investigate the influence of using software agents in low-tech multi-actor gaming simulations on their performance, and to obtain insights about the applicability of the software agents in this setting.

Acknowledgments. This research was funded through the Railway Gaming Suite program, a collaboration between ProRail and Delft University of Technology.

References

1. Meijer, S.A.: Gaming Simulations for Railways: Lessons Learned from Modeling Six Games for the Dutch Infrastructure Management. Infrastructure, Design, Signalling and Security in Railway. In: Perpinya, X. (ed.) Infrastructure Design, Signalling and Security in Railway (2012)
2. Over Prorail, http://www.prorail.nl/Over%20ProRail/Pages/default.aspx (accessed April 11, 2012)
3. Al-Ibrahim, A.: Dynamic Delay Management at Railways: A Semi-Markovian Decision Approach. Amsterdam: Thela Thesis (2010)
4. Meijer, S.A., Van der Kracht, P., Luipen, J.J.W., van Schaafsma, A.A.M.: In: The 2nd International Conference on Infrastructure Systems and Services: Developing 21st Century Infrastructure Networks, INFRA (2009)
5. Meijer, S.A., Mayer, I.S., Luipen, J., van, W.N.: Gaming Rail Cargo Management: Exploring and Validating Alternative Modes of Organization. Simulation and Gaming 43(1), 85–101 (2012)
6. Lee, Y.H., Choi, Y.C., Choi, S.H., Ujimoto, K.V.: Analysis of Survey Data on Situation Awareness of Helicopter Pilots: The Case of Helicopter Accidents in Korea. In: Proceedings of TRB Annual Meeting 2007, TRB 07-0346 (2007)
7. Banbury, S., Tremblay, S. (eds.): A Cognitive Approach to Situation Awareness: Theory, Measurement and Application. Ashgate & Town, Aldershot (2004)
8. Endsley, M.R.: Towards a Theory of Situation Awareness in Dynamic Systems. Human Factors 37(1), 32–64 (1995)
9. Endsley, M.R.: Design and Evaluation for Situation Awareness Enhancement. In: Proceedings of the Human Factors Society 32nd Annual Meeting (1988)
10. Gentner, D.: Mental Models. Psychology of International Encyclopedia of the Social & Behavioral Sciences, 9683 – 9687 (2001)
11. Endsley, M.R., Bolté, B., Jones, D.G.: Designing for Situation Awareness. Taylor & Francis Group, New York (2003)
12. Jonker, C.M., Riemsdijk, M.B., van, V.B.: Shared Mental Models: A Conceptual Analysis. In: Proceedings of 9th International Conference on Autonomous Agents and Multiagent Systems, AAMAS 2010 (2010)
13. Hoogendoorn, M., Lambalgen, R., van, T.J.: Modeling Situation Awareness in Human-Like Agents using Mental Models. In: Proceedings of the 22nd International Joint Conference on Artificial Intelligence, IJCAI 2011 (2011)
14. McCarley, J.S., Wickens, C.D., Goh, J., Horrey, W.J.: A Computational Model of Attention/Situation Awareness. In: Proceedings of the 46th Annual Meeting of the Human Factors and Ergonomics Society (2002)
15. Rousseau, R., Tremblay, S., Breton, R.: Defining and Modeling Situation Awareness: A Critical Review. In: Banbury, S., Tremblay, S. (eds.) A Cognitive Approach to Situation Awareness: Theory, Measurement and Application, Ashgate & Town, Aldershot (2004)

16. So, R., Sonenberg, L.: Situation Awareness in Intelligent Agents: Foundations for a Theory of Proactive Agent Behavior. In: Proceedings of the IEEE/WIC/ACM International Conference on Intelligent Agent Technology, IAT 2004 (2004)
17. McLeod, R.W., Walker, G.H., Moray, N.: Analysing and Modelling Train Driver Performance. Applied Ergonomics 36(6), 671–680 (2005)
18. Hamilton, W.I., Clarke, T.: Driver Performance Modelling and Its Practical Application To Railway Safety. Applied Ergonomics 36(6), 661–670 (2005)
19. McGuinness, B., Foy, L.: A Subjective Measure of SA: The Crew Awareness Rating Scale (CARS). In: Proceedings of the First Human Performance, Situation Awareness, and Automation Conference (2000)
20. Visser, W., Aydoğan, R., Hindriks, K.V., Jonker, C.M.: Framework for Qualitative Multi-Criteria Preferences. In: Proceedings of the 4th International Conference on Agents and Artificial Intelligence, ICAART 2012 (2012)
21. Klein, M., Faratin, P., Sayama, H., Bar-Yam, Y.: Protocols for Negotiating Complex Contracts. IEEE Intelligent Systems 18, 32–38 (2003)

Representing Qualitative Aspects of Vehicle Purchase Decision-Making in a Simulation Game on Alternative Fuel and Vehicle Transitions

Joel Bremson

Institute of Transportation Studies, UC Davis
jbremson@ucdavis.edu

Abstract. For a serious game on large-scale vehicle and fuel market transitioning to alternative vehicles a plausible representation of vehicle purchase was required. Vehicle buyers choose cars based on instrumental, hedonic, and symbolic criteria. Asking a game player to make a major purchase of that complexity with imaginary money strains game credibility. A utility function was used to handle this requirement. This approach was effective for simulating the diversity of the people and vehicles in that market. It may be effective for other game representations of difficult decision-making processes.

1   Introduction

This paper addresses the issue of creating a game play motivation in cases where an accurate representation of a process or behavior is difficult, due to constraints of the game media. It uses an actual example of a difficult representation to describe the method. A central assumption of serious games is that players will act similarly to how they would react in reality. However, achieving genuine verisimilitude in a game is impossible. Game designers must balance the needs for scenario accuracy against the need for engaging play dynamics. Difficult representations are those in which the constraints of the game media (e.g. computer) cannot easily communicate important dimensions of a representation (e.g. emotions).

To explore the potential of serious games as a policy analysis tool for alternative vehicle and fuel transition planning, I developed a serious game called *Autopia* (http://autopigame.com)[1]. Autopia is a three-sided, computer based, market simulation composed of vehicle producers (VP), fuel producers, and consumers. In the game, VPs build and sell vehicles, picking technologies (e.g. hybrid) seeking to outsell their competitors. Fuel producers similarly seek to gauge the fuel market and invest in resources they think will maximize their profits. Since profit maximization is a common player motivation in games the producer game objective was easy to design: make as much money as you can. Consumer players, in contrast, who represent large market segments sharing common income levels and vehicle preferences, have no obvious, dominating, player motivation as do the producer players.

Real consumers seek cars that not only meet their utilitarian needs but also their emotional (e.g. driving experience) and social (e.g. peer status) desires. Vehicle purchase decisions are complex[2], [3], [4]. This complexity needed to be somehow

S.A. Meijer and R. Smeds (Eds.): ISAGA 2013, LNCS 8264, pp. 201–205, 2014.

represented in the game. A vehicle is described in the game as a line item with the following characteristics: *name, mpg (kpl), style, performance, price,* and *drivetrain* (see *Table 1*). Mapping the complexity onto the consumers' purchase process had to work within the limits of the vehicle description.

This paper describes the essence of my approach to this problem. It covers the overall representation of the *consumer* player, the *vehicle,* which is the object of central interest to the consumer players, and the implementation details of the utility function.

1.1   Consumer Model

There were two objectives behind the design of the consumer model. First, the model needed to reflect a multi-dimensional decision process. The consumer game had to be more than a pure accounting exercise – the buying rationale for vehicles had to be deeper than that of a business fleet buyer with purely utilitarian concerns. The consumer player model needed to include the symbolic and hedonic qualities of the vehicle purchase decision to simulate the conspicuous consumption characteristic of the vehicle market i.e. *why does someone buy a prestige vehicle when there are utility-equivalent vehicles for a fraction of the price?* The S* represents the appeal of a vehicle as seen by a particular market demographic. It is the proxy value for the symbolic and hedonic aspects of the vehicle.

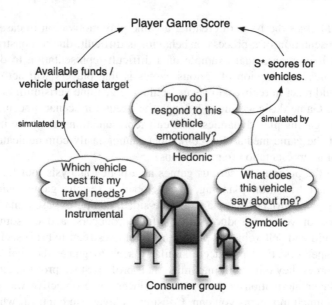

Fig. 1. The consumer simulation – translating an irrational economic decision into a simulation game model

The second design objective for the consumer was to enforce the given identity of the consumer onto the human player. I did not want to let the consumer decide that he was only going to buy expensive electric vehicles and let most of his drivers go car-less, for example. The consumer score element was used to give players a reason to follow the given scenario rather than to strike out on their own narrative. The score was based primarily on the player's ability to supply an adequate number of vehicles to his drivers (given information) and secondarily on the S* scores of the vehicles he acquired for them[1]. Consumer players were told they would maximize their game score by covering their vehicle acquisition goals with the best vehicles (S*) available, given their budgetary constraints. The scoring system was effective in encouraging player fidelity to their game consumer identities.

1.2   Vehicle Model

A *vehicle* (Fig. 2) represents an automobile line as built by a VP. It is specified by the attributes: drivetrain (e.g. gas), production cost, production volume, mpg, and the conceptual values of style, and performance. Style(s) is a quantitative proxy for the symbolic value of the vehicle, while performance(p) represents its hedonic components (Fig. 1). The drivetrain type determines a base vehicle price(d) and mpg(b). The VP chooses *style* and *performance* attributes of the vehicle in order to appeal to his target market, which can be set from 0 to 60. A *style* 10, *performance* 10, vehicle corresponds to a basic Toyota Camry, for reference. The style and performance attributes affect the production cost and mpg of the vehicle. The VP also sets a production volume (n) for the vehicle which indicates a corresponding volume multiplier (v), and determines the cost of the producing the vehicle run.

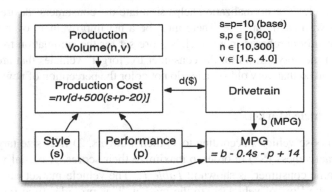

Fig. 2. A vehicle is composed of static elements and dynamic relationships

1.3   Methodology

A simple linear utility function can be written:

$$U = Bx \tag{1}$$

where B is a vector of coefficients and x a vector of values. In the game, the B values represent consumer preferences for the quantitative, intrinsic vehicle properties *style, performance*, and *mpg (kpl)*. The values of the **B** coefficients, are positive and sum to one ($\Sigma\ B_i = 1$) The **x** vector contains the corresponding attributes of the vehicle instance.

The B vector, uniquely assigned to each consumer player remains constant throughout the game. The corresponding x values are also fixed attributes of the vehicle. The x values are normalized relative to the last three turns of the consumer's purchase history. Normalization scales the vehicle attributes so they can be fairly compared. Finally, a filter function, $\lambda(B,x)$, is used to penalize unlikely vehicles. Further details on the function are available elsewhere [1].

The *S** score for a vehicle *x* is calculated:

$$S_{jx} = 10 \times \lambda(\boldsymbol{B}, \boldsymbol{x}) \times \sum_i B_{ij} \frac{(x_i - \mu_{ij})}{\sigma_{ij}} \tag{2}$$

$\quad$ S_{jx} $\quad$ score (S*) for consumer *j*, vehicle *x*
$\quad$ B_{ij} $\quad$ percent coefficient for attribute *i* for consumer *j*
$\quad$ x_i $\quad$ value of attribute *i* for vehicle *x* (e.g. style)
$\quad$ μ_{ij} $\quad$ mean of attribute *I*, for con. *j*, for the last 3 turns
$\quad$ σ_{ij} $\quad$ s.d. for attribute *i* of consumer *j* for the last 3 turns
$\quad$ λ $\quad$ filter function for extreme vehicles using $(\boldsymbol{B}, \boldsymbol{x})$

The Σ portion sums over the consumer's style, performance, and mpg vector (**B**), multiplying them by vehicle scores normalized over the last three turns. Normalizing these scores relative to the consumer's recent purchase history makes the attribute scores comparable. The normalization helps simulate the consumers' desire to improve their vehicles with each purchase. There must be a net improvement over what a consumer has recently purchased in a vehicle's score set for the summation to be positive. The three-turn memory allows for the consumer to "forget" vehicles that are more than twelve years old so that very old vehicles do not color the perception of new ones.

1.4   The Vehicle Market

Consumers choose vehicles according to 1) their budgets, 2) fleet size targets, and 3) and their attractiveness (S*) in order to maximize their scores. A partial vehicle market set, for some consumer, is shown in *Table 1*. The vehicle market runs on a timer that manages the flow of vehicles into the market. This provides time for buyers and sellers to negotiate, and makes the consumers prioritize their selections. The timer mechanism is integral to the workings of the game[1].

Table 1. Partial vehicle selection set as seen by particular consumer player

Name	Type	MPG	Style	Perf.	Price	#	S*
AX 2	Gas	43	2	2	11.2	190	48
GT H	Hybrid	60	2	2	17.5	150	61
GT D	Diesel	42	5	5	21.9	250	69

2   Discussion

The purchase of a new car is a major decision. It involves not only the utilitarian basis for the vehicle purchase, but also complex psychological factors [5]. A buyer asks: How do I feel about the way it drives? What does this car say about me? Can I afford it? It is a purchase that often entails the resolution of a conflicting set of priorities and constraints.

It is naïve to believe that people will buy virtual cars the same way they would buy a real car. Instead, I sought to make VPs and consumers make hard choices. In balancing price, mpg, availability, and S*, there is no obvious formula for the consumer player to choose his vehicles. For example, a consumer may have to choose between two closely priced vehicles, one with a low S*, high mpg, and another with a high S* and low mpg. The higher S* score vehicle will return a higher immediate score, but the higher mpg car will lower fuel costs, allowing the consumer to buy cars with higher S* score in future turns. The S* score helps to create space for game narratives to develop[6]. Discovering likely storylines of how these future markets may operate was a key research objective.

3   Conclusion

To represent actual vehicle purchase behavior by individuals in a mass-market simulation game I used a utility function to give consumer players individualized responses to the vehicles. This utility function creates a diverse set of reactions to the vehicles which drives vehicle market diversity. The consumer player's game objectives are to maximize his score by 1) obtaining the desired number of vehicles and 2) maximizing the S* scores of his purchases. The approach was effective in terms of player engagement. The game as a whole was successful in developing results similar to other predictive approaches.

References

[1] Bremson, J.: Using Gaming Simulation to Explore Long Range Fuel and Vehicle Transitions, UC Davis (2012)
[2] Schuitema, G., Anable, J., Skippon, S., Kinnear, N.: The role of instrumental, hedonic and symbolic attributes in the intention to adopt electric vehicles. Transportation Research Part A: Policy and Practice
[3] Turrentine, T.S., Kurani, K.S.: Car buyers and fuel economy? Energy Policy 35(2), 1213–1223 (2007)
[4] Bagwell, L.S., Bernheim, B.D.: Veblen effects in a theory of conspicuous consumption. The American Economic Review, 349–373 (1996)
[5] Kurani, K.S., Turrentine, T.: Automobile Buyer Decisions about Fuel Economy and Fuel Efficiency. Institute of Transportation Studies, UC Davis (September 2004)
[6] Abt, C.C.: Serious games. Viking Press, New York (1971)

Using Gamification to Enhance Staff Motivation
in Logistics

Jan Hense[1], Markus Klevers[2], Michael Sailer[1],
Tim Horenburg[2], Heinz Mandl[1], and Willibald Günthner[2]

[1] Ludwig-Maximilians-Universität München,
Empirical Education and Educational Psychology, Germany
[2] Technische Universität München, Institute for Materials Handling,
Material Flow and Logistics, Germany

1   Staff Motivation as a Key Challenge in Logistics

Logistics is concerned with effectively managing the flow of materials and supplies for production, commerce and other purposes (Christopher, 2003). *Transport logistics* deals with resource flows on a large scale level, as it involves transport by land, water, and air. A second domain of logistics is *intralogistics*, which is concerned with the internal handling of materials and supplies within specific production sites or intermediate storage facilities (Arnold, 2006). This paper focuses on intralogistics or, more specifically, on one of its central tasks, order picking.

Despite ongoing automation efforts, order picking still frequently involves intensive and repetitive manual labour. For fulfilling a customer order, workers typically receive lists of items to be picked from storage and combined in a shipment. Orders have to be fulfilled under time constraints with as few errors as possible in shifts which can easily involve dozens of orders. Due to these challenges and context conditions, and taking into account that order picking is typically performed by low-paid unskilled workers, it is not surprising that staff motivation and high turnover rates are recurrent problems for efficiency in intralogistics. However, most optimization approaches in order picking concentrate on technical aspects, leaving out the human factor (cf. Coffey, 1999).

This paper introduces gamification as an innovative approach to enhance staff motivation in intralogistics. Gamification is a recent trend (originally from marketing) that quickly spread to other areas of application such as education and training, traffic control, or influencing environmental behaviour. Conceptually, gamification denotes the application of game elements for engagement, motivation, learning, or problem-solving purposes in non-gaming, real world contexts (cf. Kapp, 2012, p. 10). As games continually succeed in luring players into investing large amounts of time and effort, it is expected that some of the mechanisms making them effective entertainment devices can also be used in non-gaming environments.

This paper presents the theoretical background and concept of "GameLog" (Gamification in intralogistics – Fostering motivation and productivity in order picking), which is aimed at developing a gamification approach for enhancing motivation in intralogistics. We first analyze current approaches to staff motivation in logistics

S.A. Meijer and R. Smeds (Eds.): ISAGA 2013, LNCS 8264, pp. 206–213, 2014.
© Springer International Publishing Switzerland 2014

(section 2), afterwards discuss psychological perspectives on fostering motivation in logistics (section 3) and then introduce gamification and analyze its potential for motivation in logistics (section 4). Subsequently, we describe the GameLog project in detail (section 5) and conclude by giving an outlook on its expected outcomes from practical and research perspectives.

2   Current Approaches to Staff Motivation in Logistics

Workers in conventional intralogistical processes like manual order picking (see Figure 1) or operating fork lifters are faced with the monotonous fulfilment of steady, recurring tasks. This can lead to fatigue and especially a loss of motivation in the long-term (ten Hompel, Sadowsky & Beck, 2011). This is supported by a case study from 2012 in which the motivation of workers in intralogistics is specified as very low compared to other business tasks (Link, Müller-Dauppert & Jung, 2012).

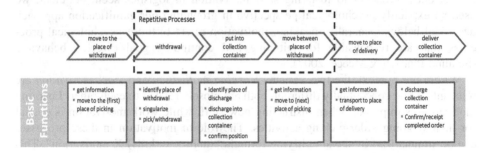

Fig. 1. Process Overview of manual order picking

Intrinsic and extrinsic motivation can be distinguished while designing a motivation system for logistic processes (see chapter 3). The most important variables (Pfohl, 2004a) within extrinsic motivation salary and working time are primarily the focus of companies' management practices. Those salary-based incentive systems can be divided into performance-related and potential-related salary systems (Wagner, 1995). While potential-related systems take the qualification for the certain work task as a basis, performance-related systems rely on surveyed key performance indicators and their correlation to the salary (Pfohl, 2004a). Thus, performance measurement must lead to methodically accepted and reproducible results. Objective measurement is a basic prerequisite for a salary-based incentive system (Pulverich & Schietinger, 2009). Additionally, a transparent composition of basic salary and bonus is essential for the success of the system (Zaunmüller, 2005).

Most production companies just concentrate on extrinsic monetary incentives to increase motivation, but those incentives are commonly considered short-term instruments (Pfohl, 2004a). In the long-term, motivation-enhancing tools like job rotation, job enlargement, job enrichment and group work (Jünemann & Schmidt, 2000) are rarely used in intralogistics (Link et al., 2012). Comprehensive intrinsic models are rarely found. The only findings that could be made while reviewing the literature and applying the research for the GameLog project were the creation of communication areas such as coffee corners to improve the corporate atmosphere, the honouring of staff with innovation prices for good ideas and the sensitization for the produced good to emotionalize the worker and create a certain level of enthusiasm (Bundesverband Materialwirtschaft, Einkauf und Logistik, 2008). A comprehensive incentive system directly connected to the working process and the measured performance indicators could not be found while working on this research project, although this could influence the motivation of staff in intralogistics more than a simple extrinsic system (Link et al., 2012; Pfohl, 2004b).

3   Psychological Perspectives on Fostering Motivation in Logistics

As current approaches to fostering staff motivation in logistics seem deficient, we used an explicitly psychological perspective in grounding our gamification approach described below. Generally speaking, motivation refers to those psychological processes that are responsible for initiating and continuing goal directed behaviors (Schunk, Pintrich & Meece, 2007).

Within our context, the two variants *learning motivation* and *work motivation* are relevant. While conceptually different, both are closely related to each other. Learning motivation is important when instructing new staff, while work motivation is crucial for their ongoing order-picking activities. The role of motivation in these processes can be summarized by the simplifying formula "(ability + skills) X motivation". This expresses that motivation is an essential component for realizing a person's potential abilities and skills in a given situation.

An important distinction in motivation research concerns *intrinsic and extrinsic motivation* (Ryan & Deci, 2000). While extrinsic motivation relies on incentives or expected consequences of an action, intrinsic motivation stems from fulfilling the action itself. Here, contents and execution of an action are so attractive that no further external motivational sources are needed. Empirically, it could be shown that intrinsic motivation is positively associated with learning and work outcomes, while extrinsic motivators do not necessarily result in better performance. In fact, existing intrinsic motivation can be corrupted by additionally providing external motivators. As the manual and repetitive tasks encountered in intralogistics offer relatively little opportunity for intrinsic motivation, we expect that gamification can provide additional options for making order picking more attractive.

In motivation research, *five principal perspectives* can be differentiated. These do not necessarily contradict each other but can become relevant in varying degrees in different contexts (Krapp, 1993). They can also be used to analyze possible motivational effects of different gamification elements (cf. Section 4).

1. The *trait perspective* investigates individual characteristics as sources of motivation, which are relatively stable over time and contexts. Corresponding

research tries to identify general classes of motives, needs and characteristics, such as achievement motive, need for recognition, sensation seeking, or need for affiliation.

2. In the *behaviourist learning perspective*, motivation is interpreted as the result of previous experiences. Therefore, past positive and negative reinforcements influence the probability of a specific behaviour in the future. Examples are providing monetary incentives, or positive and negative feedback.

3. The *cognitive perspective* understands motivation as a rational deliberation of ends and means, and emphasizes the role of internal processes such as expectancies, estimation, and assessment. Accordingly, motivation is dependent upon situation-specific goals, expectancies regarding the consequences of one's actions and the subjective value of these consequences.

4. *Self determination theory* provides a further perspective in motivation research. It focuses on the three universal psychological needs for competence, autonomy, and social relatedness. According to this perspective, people will be motivated to work and learn if they encounter feelings of being competent in dealing with a situation or task, it they are free to make their own choices, and if they are part of a community with relevant others.

5. Contrary to the previous approaches, the *perspective of interest* emphasizes individual preferences and content aspects. It is expected that motivation results from the specific relation of a person to the contents or subject matter of a task. Ideally, this can lead to feelings of flow, i.e. of being fully immersed in an activity.

Given the above analysis of current approaches to staff motivation in logistics, it is evident that the predominant approach is behaviourist. Most often we find incentive systems based on performance measures and predefined time standards, which are subject to dynamic adaption to normal performance. As elaborated in the following section, we expect that our gamification approach will open additional opportunities for increased motivational leverage in intralogistics.

4   Gamification as an Innovative Approach to Enhance Motivation

Because of the broad spectrum of gamification variations, there is no universal definition of the term. Deterding, Dixon, Khaled and Nacke (2011) propose a working definition for gamification as "the use of game design elements in non-game contexts" (Deterding et al., 2011, p. 2). The simplicity of this definition bears a potential risk of trivializing the gamification phenomenon. It is more than adding game elements like points, badges and leader boards, it is also about the use of game-design techniques (Werbach & Hunter, 2012).

Depending on their level of abstraction, game elements – the tools to create gamification scenarios – can be subdivided into three non exhaustive categories. (1) *Dynamics* are the highest level of abstraction and stand for the big picture of a gamification system, yet they cannot be added directly (Werbach & Hunter, 2012).

Dynamics can be constraints, emotions, narrative, progression or relationships. (2) *Mechanics* are basic gamification processes that can be challenges, chance, competition, cooperation, feedback or rewards. (3) *Components* are specific forms of elements, which arise from the dynamics or mechanics. These components can be achievements, avatars, collections, levels, quests or virtual goods (Werbach & Hunter, 2012). Levels (components), for example, give the player feedback (mechanics) and create a sense of progression (dynamics).

To show how gamification can address staff motivation (in logistics), exemplary gamification elements will be considered more precisely in regard to the psychological context in which they function. Therefore, the above-mentioned perspectives will be used.

6. From a *trait perspective*, the need for self-fulfilment, recognition and affiliation can be seen as stable sources of motivation. By creating a strong attachment to a meaningful and awe-inspiring story that personally involves the player, the need for self-fulfilment can be met. This so-called epic meaning (cf. McGonigal, 2011) gives the player the feeling of doing something meaningful and important. Recognition and affiliation can be illustrated by badges. They work as virtual status symbols and function as group identification by communicating shared experiences and activities (Antin & Churchill, 2011).

7. A quite common principle in gamification is reinforcement and punishment. In the sense of a *behaviourist learning perspective*, this can be called operant conditioning. Leveling up or loosing a virtual life can be examples of that. Here, the role of immediate reinforcing feedback is an important element, which should be considered for the effective design of motivating gamification scenarios.

8. From a *cognitive perspective*, motivation depends on means-ends analysis. Clear goals and a high value of consequences can facilitate motivation. By providing a goal in form of a quest, the players experience challenges with clear objectives and rewards. Within these quests, the player has to use problem-solving activities to choose between potential solutions or alternative paths (Hense & Mandl, 2012). Additionally, the value of consequences can be supported by badges because they show other users what a player has performed and what the player is capable of (Antin & Churchill, 2011).

9. Being in control and master a situation fosters the players' self-efficacy, which relates to the feeling of competence (Hense & Mandl, 2012). Offering different opportunities and choices can be a way to provide autonomy. Relatedness refers to options for cooperation, as well as possibilities to share achievements and to give the player the feeling of being part of a community (cf. Antin & Churchill, 2011). These psychological needs for competence, autonomy, and relatedness are crucial for intrinsic motivation, as a *self-determination perspective* suggests.

10. Gamification scenarios should offer many choices. Regarding the story and the resultant quests, in particular, players should have the opportunity to hit their own preferences. This can foster intrinsic motivation and facilitate flow. From a *perspective of interest*, this relation between the player and the context is crucial for motivation.

To foster staff motivation in logistics, it is important to look trough the lens of more than one of these perspectives when designing a gamification system. The next section introduces the interdisciplinary GameLog project, which aims to implement the above-mentioned concepts in logistics.

5   The GameLog Project

The GameLog research project as an interdisciplinary approach combines perceptions and problem-solving methods from the fields of Logistics, Motivational Psychology and Gaming Science. It is operated by the Institute for Material Handling Material Flow Logistics of the Technische Universität München and the chair for Empirical Education and Educational Psychology of the Ludwig-Maximilians-Universität München. The project covers both theoretical basic research and applied science. Acquired insights will be implemented in a test environment for functional testing and feasibility studies and close cooperation with the participating industrial companies will be maintained to obtain an application-oriented and viable result.

The project pursues two major objectives, one applied and one research objective. On the one hand, the feasibility of a value-adding integration of professional gaming elements into intralogistical processes should be evaluated. On the other hand, a gamification system for order picking (see Fig.1) should be implemented in a laboratory environment and examined in trials with test subjects to see how it influences a user's motivation. The GameLog project is divided into 9 major work packages: (1) Analysis of current approaches to staff motivation in logistics; (2) Feasibility study of gamification elements in order picking processes; (3) Development and evaluation of gaming concepts; (4) Development of story, mechanics and reward structure; (5) Selection of soft- and hardware; (6) Development and implementation of a prototype test environment; (7) Evaluation of the test environment; (8) Validation and improvement of the test environment; (9) Documentation and Transfer of the project results. After assessing the test environment, we expect to be able to implement the gamification system in other order picking processes of our project partners as well.

6   Outlook

Gamification has quickly become a popular trend in many contexts recently. While examples of uses for a multitude of goals in diverse settings are abundant, fostering staff motivation in logistics is still an innovative application. We expect that our project will bring forth results on several levels.

For the practice of intralogistics, we expect to develop readily applicable solutions for alleviating motivational problems in order picking. It is anticipated that this can contribute to an increased productivity and reduced costs for breaking in new staff.

On a research level, we intend to gain detailed insights into the general applicability of gamification approaches in labour contexts. In doing so, we consider gamification not as a monolithic construct. Instead, our approach is to differentiate between specific gamification elements and analyze their respective potentials and limits within a given practical labour setting. Beyond the general question 'will it work?', we aim to address the question 'what gamification elements work by which motivational mechanisms in a given context?' on a conceptual an empirical level.

On a general note, we share the expectation that gamification has an inherent potential for positively impacting learning and behaviour. However, as noted by others (Deterding et al., 2011), not games themselves are the solution, but well-designed games. This emphasizes the need for a well-planned approach grounded in gamification and psychological theory, if one seeks to fully realize the potentials of gamification for motivation.

Acknowledgements. Work on this paper was partly funded by the German Federal Ministry of Economics and Technology via the German Federal Logistics Association (grant no. 456 ZN)

References

1. Antin, J., Churchill, E.F.: Badges in Social Media: A Social Psychological Perspective. In: Proceedings of the Conference of Human-Computer Interaction. ACM, Vancouver (2011)
2. Arnold, D. (ed.): Intralogistik. Potentiale, Perspektiven, Prognosen (Intralogistics. Potentials, perspectives, prognoses). Springer, Berlin (2006)
3. Bundesverband Materialwirtschaft, Einkauf und Logistik, Best Practice in Einkauf und Logistik (Best Practice in purchasing and logistics) (2nd ed.). Gabler, Wiesbaden (2008)
4. Christopher, M.: New directions in logistics. In: Waters, D. (ed.) Global Logistics and Distribution Planning, 4th edn., pp. 22–32. Kogan Page, London (2003)
5. Coffey, D.: Zero in on Picking. Logistics & Transport Focus 1(4), 22–25 (1999)
6. Deterding, S., Dixon, D., Khaled, R., Nacke, L.: From Game Design Elements to Gamefulness: Defining "Gamification". In: Proceedings of the 15th International Academic MindTrek Conference: Envisioning Future Media Environments. ACM, Tampere (2011)
7. Hense, J., Mandl, H.: Learning in or with games? Quality criteria for digital learning games from the perspectives of learning, emotion, and motivation theory. In: Sampson, D.G., Spector, J.M., Ifenthaler, D., Isaias, P. (eds.) Proceedings of the IADIS International Conference on Cognition and Exploratory Learning in the Digital Age, pp. 19–26. IADIS, Madrid (2012)
8. Jünemann, R., Schmidt, T.: Materialflußsysteme – Systemtechnische Grundlagen (Material flow systems – Basics of system technology). Springer, Berlin (2000)
9. Kapp, K.M.: The Gamification of learning and instruction. Pfeiffer, San Francisco (2012)
10. Krapp, A.: Die Psychologie der Lernmotivation (The psychology of learning motivation). Zeitschrift für Pädagogik (Journal of education) 39(2), 187–206 (1993)
11. Link, I., Müller-Dauppert, B., Jung, K.: Motivationsstudie 2012: Mitarbeitermotivation in der Logistik (Motivation study 2012: Staff motivation in logistics). Miebach Consulting, Franfurt a. M (2012)
12. McGonigal, J.: Reality is broken: Why games make us better and how they can change the world. The Penguin Press, New York (2011)
13. Pfohl, H.-C.: Logistikmanagement – Konzeption und Funktionen (Logistics management – Concept and functions). Springer, Berlin (2004a)

14. Pfohl, H.-C. (Hrsg.): Personalführung in der Logistik – Innovative Ansätze und praktische Lösungen (Personnel management in logistics. Innovative approaches and practical solutions). Deutscher Verkehrs-Verlag, Hamburg (2004b)
15. Pulverich, M., Schietinger, J. (eds.): Handbuch Kommissionierung – Effizient picken und packen (Handbook order picking – Efficient picking and packaging). Heinrich Vogel, München (2009)
16. Ryan, R.M., Deci, E.L.: Intrinsic and extrinsic motivation: Classic definitions and new directions. Contemporary Educational Psychology 25, 54–76 (2000)
17. Schunk, D.H., Pintrich, P.R., Meece, J.L.: Motivation in education. Theory, research, and applications. Prentice Hall, Upper Saddle River (2007)
18. ten Hompel, M., Sadowsky, V., Beck, M.: Kommissionierung: Materialflusssysteme 2 – Planung und Berechnung der Kommissionierung in der Logistik (Order picking: Material flow systems 2 – Planning and calculation of order picking in logistics). Springer, Berlin (2011)
19. Wagner, U.: Entgeltdifferenzierung in logistischen Bereichen (Differentiation of wages in logistics). Deutscher Universitätsverlag, Wiesbaden (1995)
20. Werbach, K., Hunter, D.: For the Win: How Game Thinking Can Revolutionize Your Business. Wharton Digital Press, Philadelphia (2012)
21. Zaunmüller, H.: Anreizsysteme für das Wissensmanagement in KMU (Incentive systems for knowledge management in SMEs). Deutscher Universitätsverlag, Wiesbaden (2005)

A Distributed Barge Planning Game

Martijn Mes, Maria-Eugenia Iacob, and Jos van Hillegersberg

Centre for Telematics and Information Technology
University of Twente, Enschede, The Netherlands

Abstract. In this paper, we address a complex issue in the coordination of supply chains: the optimization of the alignment of barge and terminal operations in the Port of Rotterdam. Our research goal is to design a distributed multi-agent and service-oriented system architecture, which solves the barge handling problem through information exchange and a decision support system based on intelligent alignment of proposals. In order to validate this solution, we implement it by means of both a system and a management game, using web-service technology. We report our experiences with the game throughout its validation with domain experts.

1   Introduction

In this paper we address a complex issue in the coordination of supply chains, the optimization of the alignment of barge and terminal operations in the Port of Rotterdam, also called the barge handling problem. The Port of Rotterdam considers this problem as the most urgent problem in container barge hinterland transport. The poor alignment of barge and terminal operations leads to high direct costs and has even more indirect effects, such as environmental pressure, and congestion on the road and rail infrastructure. Solving the problem improves the hinterland connectivity and thereby the attractiveness of the port of Rotterdam significantly.

In the harbour, the 30 container terminals are visited daily by about 60 barges. Every barge visits on average eight container terminals to load and unload containers. For the handling of ships, appointments are made between terminal and barge operators. In the present situation, appointments are made by telephone, fax, and e-mail. Unfortunately, it happens frequently that appointments are not (or cannot) be met by either the barge or the terminal operator. In addition, the fact that barges usually visit multiple terminals creates dependencies between activities performed at different terminals. Thus, a disruption at one terminal can propagate through the port and disturb the operations of other barge and terminal operators. The result is that barge operators face uncertain waiting and handling times at terminals, and that terminals deal with uncertain arrival times of barges and idle time of their quay resources.

Besides the unreliability of appointments, the current 'manual' way of planning also results in strategic behaviour. For example, barges may announce a wrong number of containers to handle in order to obtain more convenient time slots, and terminal operators respond by creating queues of barges to prevent idle times at their quays.

S.A. Meijer and R. Smeds (Eds.): ISAGA 2013, LNCS 8264, pp. 214–221, 2014.
© Springer International Publishing Switzerland 2014

This type of behaviour makes the alignment process even more uncertain and deteriorates the relationships between the terminal and the barge operators.

All the considerations above suggest that a distributed information system for the automated handling of the barge planning problem may significantly improve the situation, since such a system can increase the reliability of appointments, prevent opportunistic behaviour, and become and acceptable solution for all parties involved (as it will be explained in Section 2). Subsequently, the performance of both barges and terminals may improve. This is also the main contribution of this paper. Our research goal is to design a distributed multi-agent and service-oriented system architecture, which solves the barge handling problem through information exchange, and provides decision support based on intelligent alignment of proposals. We build on earlier research [1] in which a conceptual foundation (in terms of optimization algorithms) for this system was developed, evaluated, and demonstrated [2]. In order to validate and test the proposed architecture, we implement this architecture by means of both a system and a management game, using model-driven web-service technology. We also report our experiences during this game's validation with domain experts.

A series of very successful studies (e.g., [3], [4], [6]) have contributed to the recognition of the design science research methodology as valid IS paradigm. This methodology [6] distinguishes between five research activities, to which we adhere in this paper. With this section covering research activity 1 and 2, the remainder of this paper is organised as follows. In Section 2, we discuss the architecture of the future dynamic barge planning system (research activity 3). Section 3 presents the main contribution of the paper, i.e., the design and implementation of a management game based on the distributed system architecture presented in Section 2 (research activity 4). Section 4 (research activity 5) is concerned with the validation of this game (research activity 4). The paper ends with conclusions, and pointers to future work (Section 5).

2   The Architecture

Before presenting the proposed architecture, we first summarize the most important requirements the future system must meet. It has to support the involved parties in optimizing their operations, and the conditions for adopting the new system have to be acceptable. Typically, for this problem we have to deal with different competing companies having different and conflicting objectives. In this business environment there is neither a clear hierarchy between companies nor dominant players. Also, no contractual relationships between terminals and barges exist, which means that no performance can be contractually enforced. In addition, this is a highly dynamic environment, i.e., information becomes known over time, and disturbances (may) take place. Due to the above characteristics, central coordination of all activities in the port (via a trusted third party or a control centre) is not an acceptable option for two main reasons. First, each party is reluctant to share information that could undermine its competitive position. Second, each party wants to have control on its own operations. Therefore, we have chosen for a distributed system in which the control of the process is assigned to the individual actors involved in the network. The proposed architecture (shown in Fig. 1) allows actors to plan their operations efficiently in such a way that the system is not unacceptable up-front: participants share only limited information and they keep autonomy over their own operations. The basic concept is a Multi-Agent System in which every party is represented by an agent (a piece of software). Together, the agents coordinate the barge and terminal activities in the port.

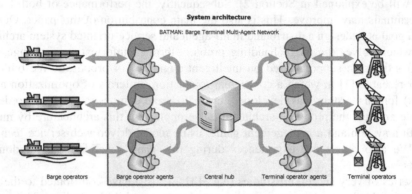

Fig. 1. Simplified system architecture

The sole core function of the hub is to facilitate the exchange and routing of messages between Barge Operator Agents (BOAs) and Terminal Operator Agents (TOAs). This exchange is carried out in two phases and is initiated by a BOA that has to plan a so-called rotation, i.e., a sequence of terminals to visit. In the first phase (Fig. 2, top) the BOA sends information about the numbers of containers that must be loaded/unloaded at each terminal in the rotation, and requests from all terminals a so-called *service time profile* (STP). The STP calculated and issued by a TOA for a particular barge B and a terminal T, denotes the maximum departure time of B (after being serviced) from T, for every possible arrival time of B at T during a certain time period.

The idea behind using STPs is that terminals are not giving away competitive sensitive information (e.g., a high service time might indicate many visits at this terminal, but could also mean that there is no crew scheduled at this time). But still, it provides enough information for barges to plan their rotations efficiently.

Based on STPs received from all TOAs, the BOA calculates the best five rotations. For more information on the algorithm to compute the STPs and the algorithm to determine the optimal rotations using these STPs, we refer to [2]. The barge operator planner may choose one of the proposed rotations. Consequently, the BOA requests appointments with the respective terminals which constitutes the second phase in the planning process (Fig. 2, bottom). In case one or more terminals are not able to confirm the requested appointments (due to the fact that, in the meantime, appointments might have been made for other barges, which could invalidate previously issued STPs), the whole rotation is cancelled, and the process starts all over again, until a rotation can be completely booked. Due to space limitations we do not go here into further details regarding the exact design of the planning and interaction algorithms.

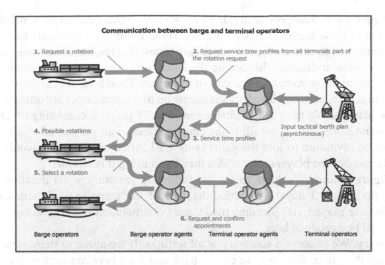

Fig. 2. The interaction protocol

The hub has been implemented by means of Enterprise Service Bus (ESB) middleware software, and has the following functionality: intelligent routing of messages, security (authentication and authorization of all agents), and monitoring. The agents (both TOAs and BOAs) have been implemented as web services.

3   The Game

To gain acceptance (from both terminal and barge operators) for the designed system and to validate its functionality, we have developed a management game (available at www.bat-man.nl/game) in which we reuse the majority of the implemented system components. In terms of software architecture, the game version of the system has been slightly simplified in order to increase the interaction speed of the players within the system. Also, to make the gaming experience more pleasant and accessible, the game offers multiple types of user interfaces (laptop, tablet and smart phone).

The game is organized by a game master and played over the Internet. The game master has to configure the game and then invite a group of players to join the game. Within the game, the group can play multiple rounds where we can use different planning strategies. After playing all rounds, we can compare the scores of players within rounds, but also the overall scores (sum of scores within each round) for each of the rounds. The latter comparison allows us compare the performance of different planning strategies. We now describe the steps that are to be carried out during a game in more detail.

1. **Configure port.** The port is divided into several regions called terminal groups. For each of these terminal groups, we set (i) the number of terminals each player has to visit within this group, (ii) the closing times, (iii) the handling times, and (iv) initial terminal utilization. Regarding the latter, it is not realistic to assume empty schedules for the terminals at the start of the game. Therefore, we randomly fill the terminal schedules with virtual appointments up to a given target utilization.

2. **Invite players.** We have a list suitable for up to 25 players, consisting of 25 barge names and icons. Either, we fill in the email address of all players after which they receive an invitation to join the game (with URL, username and password), or we simply number the players after which they login using this number.

3. **Configure round.** We have to set the following parameters: (i) duration in the game time (e.g., 3 days), (ii) actual duration of the game (e.g., 5 minutes), (iii) rounds to be played, (iv) planning mode, and (v) simulation mode. The last two settings will be explained later.

4. **Summary.** We observe a summary of all settings. If we agree to these settings we can start the game. Note that we can go back and forth between each of these steps as long as we didn't start the game. In addition we can save the game in each of these steps so we can replay the game some later time.

5. **Planning phase.** After logging in, players plan their rotation, which we explain later on, and confirm the plan of their choice. When all players confirmed their planning, the game master can end the planning phase thereby starting the simulation phase.

6. **Simulation phase.** In the simulation phase a clock is running and periodically all indicators, positions, performances, animation etc. are updated. On a map of the Port of Rotterdam (Fig. 3), we can follow the position of barges. In addition, the progress of all players is shown together with an estimate of their final score. Besides the map, there are other screens available with overview of terminal performance (utilization, fragmentation of appointments) and barge performance (handling time, sailing time, waiting time, all indicators are shown as planned, actual, and optimal).

7. **Completion of a round.** When all players completed their rotation or we are at the end of the simulation time, we finish the round and go to the scoring screen. Scoring of players is based on the difference in length of stay in the port between (i) their optimal plan (computed by the routing algorithm) and (ii) their actual rotation. We use this deviation from optimum as scoring criteria because the optimal length of stay in the port might differ per player. We keep track of this score in each round of the game. Within a round, we have a ranking of players based on this score. After playing all rounds, we display the score for all players over all rounds as well as the sum of scores for each player for each of the rounds. This way we can observe whether the availability of extra information results in higher scores. The game master can now start the next round and go back to the planning phase.

Fig. 3. Screen capture of the game

There are four types of rounds that can be played during a game and can be compared with respect to the planning performance. We describe them below.

1. The player choses the order in which terminals are visited without making an appointment with them, and without having information on their utilization.
2. The player choses the order in which terminals are visited and also makes appointments with them. As in type 1, no information on the utilization of these terminals is available. To make an appointment, the player asks the terminal whether it can handle the barge at a certain arrival time. The terminal's answer could be yes or no.
3. The player choses the order in which terminals are visited and makes appointments with these them. The player can now gain insight into the utilization of these terminals by requesting their STPs.
4. The player gets decision support from the barge operator agent by receiving a set of efficient rotations, together with various performance indicators of these plans. Now the player only has to decide which rotation to use.

By playing these four rounds, we demonstrate (i) more information on available terminal capacity results in better routes, (ii) the use of our decision support system results in the best routes, and (iii) overall increase in performance is achieved without central coordination; players maintain their autonomy.

4   Verification and Validation of the Game

The game has two main purposes (i) to familiarize students and professionals with the challenges of routing and scheduling problems and (ii) to illustrate possible new ways of planning within the port of Rotterdam. For both objectives, extensive validation of the game is important. We use several steps to come up with a valid game implementation. Here we make a distinction between the validation of the system architecture, of the algorithms, and of the game itself. The development methodology we followed and the game itself also provided opportunities for verification and validation. We used the SCRUM agile software development approach. The four weekly sprint review meetings were used to verify whether the implementation meets our requirements and obvious mistakes where found and placed on the product backlog to be fixed in a later sprint. The game itself is also a useful tool to validate the system architecture and the algorithms, as the game is basically a simulation layer on top of the original system. By playing the game, we observe the added value of the implemented algorithms and the user friendliness of our decision support system.

The validation of the application architecture focused on whether all required messages are sent and received, whether the response times are reasonable, and whether the application reacts properly on 'ill defined' messages and other types of exceptions. For this, we used the game with varying scenario's (planning horizon, number of players, number of terminal visits, terminal utilization, etc.). After extensive testing we conclude that the application architecture requires some small modifications for the gaming environment to reduce the response times. The reason for this is that in the game all players plan their rotation exactly at the same time, which is not likely to occur in practice. There are two algorithms used in the game: the barge operator agent uses a routing algorithm and the terminal operator agent uses an algorithm to compute the STPs. We implemented both algorithms as separate web services such that we can separately test them outside the game. In addition, we compared the output of our implementation to the original implementations of [2], who in turn benchmarked the algorithms against centralized planning methodologies.

To validate the game itself, we again used (i) manual testing under normal circumstances, (ii) extreme condition tests and (iii) sensitivity tests. Regarding the manual test, we play rounds with simplified settings such that we can compute the KPI's, such as the final game score, by hand and compare it with the results from the game. Extreme condition tests are carried out by simulating the model after setting certain variables (e.g., amount of players, number of visits per region, time-windows) to an extremely high or extremely low value and examining the behaviour of key variables. Results of these tests reveal evidence of high structural validity. Due to space limitations, the results of these tests are not shown in this paper. After the extreme-condition tests, a series of sensitivity runs were made to determine whether the sensitivity of the base model was within acceptable limits. The sensitivity tests were performed by playing with the same key variables, but varying them around given default settings (resembling reality). The results indicate that the model has a meaningful and reasonable level of sensitivity to these parameters. Finally, we played numerous rounds with the project team, which also consists of several field experts, such as a terminal operator. In addition, these meetings were also visited by a representative of the port authority and a representative of a group of barge operators. We also organized gaming sessions at various national events, again with the presence of many field experts. After each round, we improved the game using feedback from the players. We are now ready to take the final and most important step, namely to organize gaming sessions for the target audience, i.e., the barge and terminal operators, and to assess their reactions.

5   Conclusion

In this paper we proposed a solution for the barge handling problem in the port of Rotterdam, which has been implemented in a distributed multi-agent planning system and a management game. The system consists primarily of several intelligent barge and terminal software agents and a hub that is responsible for the routing of messages between the interacting agents. The system architecture and the game have been tested and validated in several ways. The results of the tests indicate that the overall performance of the proposed solution is satisfactory.

We foresee two directions for further work. First, we want to improve the game itself by making the four planning options also available within the simulation phase. Instead of passively observing possible deviations from the plans (e.g., due to unforeseen waiting times), we can now change our plans dynamically. Second, we want to demonstrate the usability of our approach by organizing various gaming sessions with the target audience and by analysing the change in mental models of the players.

References

1. Douma, A., Schutten, M., Schuur, P.: Waiting profiles: An efficient protocol for enabling distributed planning of container barge rotations along terminals in the port of Rotterdam. Transportation Research Part C 17(2), 133–148 (2009)
2. Douma, A., Schuur, P., Schutten, J.: Aligning barge and terminal operations using service-time profiles. Flexible Services and Manufacturing Journal 23(4), 385–421 (2011)
3. Gregor, S., Jones, D.: Anatomy of a Design Theory. JAIS 8(5), 312–335 (2007)
4. Hevner, A.R., March, S.T., Park, J.: Design research in information systems research. MIS Quarterly 28(1), 75–105 (2004)
5. Malandraki, C., Dial, R.: A restricted dynamic programming heuristic algorithm for the time dependent traveling salesman problem. European Journal of Operational Research 90(1), 45–55 (1996)
6. Peffers, K., Tuunanen, T., Rothenberger, M., Chatterjee, S.: A Design Science Research Methodology for Information Systems Research. Journal of Management Information Systems 24(3), 45–77 (2008)

A Prediction Market Game
to Route Selection under Uncertainty

Hajime Mizuyama, Shuhei Torigai, and Michiko Anse

Dept. of Industrial and Systems Engineering, Aoyama Gakuin University
mizuyama@ise.aoyama.ac.jp

Abstract. This paper addresses a route selection problem under uncertainty. The structure of the problem can be captured as an ordinal shortest path problem of a directed graph. However, the length of each arc of the graph is an uncertain random variable and its probability distribution is unknown to the decision maker; instead, information on the distribution is dispersed among the crowd. Under this set of circumstances, this paper provides a prediction market game for gathering the dispersed information from the crowd and thereby solving the reformulated problem. Further, the proposed gaming approach is applied to a simple real-life problem to understand how it works.

1 Introduction

Route selection decisions need to be made in various situations. For example, when delivering relief goods to a disaster-stricken area by truck, the driver must choose an appropriate route to the area for the mission. If the available road network has been captured as a directed graph and the time required to drive along each arc of the graph has been evaluated, the route selection decision can be modeled as an ordinal shortest path problem, and its solution can be easily obtained, for example, by Dijkstra's algorithm [1]. However, if the disaster is so severe that the road network is damaged to some degree, the situation can be different. In other words, the shortest path obtained based on the graph representing the road network before the disaster happened may no longer be the shortest and can even be unreachable. Thus, in this situation, the route selection decision involves not only solving a shortest path problem but also reformulating the problem itself by gathering information on the status of the road network. This composite problem is quite cumbersome, and an effective supporting tool is strongly demanded.

Under these circumstances, it is unlikely that any single person has all the necessary information about the entire road network, but rather the information is likely to be dispersed among different people. Therefore, crowdsourcing can be an effective approach for gathering the information [2]. Further, in order to collect the dispersed information from the crowd, a prediction market can be utilized [3-6]. A prediction market is a market for prediction securities whose worth depends on the unknown realized value of some random variable of interest, and thus the market price of the security provides a dynamic forecast of the random variable, reflecting the collective

S.A. Meijer and R. Smeds (Eds.): ISAGA 2013, LNCS 8264, pp. 222–229, 2014.

knowledge of the participants. This approach has been successfully applied not only to forecasting problems but also to a knapsack problem [7]. Thus, in this study, we develop a prediction market game for addressing the composite route selection problem under uncertainty, where reformulating a shortest path problem and resolving it need to be dealt with simultaneously. We also report the results of the proposed gaming approach applied to a simple real-life problem to understand how it works.

2   Route Selection Problem under Uncertainty

The structure of the route selection problem considered in this paper can be captured as an ordinal shortest path problem on a directed graph $G = (V, A)$, where V is the set of nodes and A is the set of arcs; that is, the topology of the available road network is known and is modeled as a directed graph G. The original location and the destination are represented as v_O and v_D ($\in V$), respectively, and the set of possible routes or paths from v_O to v_D, each of which is a sequence of consecutive arcs without cycles bridging the nodes v_O and v_D, is denoted as R.

What makes the problem cumbersome is that the length of each arc a_i ($\in A$) is an uncertain random variable and its distribution is unknown to the decision maker. Since the length of each arc is a random variable, which route is the shortest may also be probabilistic. Thus, the problem is to estimate for each route r_j ($\in R$) the probability that it will be the shortest.

When a part of the road network represented by the arc a_i has been damaged and has become no longer available, the situation can be modeled either by a topological change of the graph G or by considerably extending the length of the arc a_i. In other words, the situation can be addressed by the formulation provided above by taking the second option. Thus, it can be seen that the problem formulation here is more general than it first appears.

3   Prediction Market Game for Addressing the Problem

3.1   Design of Securities

This paper utilizes a prediction market game, where players buy and sell prediction securities, for gathering dispersed information on the problem from the players. A simplest ways of designing prediction securities for the game would be to introduce a winner-take-all security for each route r_j ($\in R$), to which a fixed payoff amount will be given if and only if r_j is confirmed to be the shortest by a post-hoc evaluation. Hereafter, this is called route security r_j.

In many cases, a player is knowledgeable about only a limited area of the road network and what needs to be aggregated through the prediction market is such local knowledge. However, when the players are to trade route securities, they must be capable of comparing road conditions for one entire route with that for other complete routes in R. This means that route securities are not suitable for aggregating local knowledge. Thus, this paper introduces a winner-take-all security to each arc a_i ($\in$ **A**) instead of each route, to which a fixed payoff amount will be given if and only if a_i is included in the shortest path identified by a post-hoc evaluation. Hereafter, this is called arc security a_i.

3.2 Central Market Maker for Arc Securities

In order to assure sufficient liquidity for arc securities, we utilize a computerized central market maker system as the market institution of the game. A central market maker (CMM) accepts any bid/ask requests from players as long as they agree with the price offered by the CMM.

One of the most popular CMM algorithms for a prediction market would be the logarithmic market scoring rule (LMSR) proposed by Hanson [8, 9]. Suppose that there are N mutually exclusive and collectively exhaustive possible events, and a set of winner-take-all securities are assigned to the events. Further, the securities are traded among K players, and player k has q_{kn} units of the security corresponding to nth event. Then, the entire quantity of securities sold so far to all the players is given by

$$Q_n = \sum_{k=1}^{K} q_{kn} \qquad (1)$$

LMSR defines a cost function based on this variable as

$$C(\mathbf{Q}) = b \cdot \log\left[\sum_{n=1}^{N} \exp(Q_n / b) \right] \qquad (2)$$

where $\mathbf{Q} = (Q_1, Q_2, \ldots, Q_N)$, and b is a parameter controlling the sensitivity. When a player buys $\Delta\mathbf{q}$ units of the securities, LMSR determines how much to charge using the cost function as

$$\text{Cost} = C(\mathbf{Q} + \Delta\mathbf{q}) - C(\mathbf{Q}) \qquad (3)$$

Thus, the unitary price of the nth security is given by

$$p_n = \frac{dC(\mathbf{Q})}{dQ_n} = \frac{\exp(Q_n / b)}{\sum_{i=1}^{N} \exp(Q_i / b)} \qquad (4)$$

Unfortunately, LMSR cannot be directly applied to arc securities, because they do not correspond to a set of mutually exclusive and collectively exhaustive events. On the other hand, the events corresponding to route securities satisfy this condition. Thus, we propose to run LMSR for route securities behind the scenes, and to treat each arc security as a set of the route securities containing the arc. In other words, the price of an arc security is calculated from those of the route securities as

$$p_i^a = \sum_{a_i \in r_j} p_j^r \tag{5}$$

where p_i^a and p_j^r are the prices of arc security a_i and route security r_j, respectively, and where the notation $a_i \in r_j$ means that arc a_i is included in route r_j.

4 Gaming Experiments

4.1 Game Concept

In order to study how the proposed approach works in practice, a simple prototype prediction market game platform was developed as a web application, and the gaming approach is experimented on the platform. The players in the experiments were 18 undergraduate students studying at the Sagamihara campus of Aoyama Gakuin University. They were grouped into three teams, A, B, and C, each consisting of six students, and each team was asked to evaluate possible routes from the nearest train station Fuchinobe to the front gate of the campus by interactively playing a prediction market game on the prototype platform.

The road network between the station and the gate is depicted in Fig. 1. We note there are ten possible routes, r_1, r_2, ..., r_{10}, from the station to the gate; these routes are summarized in Table 1. All the players were well aware that the amount of time required to walk through each route differs significantly depending on whether it is a weekday morning, because on weekday mornings, the routes are full of students heading to the campus. Further, the degree of congestion, and thereby, the walking speed, differs among the routes. Thus, two situations, HC where congestion is high (weekday mornings) and LC where it is low (other times), were considered in the experiments.

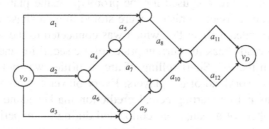

Fig. 1. Example road network

Before conducting the experiments, the transit time of each route was measured by actually walking through the route eight times under both traffic conditions. Further, the probability that the route will be the shortest in terms of transit time was calculated with the Monte Carlo method. The results are shown in Table 2.

Table 1. Possible routes from station to campus

Route	Included arcs	Route	Included arcs
r_1	$a_1 - a_8 - a_{11}$	r_6	$a_2 - a_4 - a_7 - a_{10} - a_{12}$
r_2	$a_1 - a_8 - a_{12}$	r_7	$a_2 - a_4 - a_5 - a_8 - a_{11}$
r_3	$a_2 - a_6 - a_9 - a_{10} - a_{11}$	r_8	$a_2 - a_4 - a_5 - a_8 - a_{12}$
r_4	$a_2 - a_6 - a_9 - a_{10} - a_{12}$	r_9	$a_3 - a_9 - a_{10} - a_{11}$
r_5	$a_2 - a_4 - a_7 - a_{10} - a_{11}$	r_{10}	$a_3 - a_9 - a_{10} - a_{11}$

Table 2. The required transit time and the probability of being the shortest of each route

Route	LC situation			HC situation		
	Mean (s)	Std. dev. (s)	Prob. (%)	Mean (s)	Std. dev. (s)	Prob. (%)
r_1	661	54	0.2	671	61	1.0
r_2	592	56	1.4	631	67	3.5
r_3	491	22	5.3	627	66	3.7
r_4	453	42	42.4	579	61	9.4
r_5	533	50	5.0	560	56	13.2
r_6	470	45	27.4	529	56	26.0
r_7	550	49	3.0	548	58	17.7
r_8	479	31	15.3	545	81	25.2
r_9	651	31	0.0	686	35	0.1
r_{10}	582	14	0.0	652	39	0.3

4.2   Game Implementation

A client–server architecture was used for the prototype game platform. The players' assets as well as their transaction history were stored in a database on the server PC. Each player was provided a client PC, which was connected to the server PC through a LAN. He or she could check the current prices of arc securities and trade them from the web browser on the PC. Short selling of arc securities was not allowed so as to reduce the cognitive workload of the players. Every player experienced several practice market sessions before starting actual prediction market game experiments. Although all the members of a team were collocated during the experiments, they were not allowed to directly communicate in order to limit the information channel to the market game.

Each team played two market sessions corresponding to high- and low-congestion situations. The value of the liquidity parameter b was set to 100 for all sessions. At the beginning of each market session, every team member was provided an initial endowment of P\$1000, where P\$ was the unit of play money used in the game. Further, five pieces of every arc security were also given only to the members of team C to make it easier for them to sell arc securities. No preset limit was imposed on the length of a market session, but the session was terminated when no one wanted to conduct further transactions. The amount of posterior payoff was set to P\$100, and was given at the end of a market session to a unit of each arc security contained in the route having the highest probability of being the shortest, as shown in Table 2. The winner of the game was the player having the most posterior wealth including the payoff.

Table 3. Final price of each route security

Route	LC situation			HC situation		
	Team A	Team B	Team C	Team A	Team B	Team C
r_1	6.4	6.0	1.6	8.8	7.6	4.6
r_2	8.3	7.6	4.4	11.0	8.0	5.6
r_3	12.7	12.8	11.8	8.8	8.9	6.8
r_4	16.4	16.3	31.5	11.1	9.2	8.3
r_5	8.7	9.5	5.7	9.0	12.2	13.9
r_6	11.2	12.1	15.2	11.4	12.7	17.1
r_7	7.6	9.0	3.6	10.0	13.1	16.1
r_8	9.9	11.5	9.6	12.5	13.7	19.9
r_9	8.2	6.7	4.5	7.7	7.1	3.5
r_{10}	10.6	8.5	12.1	9.7	7.4	4.3

4.3   Game Results and Discussion

The final market prices of the route securities are compared with their theoretical values calculated from the probabilities provided in Table 2. If these values are linearly correlated, the proposed gaming approach can be judged to have worked properly. The results are shown in Fig. 2 and Fig. 3. We first note that Pearson's correlation coefficient is satisfactorily high for all the cases. Further, its 95% confidence interval is (0.35, 0.95), (0.51, 0.97), and (0.60, 0.97) in LC conditions, and (0.13, 0.92), (0.79, 0.99), and (0.90, 0.99) in HC conditions for teams A, B, and C, respectively. The sensitivity of the market price is not sufficient for teams A and B, but it is significantly improved for team C. This is because arc securities are given at the beginning, and hence selling securities is made easier for the players. Some players may be confident of whether some particular arcs will be included in the shortest route, but others may only be confident of whether some particular arcs will not be included in the shortest route. In the case of team C, the latter players are also given a means, i.e., selling securities, to express their knowledge.

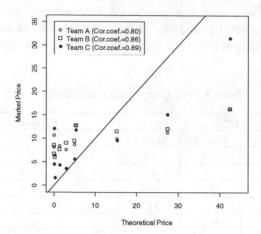

Fig. 2. Final market price and the corresponding theoretical value of each route (LC situation)

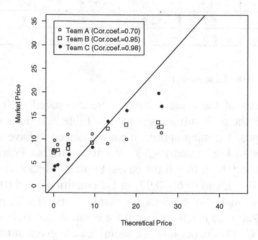

Fig. 3. Final market price and the corresponding theoretical value of each route (HC situation)

5   Conclusions

In this study, we first formulated a route selection problem under uncertainty, the structure of which can be captured as an ordinal shortest path problem of a directed graph while the length of each arc of the graph is a random variable following an unknown distribution. We then pointed out that aggregating information on the distribution and identifying the shortest path according to the information should be addressed simultaneously. Then, we proposed a prediction market game for addressing the composite route selection problem and developed a simple prototype platform for the game. Further, the proposed gaming approach is tested on the platform to understand the mechanism of the approach for a real example problem. We confirmed that this approach can produce satisfactory results. Future research directions include extending the CMM algorithm to a large-scale problem, incorporating topological uncertainty, and designing appropriate incentives for participation. The current CMM algorithm assumes that all the possible routes can be enumerated, but this would be difficult for a large-scale problem. Hence, how to extend the algorithm to such a case is an important issue. The current system also assumes that the topology of the road network is fixed. However, incorporating the ability to add new arcs and nodes during a market session will extend its applicability. Further, in order to use this approach for a practical problem, devising a method to attract knowledgeable players will be important.

Acknowledgments. This research was partially supported by the Japan Society for the Promotion of Science, Grant-in-Aid for Scientific Research (B) 20310087.

References

1. Dijkstra, E.W.: A Note on Two Problems in Connexion with Graphs. Numerische Mathematik 1, 269–271 (1959)
2. Estelles-Arolas, E., Gonzalez-Ladron-de-Guevara, F.: Towards an Integrated Crowdsourcing Definition. Journal of Information Science 38, 189–200 (2012)
3. Plott, C.R.: Markets as Information Gathering Tools. Southern Economic Journal 67, 1–15 (2000)
4. Wolfers, J., Zitzewitz, E.: Prediction Markets. Journal of Economic Perspectives 18, 107–126 (2004)
5. Tziralis, G., Tatsiopoulos, I.: Prediction Markets: An Extended Literature Review. Journal of Prediction Markets 1, 75–91 (2007)
6. Pennock, D.M., Lawrence, S., Giles, C.L., Nielsen, F.A.: The Real Power of Artificial Markets. Science 291, 987–988 (2001)
7. Meloso, D., Copic, J., Bossaerts, P.: Promoting Intellectual Discovery, Patents Versus Markets. Science 323, 1335–1339 (2009)
8. Hanson, R.: Combinatorial Information Market Design. Information Systems Frontiers 5, 107–119 (2003)
9. Hanson, R.: Logarithmic Market Scoring Rules for Modular Combinatorial Information Aggregation. Journal of Prediction Markets 1, 3–15 (2007)

Parameterised Business Simulation Game Development for Education in Supply Chain Management and Logistics

Luiz Antonio Titton

Universidade de Sao Paulo, Brazil

Abstract. This paper examines the development of a business simulation game for training and education in the area of supply chain management. The paper begins by identifying the need for an apparatus that could be used in many disciplines, minimising the learning time with regard to the simulator with reasonable parameterisation, followed by a brief conclusion about the available games. Fidelity and embodied experiences are needs that are effectively detected in the design process, demonstrating the relevance of these aspects. One topic of interest is that the effects of the main functions of management (marketing, finance, and production) were minimised in this game to make decisions on logistics with higher relevance. This paper describes the process that was used to design the simulator and draws the first conclusions about interface, usability, technical functionality and potential adoption in an educational context.

Keywords: Business simulation game, supply chain management simulation game, logistic simulation game, education based on simulation.

1   Introduction

Business simulation games (BSGs) are widely used in technical and managerial skill training. In particular, logistics is perceived as a relevant activity in numerous industries, a factor that justifies the use of these instruments to support this type of learning. By studying logistics, students access the knowledge and techniques structured in disciplines that eventually make use of simulators, not only to illustrate the learned concepts but also to increase their motivation and interest level [1].

Among the various classifications of BSGs, the distinction between total and functional simulations is particularly important. Whereas the first type of simulation covers a wide range of management functions (for example, finance, marketing, production, etc.), the second type has a unique emphasis on one discipline [2].

Although numerous management games of the first type are available to students and teachers of management, the number of games to teach/learn specific management skills is small. [3]

Because of the limited variety and quantity of games that are targeted for each discipline, teachers are unable to conduct an extensive analysis before selecting the most appropriate products. In addition, from the point of view of the course coordinators, the purchase of products from multiple vendors creates problems related to high costs and variations in quality and usability, interface and other features.

S.A. Meijer and R. Smeds (Eds.): ISAGA 2013, LNCS 8264, pp. 230–236, 2014.

With regard to productivity in the learning process, learning about the function of each copy of the available games hinders the adoption of additional games targeted specifically to each discipline. When the user learns about the functioning of a particular game, little is reused in the following case. That difficulty creates different attitudes among teachers and students. In this study, we observed a tendency for teachers to be reluctant to adopt new games, even if the games appeared to be the most appropriate. For students, the learning process that is repeated for new games can become a routine that diverts attention from the content of the discipline.

The proposal conceived by this work was to design and produce a simulator that integrates various aspects of logistics concepts with a level of parameterisation that enables teachers to set the scene and to direct the operation of the system to meet educational goals. Additionally, this system was designed with the clear intention that the same virtual environment could be reused in various disciplines for different uses. The ability of teachers to configure the simulator can potentially offer benefits to students, who can apply the previous knowledge acquired from the simulator functionalities to new course objectives In addition, course coordinators can achieve uniformity across disciplines by using a common tool to support teaching and learning.

The survey used in this paper was conducted in Brazil, a country with nearly continental dimensions and in which a high percentage of logistics spending occurs through the highway that connects more than 5500 municipalities, in many cases only by land.

2   Objectified Conceptual Content

As prior procedures in designing the game, the paper sought to identify the logistics concepts that steer the resulting product and to determine any desired traits. Through consultation with teachers in disciplines involving logistics, a survey was conducted to answer the following questions: What reference books are used? What is the content of the plan of the discipline? What trials would be perceived as interesting enough to justify the use of a simulator as a support tool for teaching? We interviewed five teachers from different educational institutions, using semi-structured interviews so that the qualitative data collection occurred naturally and with encouragement for suggestions.

Importantly, the proposed simulator is not designed to replace existing methods; therefore, it was essential that the formal content represented by books and handouts was not replaced. Rather, the simulator serves to illustrate or allow students to experience exactly the existing material. The next step was to map the concepts of the chapters listed in the books that were adopted by teachers. The result was a list of concepts that have been reserved for later comparison with the available games. At that point, it was concluded that the concepts were directly related to logistics performance, i.e., the entire learning process was aimed toward using the knowledge of concepts to achieve better performances. This finding, although intuitively predictable, was applicable to the existing feature in simulation games, that is, the component of playful competition between teams. During the application of BSG activity, participants compete for the best performance, which illustrates the outlook that the correct way to measure the effectiveness of decisions is through performance indicators. In this case, the performance measures proposed by Bowersox, Closs and Cooper [4] responded to all the issues that were mentioned by teachers and that were constant in their teaching plans through dimensions that include cost, customer service, productivity, quality, and asset management measures. Each dimension has specific measures. Notably, this book [4] is adopted by all teachers consulted.

3   Simulation Games Available

The next step involved research to discover all the logistics simulation games that were available to teachers through any means. The initial list was obtained from teachers and then expanded with searches of scientific research databases, search engines, books, etc. Twenty-four games were listed and classified according to the criteria established for inclusion (the measures of logistics performance).

Based on a descriptive analysis of the specimens using the model proposed by Klabbers [5], it was possible to identify two relevant aspects as follows.

First, some games include very important decisions in areas other than logistics. As a consequence, the performance indicators are affected by these decisions. For example, higher spending on marketing produces demand and enables larger-scale logistics operations, which can dilute fixed costs. In finance, ruses to obtain financing from a company's own resources can produce simulated, artificially reduced logistics costs.

Second, not all of the games are realistic. Some games represent distant places with another reality, especially outside the country. The teachers consistently observed that the available simulators do not take into account local conditions and present playful scenarios that are unrelated to what actually occurs in professional activity. The teachers indicated that in post-graduate courses, students show a lack of seriousness in activities with simulators because of the use of models that are far from reality and that often include unnecessary playful elements.

4   Desk Model: Fidelity and Embodied Experiences Added

At this point in the work, it was already clear that the design of the game logistics must strongly consider the need for the experience to be as close as possible to reality, requiring the inclusion of recognisable elements of students' daily life. Thus, from the beginning, the development of the system attempted to ensure that distance maps and journey times were real. Toward this end, we adopted the access maps.google as the basis for all development. This action was performed according to the unpaid use of access points required to represent the locations of effective elements of the links in the supply chain. The game's scenario was defined as being exactly that way in the real world.

The next step was to create a model that would include all performance measures defined. This model was translated into a web program. The result was a complete integration into the Internet environment between the simulation game and the platform offered by the company Google.

The model begins from an initial position in which participants are organised into teams representing each of the company's logistics operations. The starting address of all these companies is the address of the school. The participants' first mission, to find a company site that they deem is the most appropriate in the market, is conducted using baseline data of 70 clients and their average annual demand. The cost of this distribution centre is fixed, and five predefined sizes are available. Each distribution centre includes parking to accommodate vehicles, a deposit for the products, and office facilities. The address must exist in reality to ensure that the centre can be effectively located on Google maps.

The system has a list of vehicles with characteristics found in the market. For the purposes of financial decisions that did not affect the indicators of logistics companies, all vehicles have the same credit line with identical costs. We created some restrictions on vehicle access; for example, in some cities, only vehicles with a payload of less than 1600 kg are permitted. Each vehicle has different characteristics and consumption per kilometre per tonne transported. Thus, the call for services in distant cities that limit the traffic of heavy vehicles necessarily leads to the creation of local transposition facilities to load payloads into an urban vehicle. This process requires an additional building to be positioned by the participants with an extra cost.

The participants recorded delivery routes that were allocated per vehicle and the assigned clients to be served. At the end of each trip, the vehicle returns to its distribution centre and recharges to fulfil all deliveries. Partial deliveries occur when the vehicle load is not sufficient to fully meet the request, in which case the vehicle returns to the complement. If a route does not have a customer order, the system automatically diverts the route to the next customer. The delivery order can be changed by the participant within each route, and customers can be relocated to other routes.

Concern that marketing actions could produce undesirable effects in the model led to the adoption of a product that was not likely to increase demand produced by the participants actions in the simulator. Thus, we adopted a product used for cleaning machinery used in clinical analysis, specifically in blood tests. This product, which actually exists, has a consumption that is directly related to the population size of a city; i.e., it was estimated that a population makes on average three annual exams, with some seasonality that varies between regions, and thus has an expected consumption. To experience some logistics effects (for example, the bull-whip effect), the occurrence of a localised epidemic causes the peak demand that is led by the teacher during activities.

Before beginning the activities, the teacher will indicate the number of supply chain levels and determine the companies that will occupy each link. Although teams can be assigned to any link, the intermediate links are more appropriate based on inputs and outputs.

The company may also have an internal process of tagging features that turns a logistics operation into a simple industrial process. Thus, the need for additional inputs results in dimensions of decision-making.

The constraint that a driver has a maximum number of working hours per day was added to the model. In addition, in calculating the travel time, it was assumed that the average speed of the simulated transportation vehicles is 75% of the passenger speeds indicated by Google. The Google's default is the velocity of a passenger vehicle.

The operating system is formed by cycles in which the company receives orders from its customers and completes the orders with available stock that is supplemented by acquisitions. Negotiations can be made with suppliers or competitors as long as this option is activated by the teacher.

Another feature of the system is that the purchase order can be released by the teacher to skip a previous link; i.e., it is possible that the company acquires the supplier's products directly from their supplier.

The desk model was produced to integrate scenario, roles, rules, accounting system, logical models, indicators, symbology, decision sequence and linkage as proposed by Angelides & Ray [2]. After that, it was presented to five specialists, who included two logistics operators and three new teachers in this area, with only one question: "Does this model represent effectively the logistics activity?" The responses generated several changes to the model, including the following: limited financial resources for business start-up operations, a random delay in the routes, and the lifetime of the vehicles. This last topic is directly related to customer service because in some cases, this factor is relevant.

The product value was set at a monetary unit throughout the supply chain and the value accounted became only the cost of shipping. In the case of added processes (in companies that have some internal process), the increase in value was added to the shipping because it is only a labelling. The quality of service was associated with on-time delivery and the age of the vehicle.

Thus, performance can be measured in equal conditions for all companies seeking efficiency measured in monetary units directly related to logistics operations.

Because there are not necessarily humans occupying companies in all links, a button was added to the model to automatically act on decisions. In this case, the choice of supplier was based on a two-dimensional array that considers the cost and quality of service. Each company classifies the quality of its suppliers based on a historical series of previous events.

5   The Logistic Simulation Game

The main objective of the game is to simulate a scenario in which students could experience supply chain management. In the default scenario, three vendors supply raw materials to the simulated companies, which are managed by the students. These vendors are located at different distances from the simulated companies and have different shipping prices but the same cost for materials. All simulated companies are located at the same address, which is the address of the school. The companies compete for a market of 60-70 clients located at distances of 100 to 1500 km from their current location, each having distinct demands for products. There is no industrial processing of raw materials, and the materials are only available in small packages. The identity of the product, in fact, has no importance, but for a reference, the product is said to be a component used to clean analytical laboratory equipment after processing human fluids. As a result, this product experiences a demand relative to each city's population, and extra demand may occur when an epidemic occurs. Because all of the locations are real, they can be seen on a map generated by Google Maps.

Many decisions can be made, and a few of these decisions are described here. The decisions include changing the company to a new address located anywhere that the team feels to be closer to the clients, thus giving less total cost for transportation; buying or selling distribution centers where the product is stocked; buying or selling trucks; and hiring more truck drivers.

During each round, which represents a month, the clients send their needs for the next month to all of the companies, receive a price quotation and buy considering price and quality. These clients are performed by the software. Price is easily understood because the lower it is, the more items will be sold, but quality is measured by how quickly at the beginning of the next month the company receives the materials and by how many times the truck stops for delivery. This process is affected by the age of the trucks, the quantity of truck drivers and the training they have received, the road conditions, and many other factors that could delay a delivery.

The teams create a route to serve each group of clients before offering their final price because the traveling distances are significant and affect the cost. However, some of the clients on each route are not going to buy from the company. The team may then choose not to answer calls from regions where there is a high risk of not being the chosen vendor.

A client can sometimes make an extra order to service demand resulting from an epidemic. In this case, the company can answer in a short period of time. Because rounds may happen weekly, these urgent calls force the team to be more participative. For example, these calls may occur on a Saturday night and have a turn-around time of 5 hours. These calls are made to the president of the team via email, whereas regular calls are visible in the system.

6   Implementation and Tests

The software was implemented in 2011 in the web environment, with two applications in an MBA course directed toward logistics in the state of Minas Gerais, Brazil. The software configuration allowed five teams. Because the game did not require any simulated industry activity, there was a simple simulation of logistics operation. The users participated in six rounds related to decisions about the adequacy of company infrastructure (distribution centre location and the acquisition of fleet vehicles). These applications found some deficiencies related to usability, which were subsequently rectified.

Notably, a fully realistic game would address the issue of documentation needed for transportation in Brazil, the corresponding charges and toll rates, which in the specific case of Brazil are very costly. These aspects have not been implemented because they correspond to elements unlisted from the beginning and could increase the complexity of the simulator to the detriment of the experience of the concepts targeted in each application. Although there is still no provision to include this aspect in the system, the issue will not be ignored in the future.

In the opinion of the teachers involved in these applications, the system has great potential for use in logistics education.

The first application in a graduate course will occur in the first half of 2013 with a focus on scaling warehouses and fleet sizing. It is a discipline directed to logistics management in a class of students in the third year of the course All applications were free of cost with the sole intention of system development and the dissemination of research.

7   Conclusion

Given the aim to produce a logistics simulation game that could be used in various configurations and in different disciplines, the first applications corresponded well to the need. Desk tests continue to be conducted, and in 2013, the first application in different disciplines of the same course will test the effectiveness of the model.

Using the Google map as part of the simulator is a feature that produced a significant approximation to reality, particularly by enabling actual geographic relationships. Additionally, the registration of vehicles with their effective characteristics was an element that provided interest for the participants, who demonstrated their preference for brand manufacturers and even specific models.

New applications are needed to explore other configurations that will lead to system maturity. To make progress in this direction, it would be interesting to use another country with local characteristics.

In a future version, we study the inclusion of other modes of transportation such as trains and ships, and consequently, specific depots and corresponding terminals.

References

1. Merkuryev, Y., Bikovska, J.: Business Simulation Game Development for Education and Training in Supply Chain Management. In: Sixth Asia Modelling Symposium (2012)
2. Angelides, M.C., Ray, J.P.: A methodology for specific, total enterprise, role-playing, intelligent gaming-simulation environment development. Decision Support Systems 25, 89–108 (1999)
3. Basnet, C., Scott, J.L.: A spreadsheet based simulator experiential learning in production management. Australasian Journal of Educational Technology 20(3), 275–294 (2004), http://www.ascilite.org.au/ajet/ajet20/basnet.html
4. Bowersox, D., Closs, D., Cooper, M.B.: Supply Chain Logistics Management, p. 496. McGraw-Hill Education (2012)
5. Klabbers, J.H.G.: The Magic Circle: Principles of Gaming & Simulation, Modeling and Simulations for Learning and Instruction, 2nd edn., vol. 1. Sense Publishers (2008)

A Review of Gaming Simulation in Transportation

Jayanth Raghothama and Sebastiaan A. Meijer

Division of Traffic and Logistics, KTH, Sweden
{jayanthr,smeijer}@kth.se

Abstract. Gaming simulation has proven to be an invaluable method for experimentation and learning and exploring scenarios in various fields of policy making. In this paper, we present a case for the use of gaming simulation in transportation analysis. We also present a review of games and gaming simulation in transportation analysis. We observe that *gaming simulation is not widely used in transportation, despite its wide use in associated fields.*

1   Introduction

Simulation games can be defined as experiential, rule based interactive environments where players learn by taking actions and by experiencing the effects through feedback mechanisms built into the game [1]. With their roots in war gaming, simulation games have a long history of being used for policy analysis. They have also been extensively used as business simulation games. They have been used in studies on human cognition and behavior, and as training and pedagogical tools.

In the transportation domain, understanding travel behavior and activity is a crucial prerequisite for transportation analysis and planning, urban planning and infrastructure investment decisions. Understanding travel behavior means understanding the movement of people and goods based on preferences, activity and demand.

In the last decades many techniques to aid decision-making have been developed. Within these, there are two major styles. One has its foundations in applied mathematics, operations research and systems analysis, and focuses on formal methods and algorithms to aid the decision maker. The other set has its foundations in cognitive and social psychology and focuses on intuition, creativity and communication to aid the decision maker. While both sets of techniques have their own problems, gaming simulation is considered a hybrid of these two, borrowing the best from both worlds [2].

Transportation systems are complex in nature. They are characterized by emergent properties from the interplay of a large number of actors. These actors could be users, planners and managers of a number of transport modes within geography, linked to global transport flows of people and goods. This means that planners have to take into account all the uncertainties that result from these complex, dynamic and socio technical systems.

Gaming simulation is therefore particularly suited to transportation analysis, providing the ability to ask a range of questions on individual decision making, interaction of individuals, and the behavior of organizations across institutional levels.

S.A. Meijer and R. Smeds (Eds.): ISAGA 2013, LNCS 8264, pp. 237–244, 2014.

To further strengthen the case for gaming simulation in transportation, there is a rich history of the use of these methods in disciplines closely aligned with transportation, such as logistics and supply chain management.

In the following sections, we describe the use of gaming simulation in logistics research and the linkages between logistics and transportation. We then present a review of simulation games in transportation, and some future directions for research.

2   Gaming Simulation in Logistics

Broadly, there are three categories of simulation games. From a historical perspective, war games are among the oldest categories of games. Following World War 2, games were used widely in training exercises in business. Later, games were used in a number of areas, such as education, urban planning and so on [1,3].

Simulation games in logistics fall under the category of business games. Their history begin in the year 1955, when RAND corporation developed a business simulation game on the U.S. Air Force logistics system. The simulation, called MONOPOLOGS, required players to take the role of inventory managers of the Air Force supply system [4,5]. A popular educational game is the MIT Beer Game, which illustrates the bullwhip effect in supply chains [6] Business games have since been employed extensively and effectively as teaching tools in both management sciences and operations research [5].

Simulation games have also been used in the transportation and logistics fields, for future asset management and road maintenance tendering [7], to explore the nature of trust and bargaining power in supply chains and networks [8,9] and so on. The design methods for these games have also been generalized [10].

The development of a city economy depends on an efficient logistics service. Urban freight transport policies have significant impact on the efficiency, safety and environmental aspects of a city. Further, given that most freight nodes, distribution centers and intermodal transfer points are located in urban areas, the impact of logistics on a city's environment, congestion and livability is immense. A majority of freight is transported by road, placing further emphasis on the integration of city logistics and transportation planning [11].

3   Gaming Simulation in Transportation

In this section, we present a review of simulation games in transportation analysis. A broad search was conducted using the keywords *transportation, traffic, mobility, logistics, urban planning* in the journals Simulation and Gaming, Games and Culture, Journal of Artificial Societies and Social Simulation. Similarly, the gaming keywords *gaming, simulation gaming, virtual reality, experimental simulation* were used to search in the journals Transportation Research, parts A through F and Google. Combinations of the gaming and transportation keywords were used to search through the Scopus database. A broad web search was also conducted using Google. Results of the search on the keywords game/games were too broad to be of any relevance, due to their different meanings, for instance in game theory and political games.

The results of the searches are described below. There are quite a few entertainment games that focus directly or indirectly on transportation. There were very few games described in the literature to draw any patterns or comparisons. Game theoretic and other simulation models are being used extensively, providing scope for future development of simulation games based on these models.

3.1   Commercial and Open Source Games

Below is a brief comparison of popular commercial and free games on transportation. Most of them deal with the construction and evolution of transportation networks, based on simple economic models. These networks then have to be managed by the players.

Table 1. Popular Entertainment Games on Transportation

Game	Goal	Transport Modes	Realism
Transport Tycoon	Make as much profit as possible, transporting passengers and freight by road, rail, sea and air.	Rail, Monorail, Road, Sea, Air	Some features, such as signaling and the evolution of new modes of transport are realistic. The economic models are not.
OpenTTD [12]	Make as much profit as possible, transporting passengers and freight by road, rail, sea and air.	Trucks, Buses, Trains, Monorail, Airplanes, Ships	Some features, such as signaling, evolution of new modes of transport, and the construction of networks are realistic. The economic models are not.
Simutrans [13]	Run a successful transportation company transporting people, mail and goods	Rail, Road, Tram, Monorail, Ship, Air	Not realistic. However, the extensible design of the software means that it can be made to be.
Railroad Tycoon	Build and manage a railroad company	Rail	Not realistic
Airport Tycoon	Build and manage an airport	Air	Not realistic
SimCity [14]	Build an entire city from scratch	Road, Rail, Monorail, Elevated Rail, Ferry	Some features such as policy options and environment effects of building will be realistic, in the new version of the game scheduled for release in 2013.
Microsoft Flight Simulator [15]	Mission Oriented Goals	Air	Realistic

Games in the transportation domain fall mainly into two distinct categories. Most games are business simulations, with goal being building and managing transportation networks and companies of different modes. The first game in this genre was Transport Tycoon, and it has spawned different game series' over the years, both open source and proprietary. Airport Tycoon and Railroad Tycoon are both game series' similar to Transport Tycoon. Simutrans and OpenTTD are open source extensions of Transport Tycoon. The gameplay of these games are similar, with the player asked to build large transportation networks of different modes to transport passengers and freight. While some aspects of these games may be realistic, most of them are not. In particular, the economic and ecological models are not realistic, but the transportation aspects, such as network characteristics, scheduling and signaling tend to be realistic. However, none of these models are validated. Other games not mentioned in the comparison are Locomotion, Transport Giant, Cities in Motion [16] (unreleased) and so on.

The second category is one of simulations, primarily flight simulations. These games involve the player flying a plane. The game play is very realistic, as is the terrain which is based on actual geographies. The planes in the game are existing and pervious models of aircraft. These games also involve some aspect of traffic management, simulating the functions of air traffic controllers.

The third category is one of urban planning, or city building games in virtual environments. SecondLife [17], IBM's CityOne [18] and SimCity are all city building games. These games do not directly study transportation, but it is an essential components in all of them. Compared to the other games, SimCity has been used more often for research purposes, as a pedagogical tool for urban planning [19,20] and in envisioning sustainable cities and so on. [21]

3.2   Simulation Games

Despite the benefits of simulation games for transportation, they have not been used widely in trying to understand transportation issues and solutions. Very few examples of the use of simulation games in transportation exist.

These games have been used for a range of purposes, with very little overlap among them. Backlund et al [22] studied the effectiveness of a simulation game in enhancing learning in driver education. Games have been used to collect data and conduct research on travel behavior and adaptability when fuel prices increase rapidly, and to investigate adaptive capacity in the same situation [23, 24]. Games have also been used to assess the environmental and health impacts of different modes of transportation [25]. They also been used to create appropriate traffic behaviors in various situations. Renaud et al used simulation games to train children in appropriate traffic safety behaviors [26]. Meijer et al used simulation games to explore alternative modes of organization for rail cargo management [27]. In a similar vein to the entertainment games described above, Lardinois used a simulation game to aid decision makers in the planning, management and operations of an inter city transportation system [28]. There have also been attempts at building a generalized traffic simulation game that can be used for different purposes. [29]

Simulation games have also been used in situations where transportation is not the main focus, but an essential component of the problem being addressed. A common use case is one of emergency management training, where the management of various transport modes becomes essential [30,31]. Another use case is that of urban planning, where transportation is an essential component. Reckien et al used a game to study the effects of urban sprawl [32]. King et al posit the need for a simulation game approach to regional and urban planning in third world countries such as India [33]. CARamba, a game for the Dutch road network makes clear the effects of measures on the road network.

In terms of technology, the games presented in the literature are similar. There is a wide spectrum of technological use, from paper based table top exercises, to computer aided immersive gameplay and physical cars. Most games use a combination of paper based table top exercises combined with simulations run on a computer and/or visualizations of data and results. Wood et al, Storshcnider et al, Reckien et al used simple paper based table top games to simulate their scenarios, with a few other artifacts to describe other objects in their games [30,31,32]. Renaud et al created a controlled environmental setup, with mock ups of physical layouts [26]. Meijer et al used paper based instruments, aided by computer simulations [27], while Watcharasukarn et al, Johansson et al, Lardinois et al used purely computer based gameplay [23,24,25,28]. Backlund et al used a physical car in a controlled environment to play the game [22]. Kutz et al are trying to construct a generalized immersive 3d environment, supported by computer graphics and a physical object to simulate the effect being in traffic [29].

Little attention has been paid to the validation of these simulation games. Most approaches rely on earlier work or on empirically collected data during the game sessions to validate their approaches.

3.3   Game Theory

Game theory provides transportation analysts powerful tools to solve many problems. There are a lot of examples of its use in transportation analysis, from analyzing vehicle routing problems [34] to transportation network reliability [35], to optimal parking policy [36], and so on. Zhang et al and Hollander et al present a comprehensive reviews and classification of game theoretic applications in transportation analysis [37,38]. It is observed that there is wide use of game theoretic models in transportation analysis, but simulation games remain relatively unused. It should be possible to convert the same game theoretic models into simulation games, to ask certain questions that will not be possible with the purely mathematical formulations of game theory. It should also be possible that the same models can be used as simulations to support game play.

4   Future Work

- Validation: Little attention has been paid to the validation of the simulation games. Validation methods from the gaming literature could perhaps be used to validate the games developed so far, which might lead to more interest in the use of these games in transportation analysis. These methods generally measure the correspondence between the reference system and the simulated system[39], and measure the validity of the process, structure of the model, gameplay and so on.

- Entertainment Games: Some of the entertainment games can easily be modified for realism and real world use. These games are generic and flexible enough to fit a variety of different uses without significant effort. Once validated, these games can be easily used for the same purposes as the games presented in the literature.
- Game Theory: There is a wide use of game theoretic models in transportation analysis. These models can be used to develop simulations games, so as to ask certain questions not otherwise possible. The same models can be simulated, and these simulations can be integrated into games.
- Theoretical frame for inter-operability: We have observed three different classes of games: entertainment games which can be extended for realism, simulation games that ask very specific questions and game theoretic models that describe a wide range of scenarios in transportation analysis. There is considerable overlap in the scenarios that all of these classes of games describe, and it should be possible for some of them to be integrated. Given that they are all completely different approaches, there needs to be a theoretical frame and method developed and validated for their integration.

5   Conclusions

As the challenges in transportation grow, and become ever more complex, it is necessary to use tools that are capable of addressing these new complex challenges. Gaming simulation provides the ability to ask questions on a range of issues, such as individual decision making, institutional behavior, future scenarios and policy making. Since gaming simulation has a lot of potential for use in transportation, it is important to provide an overview of its use so far in the transportation domain, and therefore set up a general research process and a future research agenda.

This paper first attempts to make a case for the use of gaming simulation in the transportation domain. We then provide a review of entertainment games that deal with transportation, and then a review of games used for research purposes. We draw upon the literature to find a significant use of game theoretic models in transportation, and posit that these models can be used as a base for building simulation games. In the last section, we point out some drawbacks in currently existing examples of simulation games in transportation, and try to provide some directions for future research.

References

1. Mayer, I.S.: The Gaming of Policy and the Politics of Gaming: A Review. Simulation & Gaming 40(6), 825–862 (2009)
2. Duke, R.D., Geurts, J.L.A.: Policy Games for Strategic Management: Pathways into the Unknown. Dutch University Press (2004)
3. Duke, R.D., Kemeny, N.K.: Keeping Score One Score Later: Two Decades of the Simulation & Games Journal. Simulation & Gaming 20(2), 165–183 (1989)
4. Jackson, J.R.: Learning from experience in business decision games. California Management Review 11, 23–29 (1959)

5. Faria, A.J., Hutchinson, D., Wellington, W.J., Gold, S.: Developments in Business Gaming: A Review of the Past 40 Years. Simulation & Gaming 40(4), 464–487 (2009)
6. Sterman, J.D.: Deterministic Chaos in an Experimental Economic System. Journal of Economic Behavior and Organization 12, 1–28 (1989)
7. Altamirano, M.A., Herder, P.M., de Jong, M.J.: Road Roles, using Gaming Simulation as Decision Technique for Future Asset Management Practices. In: Proceedings of the IEEE International Conference on Systems, Man and Cybernetics, pp. 2297–2302 (2008)
8. Meijer, S.A.: The organisation of transactions: Studying supply networks using gaming simulation. Wageningen Academic (2009) ISBN
9. Zuniga-Arias, G., Meijer, S., Ruben, R., Hofstede, G.J.: Bargaining power and revenue distribution in the Costa Ricanmango supply chain: a gaming simulation approach with local Producers. Journal of Chain and Network Sciences 7(2), 143–160 (2007)
10. Fumarola, M., van Staalduinen, J.-P., Verbraeck, A.: A Ten-Step Design Method for Simulation Games in Logistics Management. Journal of Computing and Information Science in Engineering 12(1), 011006–6 (2012)
11. Road Transport: A change of gear. European Commission Report (2010)
12. http://www.openttd.org
13. http://www.simutrans.com
14. http://www.simcity.com/
15. http://www.microsoft.com/games/fsinsider/
16. http://www.citiesinmotion.com/
17. http://secondlife.com/
18. http://www-01.ibm.com/software/solutions/soa/innov8/cityone/
19. Adams, P.C.: Teaching and Learning with SimCity 2000. Journal of Geography 97(2), 47–55 (1998)
20. Gaber, J.: Simulating Planning: Sim City as a Pedagogical Tool. Journal of Planning Education and Research 27(2), 113–121 (2007)
21. Nilsson, E.M., Jakobsson, A.: Simulated Sustainable Societies: Students' Reflections on Creating Future Cities in Computer Games. Journal of Science Education and Technology 20(1), 33–50 (2011)
22. Backlund, P., Engström, H., Johannesson, M., Lebram, M.: Games for Traffic Education: An Experimental Study of a Game-based Driving Simulator. Simulation & Gaming 41(2), 145–169 (2010)
23. Montira, W., Krumdieck, S., Green, R., Dantas, A.: Researching Travel Behavior and Adaptability: Using a Virtual Reality Role-Playing Game. Simulation & Gaming 42(1), 100–117 (2011)
24. Montira, W., Page, S., Krumdieck, S.: Virtual Reality Simulation Game Approach to Investigate Transport Adaptive Capacity for Peak Oil Planning. Transportation Research Part A: Policy and Practice 46(2), 348–367 (2012)
25. Maria, J., Küller, R.: Traffic Jam: Psychological Assessment of a Gaming Simulation. Simulation & Gaming 33(1), 67–88 (2002)
26. Lise, R., Stolovitch, H.: Simulation Gaming: An Effective Strategy for Creating Appropriate Traffic Safety Behaviors in Five-Year-Old Children. Simulation & Gaming 19(3), 328–345 (1988)
27. Meijer, S.A., Mayer, I.S., van Luipen, J., Weitenberg, N.: Gaming Rail Cargo Management: Exploring and Validating Alternative Modes of Organization. Simulation & Gaming 43(1), 85–101 (2012)
28. Lardinois, C.: Simulation and Gaming with Jet-Set: An Intercity Passenger Transportation Training Tool. Simulation & Gaming 18(1), 13–33 (1987)

29. Michael, K., Herpers, R.: Urban Traffic Simulation for Games, p. 181. ACM Press (2008)
30. Wood, C.J.B., Foster, H.D., Hardy, N.E.: Crisis Simulation and Health Care Systems. Simulation & Gaming 28(2), 198–216 (1997)
31. Stefan, S., Gerdes, J.: MS ANTWERPEN: Emergency Management Training for Low-Risk Environments. Simulation & Gaming 35(3), 394–413 (2004)
32. Reckien, D., Eisenack, K.: Urban Sprawl: Using a Game to Sensitize Stakeholders to the Interdependencies Among Actors' Preferences. Simulation & Gaming 41(2), 260–277 (2010)
33. King, R.A., Rathi, S., Sudhira, H.S.: An Approach to Regional Planning in India. International Journal of System of Systems Engineering 3(2), 117 (2012)
34. Bell, M.: Games, Heuristics, and Risk Averseness in Vehicle Routing Problems. Journal of Urban Planning and Development 130(1), 37–41 (2004)
35. Bell, M.G.H.: A Game Theory Approach to Measuring the Performance Reliability of Transport Networks. Transportation Research Part B: Methodological 34(6), 533–545 (2000)
36. Hollander, Y., Prashker, J., Mahalel, D.: Determining the Desired Amount of Parking Using Game Theory. Journal of Urban Planning and Development 132(1), 53–61 (2006)
37. He, Z., Su, Y., Peng, L., Yao, D.: A Review of Game Theory Applications in Transportation Analysis. In: 2010 International Conference On Computer and Information Application (ICCIA), pp. 152–157 (2010)
38. Yaron, H., Prashker, J.N.: The applicability of non-cooperative game theory in transport analysis. Transportation 33(5), 481–496 (2006)
39. Vincent, P., Geert, V., Gerton, H.: The Validity of Games. Simulation & Gaming 29(1), 29–30 (1998)

Part IV
Professionalism and Business in Gaming Simulation

Challenges to Designing Game-Based Business

Thomas Duus Henriksen

Department of Communication, Aalborg University, Denmark
tdh@hum.aau.dk

Abstract. The four categories labelled game-design, didactic design, organisational design and business design each constitute a set of challenges, each requiring a particular set of competencies. The key conclusion of the paper is that even though the learning game design constitutes the core of establishing game based business (GBB), the subsequent stages of development call for other kinds of competencies in order to become a viable GBB.

This paper addresses the challenges encountered when attempting to design learning game-based business (GBB). On basis of a longitudinal case study of the development of a business game, the paper aims to propose a four-category model for addressing and handling a range of key challenges when trying to develop a learning game for business purposes.

Learning games have long played a role in developing business skills, both as on-the-job-training and in formalised education. The games have developed [1], so have their use in the didactic process [2], as well as their organisational integration and means of organisational integration [3]. While these reviews and models emphasise the development of well-designed learning games, learning processes and institutional integration of both, little is known on how the development and makings such games available impacts on the suppliers. Summers [4] describe how GBB has become professionalised, but little is known on how to make successful business models based on learning games to make such games profitable.

This paper is based on a qualitative case study of the challenges encountered when attempting to develop GBB on basis of the learning game Changesetter (CS). The study was conducted as a longitudinal study from 2006-12, allowing the gradual maturation to be studied as an ethnographic, action-research-based study [see 5], using participatory observation, design experiments and designer interviews to map the development.

1 Case Study: The Development of Changesetter

Changesetter is a Danish designed learning game for teaching managers how to plan change projects and manage employee resistance towards change (www. change setter.dk). The game was originally designed to meet with training demands with a particular customer and aimed to develop an operational understanding of theoretical change management concepts from Kotter [6] and Maurer [7]. Elements of those two

S.A. Meijer and R. Smeds (Eds.): ISAGA 2013, LNCS 8264, pp. 247–252, 2014.

theories were developed into a game-based metaphor, which turned Maurer's cycle of change into a FloorBoard™ (FB) on which project boats could travel through different project phases while keeping employees from resisting and metaphorically jumping overboard. This created a tangible illustration of resisting, progress, lagging behind and abandonment, all occurring while the project sailed through its intended lane.

Each team of participants controls one project as a team effort against other teams. It is facilitated by a certified consultant and the game mechanics are handled by computers. When played, the participants discuss their options on basis of information from a computer, which also provides feedback. The FB and its figures serve as a dynamic discussion object among participants and facilitators.

The experiences form the case study showed how the development of GBB encompassed several, qualitatively different design processes, which each called for a particular, academic approach. As CS was developed over a period from 2006-12, the original game was gradually redesigned and supplemented by didactic frames for using it as a consultant tool was developed, an organisation for making the game widely available and a business model for making the game profitable. Although these four development tasks were not followed chronologically, but rather served as points of iteration, they form the basis of the 4-category model presented in this paper concerning game-, didactic-, organisational- and business design. The purpose of dividing the process into these four categories is to show how the different design tasks in developing GBB proposes its own unique, but interrelated set of challenges, and call for a different set of design competences.

2   First Challenge: Game-Design

This challenge concerns the learning game in itself, and concerns the design of a learning game that is both playable and meets with the learning objectives. This set of challenges calls for competencies in the combination of learning design and game-design in order to design a game that incorporates the academic points and theories particular to the learning objective. This part of the process is often labelled as gamification, using game-based processes to make a theory operational and explorable.

In the CS case, this was done by selecting elements from the relevant theories, using the cycle of change and resistance levels from Maurer [7] and the 8 common obstacles from Kotter [6]. These elements were designed as board positions and game-mechanics were developed to guide transitions between these positions. A case structure was added, allowing the transitions to take place between within different settings, e.g. an organisational merger. CS was first developed as a board game. The mechanics and feedback mechanisms were later computerized to ease game administration for the facilitator. While the basic game mechanics and the representational metaphor used to illustrate the core theories as board positions were fixed, the game was continuously iterated through fine-tuning of effects and scenario developments.

Handling the learning game-design challenges is the core-competency among designers, as well as the core in GBB, but even though CS offers what Malone and

Lepper [8] refers to as an endogenous relationship between academic content and game mechanics, playing the game does not necessarily facilitate the learning process. The game offers the foundation for the learning process, but the learning outcome is greatly affected by how the game is used in a game-based learning process [9].

3   Second Challenge: Didactic Design

The second challenge is all about how the learning game is being used as a part of a didactic design to meet with a set of learning objectives. This challenge calls for competencies in combination of learning design and game-didactics, and in particular on how to use learning games as tools for facilitating learning. One key discussion is the question on whether participants should be allowed to play the game in an undisturbed manner while experiencing game-flow, or if they should, according to Knowles' [10] theory on adult learning, be encouraged to reflect and incorporate own experiences. This greatly affects how a game is being didactically designed in combination with e.g. theory presentations, reflective processes, discussions and recontextualisations to participant practice, e.g. by using debriefing activities [see 11]. From his circular approach, Kolb [12] offers an iterative process that combines practical experience with reflection (see Henriksen and Lainema [2] for application).

In the CS case, the game was didactically designed to be played in iterative phases. Rather than running the game as an uninterrupted process, preceded by theory presentations and followed by reflective processes, these didactic processes were designed to be integrated with each game phase. This meant that the participant only played the game for a limited period before being asked to participate in reflective discussions, theory presentations and relate those discussions to their work experience.

When analysed on basis of Kirkpatrick's [13] four levels of course evaluation, both the game-design and the didactic design would concern improvement of the learning process. Kirkpatrick's point was to state that participation was frivolous if it did not lead to learning. Though the game- and didactic design, CS had become an effective tool for facilitating learning, but according to Kirkpatrick, learning has little relevance if it does not lead to new behaviour among the participants. This caused recontextualistion processes to be integrated into the didactic design to facilitate the use of game-points and course theories in the participants' subsequent practices. This led to the development of the CoachingBoard™ to help participants in leaving behind the fictional universe, and instead help them apply theories to their own, real-life scenarios. This development did not alter the game-design, but lead to the development of a new set of didactic materials to aid the learning process.

The challenges concerning didactic design clearly calls of competencies closely associated with adult education and process facilitation. The core is here to design a game-based process that uses an optimal mix of didactic processes to meet a learning objective.

4   Third Challenge: Organisational Design

The third challenge is to develop an organisation for using the game to meet with certain organisational challenges. This challenge calls for organisational developers who are able to integrate the game-based activity into organisational practices, as well as establishing communities for using the particular game, e.g. into business schools as curriculum activities [3]. A key challenge to building communities for using a game concerns the problem of making the game available to a broad audience.

In the CS case, a certification model was employed, mainly with the purpose of generating volume by allowing external consultants to sell CS deployments through their own sales networks. This certification model was based on a 2-day certification course, which gave consultants access to purchasing and using CS materials. This model was a solution to a continuous demand among customers to have the developers tour various courses to run the game. To solve this, the course both sought to empower consultants with the skills and encouragement to run CS.

As the distribution model moved the handling of the game-deployments handling away from the developers, the demand for a simpler game-process grew. In the early game-deployments, it became evident that even experienced consultants were not always comfortable with the idea of running a learning game, let alone a complex one. Teaching with games is not a straight forward task [15], which in the CS case led to a more extensive training program. This also caused rule-handling to be simplified and computer based, and simplification of the materials involved, thereby reaffecting both game- and didactic design considerations. The organisational integration calls for educational design competencies, allowing developers to both meet with learning objectives as and constructing new ones. It also calls for change management competencies for establishing organisational grounds to support the use of games.

5   Fourth Challenge: Business-Design

The fourth challenge is all about making money on the game, and especially on making it worthwhile to develop the game in the first place. This challenge calls for business designers who are able develop financial models, a) to ensure a proper return of investment, and b), to ensure that the game generates a continuous rather than an incidental income. The business simulation industry has undergone dramatic changes, both from technological advances, and as a professionalization of the field [4]. Management has been professionalised, and the field has also become dominated by simulation specialist while outsourcing the content production.

In the CS case, the business model was developed continuously alongside the other design processes. Two strategies are prominent in the Danish industry; the consultant strategy, by which companies sell game sessions deployed by consultants; and the product strategy, by which the companies sell products that external consultants to use in their work. CS has gradually developed been into the product strategy, thereby making money on selling materials and certification to consultants, who then sell game-deployments and other services to end users. To remain viable, a consumable materials strategy was integrated to overcome the inherent problem of this business model, namely that selling a FB only generates only a one shot income, as those materials can be used continuously. By shifting emphasis from the end user to the consultant, a sales function is outsourced to the consultants, who then add their revenue to the cost of the consumable materials. The CS brand then becomes second to the consultant who deploys the game to its end users, but at the same time allows consultants or academy programs to profile them rather than their tools. It also shifts emphasis for the game-, didactic and organisational design towards facilitating the consultant's work in the seminar room.

On basis of the experiences from the CS case study, the four categories can be illustrated as the following:

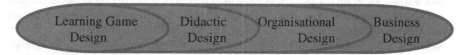

The model can be read both as chronological and elaborative. The development of CS might seem chronological, but developments in later phases had led to elaborations on previous. When moving right in the model, the previous becomes a tool for achieving the next: To the didactic design, the game becomes a didactic tool for teaching, the didacticised game becomes a tool for meeting an organisational demand, and the organisational integration of the game becomes a tool for generating profits. Findings from the CS case indicate that a late consideration of the business perspectives will cause serious problems when trying to add business to an already developed game. Instead, the business perspective should be integrated at an earlier point to inform game, didactic and organisational designs in a profitable direction. This reading of the model draws upon Kirkpatrick's four levels of evaluation and his idea of stating the higher level objectives as central; emotional satisfaction didn't matter if learning was not achieved, learning regardless if behavioural change did not occur, etc. When applied to the four levels of the model, it points to the following; if the didactic design, if the means for using the game does not facilitate learning, the well-designed learning game loses its value. A well didacticed game would lose its impact if it lacked organisational integration, e.g. if only the designers were the ones able to run the game, or the game did not fit into the goal-structure of the organisation. Finally, a well-designed, didacticised and organisationally integrated game would from a GBB perspective have little value if not supported by a business model that allowed it to generate sufficient earnings.

6   Conclusion

The case study shows how the developers had to navigate a series of qualitatively different obstacles in the process of developing CS from being a good learning game to become a successful game-based business. Analysis indicates that the design efforts and challenges are not limited to learning-game-developer competencies, but also draws upon a wider set of developer competencies. It also indicates that business perspectives sometimes are added last, but should be considered continuously.

References

1. Faria, A.J., et al.: Developments in Business Gaming: A review of the Past 40 Years. Simulation & Gaming 40, 464–487 (2009)
2. Henriksen, T.D., Lainema, T.: Three approaches to integrating learning games in business education. In: Nygaard, C., Courtney, N., Leigh, E. (eds.) Transforming University Teaching Into Learning Via Simulations and Games, p. 15. Libri Publishing, Nygaard (2012)
3. Henriksen, T.D., Løfvall, S.: Experiences and opportunities for enhancing business education with games. A review on current and past experiences with learning games at business schools. In: Nygaard, C., Courtney, N., Leigh, E. (eds.) Transforming University Teaching into Learning Via Simulations and Games, p. 15. Libri Publishing (2012)
4. Summers, G.J.: Today's Busniess Simulation Industry. Simulation & Gaming 35(2), 208–241 (2004)
5. Kemmis, S., McTaggart, R.: Participatory Research. Communicative action and the public sphere. In: Denzin, N.K., Lincoln, Y.S. (eds.) The Sage Handbook of Qualitative Research, pp. 559–604. Sage Publications, London (2005)
6. Kotter, J.P.: Leading in Change1996. Harvard Business School Press (1996)
7. Maurer, R.: Beyond the wall of resistance. Why 70% of all changes STILL fail and what you can do about it. Bard Publishing, Austin (2010)
8. Malone, T.W., Lepper, M.R.: Making Learning Fun. A Taxonomy of Intrinsic Motivations for Learning. In: Aptitude, Learning and Instruction. Lawrence Erlbaum Associates, Inc. Publishers, NJ (1987)
9. Henriksen, T.D.: A little more conversation, a little less action, please. Rethinking learning games for the organisation. In: Department of Curriculum Research, Danish School of Education, Aarhus University, Copenhagen, p. 250 (2009)
10. Knowles, M.S.: The modern practice of adult education: From pedagogy to andragogy. Prentice Hall, Englewood Cliffs (1970)
11. Petranek, C.F., Corey, S., Black, R.: Three levels of learning in simulations: Participating, debriefing, and journal writing. Simulation & Gaming 23(2), 174–185 (1992)
12. Kolb, D.: Experiential Learning: Experience as the Source of Learning and Development. Prentice Hall, Englewood Cliffs (1984)
13. Kirkpatrick, D.L.: Evaluation of training, in Training and development handbook: A guide to human resource development, R.L. Craig, Editor. McGraw-Hill, New York (1976)
14. Dukes, R.L., Fowler, S.M., DeKoven, B., Garry Shirts, R.: Simulation Gaming Exemplar. Simulation Gaming 42(5), 545–570 (2011)
15. Knotts, U., Keys, B.: Teaching Strategic Management with a Business Game. Simulation & Gaming 28(4), 377–394 (1997)

Identifying the Competencies and Capabilities
of Simulation Professionals

Elyssebeth Ellen Leigh

Simulation Australia

Simulation Australia, the national body for simulation professionals in Australia, is developing an approach to documenting the skills and knowledge used by simulation professionals. The aim is threefold. The first and most basic is to identify an irreducible set of core knowledge and skills required by anyone using simulation in a professional manner in any context. The second goal involves developing a means of aligning the work of all users of simulation with these core skills and knowledge so that relevant professional competencies can be documented and demonstrated to exist within a professional field. The third involves developing the framework for a set of formal qualifications within the Australian Qualifications Framework (AQF).

The project will face many difficulties and challenges. And there will be challengers. This chapter introduces the background to the project including the underlying models informing the initial stages of the work. It positions the ongoing research within a range of literature about the complexity of identifying the essentials of being a 'competent simulation professional'. This inevitably involves defining 'simulation' to establish some boundaries for the future work, and considering how this work will contribute to wider understanding of what it means to be a 'simulation professional'.

1   Introduction

Australia is a growing nation with a population spread across a vast land mass. It began as a number of widely separated settlements. The national, unified image we have today took a long time to build, with extended negotiations about 'federal' and 'state' responsibilities. Education was reserved as a "States' Right" so our educational systems grew apart rather than together. Economic considerations slowly altered this, and late in the 20th century came agreement about the need for a national agenda - called the Australian Qualifications Framework (AQF). The significance of all this for simulation is the emerging need to establish appropriate qualifications for educators, technicians and other specialists (e.g. business systems analysts) who work with simulation in contexts that now expect formal qualifications and proof of capability.

These needs have become evident to large manufacturing and contracting businesses as well as government departments, and Simulation Australia is centrally placed to take a lead in the development of the necessary formal qualifications.

Questions to be answered include

- What work roles are involved?
- What do they have in common?

S.A. Meijer and R. Smeds (Eds.): ISAGA 2013, LNCS 8264, pp. 253–264, 2014.
© Springer International Publishing Switzerland 2014

- How do they differ?
- What kinds of 'simulation' are involved?
- Is it possible for 'capabilities' to transfer across disciplines and industries?
- Where do concepts of 'teaching' and 'learning' belong?
- How do we align technology roles and soft skills ones?

And so the questions will go on. This chapter sets out the beginning points of the research involved. It is written at the beginning of a process to develop answers to these and many associated questions. As the final outcomes of this work will not be available for some time, the chapter outlines the current state of the problem as it exists in the specific context of Australia, and drawing on progress to date, suggests issues likely to become relevant in other contexts where formal qualifications for simulation professionals are becoming more important.

2   Background to the Project

Simulation Australia was established sixteen years ago, initially as an industry representative body. It emerged from the efforts of academic researchers and industry practitioners to establish a funded academic research facility. While the funds were not awarded, the individuals decided the value of their effort warranted continuity and the Simulation Industry Association of Australia (SIAA) was born. The scope and focus of SIAA gradually broadened from an 'industry' to a 'profession' perspective and SIAA morphed into Simulation Australia in 2010. The Professional Development Committee of SIAA had employed a part-time Learning and Development Officer who, by 2006, had produced a detailed blueprint (Garrett, 2011) for use in identifying the range of roles where simulation is a major or partial responsibility.

At the time that work began, attention was focused on the more technically oriented aspects of simulation. As it was 'industry' focused this was inevitable, since the intention was to provide for the needs of member organisations. During the ensuring years contributions from the 'soft skills' sector have increased and focus has broadened. For example educators using role-play based activity were not considered in developing the first iterations, and this will have an impact on future adjustments to the overall set of tasks to be done. However the initial work was expressed in a manner that allows relatively easy extension – or adjustment - of terminology to incorporate non-technically based contexts. One point to note here is the tendency for language to divide and separate, and the continuing need to make evident the connections among domains that initially appear diverse, divergent and dissimilar.

The SIAA pamphlet notes that
"Those employed in the field of simulation work across a diverse range of occupations and sectors. In general, individuals obtain qualifications in a relevant field and then find themselves employed in the simulation industry. . ." Which is as true of engineers as academics and consultants. Using a life cycle approach to developing and using simulation, the research identified eight workplace roles. These are listed below and formed a starting point for investigation.

They are so diverse that there was no suggestion that any one person would ever do all eight roles. However there are clear connections among all the roles in relation to the central element of simulation. And that connection is the nature of simulation and how it is uniquely different from things that are 'real'.

Eight workplace roles

1. Contribute to policy related to simulation
2. Devise strategies for the use of simulation
3. Develop specifications for simulations
4. Develop simulations
5. Commission simulations
6. Employ simulations
7. Support simulations
8. De-commission simulations

Each and all of these may be found as sub-tasks within generic positions. For example someone who 'develops simulations' may do so in engineering settings, education contexts or business settings. All of them use specific skills and knowledge as they do so, and this may be tacit and unconscious competence at work. That is expert simulation specialists may be so – and not even be aware of it.

In September 2012 the Simulation Australia PD committee agreed on the importance of developing formal documentation towards establishing simulation as a profession. Exactly what this documentation will look like, what it will address and how long it will take to complete - are not yet fully developed. However, Simulation Australia is determined to contribute to the emergence and recognition of simulation as a unique domain - a stand-alone discipline of work and research. And this includes contributing to the expansion of cross-disciplinary and inter-disciplinary activity.

The next section explores our current position regarding several questions including: what is 'simulation'? Who are 'simulation professionals'? What are 'competencies'? What is the importance of 'setting' or 'context' and 'equipment' in the context of creating and using simulation? the section begins with issues about about people and moves to relationships among jobs and technologies.

3   Who Are *Simulation* Professionals?

Consideration of this question involves settling on a position about '*what is a profession?*' Wikipedia *(2013) suggests that "a profession is a vocation founded upon specialized educational training the purpose of which is to supply objective counsel and service to others, for a direct and definite compensation, wholly apart from expectation of other business gain.* Routledge (2011) adds responsibility and accountability when exploring the professional status of web designers. And, writing in support of the USA-based Certified Modeling and Simulation Professional (CMSP) Program, Lewis and Rowe (2010) assert that a formal certification program is *the way to determine who is truly qualified to practice [a] profession.*

With this and related definitions in mind, Simulation Australia defines a Simulation Professional as – *anyone who both considers themself to be involved in simulation through their employment, and who undertakes to maintain and improve their professional knowledge and skills in the field.* Further than this, professions share a limited number of common characteristics including i) a defined body of knowledge, ii) a formal means of educating and certifying individuals as 'professional', iii) a formal means of oversighting the domain within which those operating as 'professionals' operate, and iv) a code of ethics subscribed to by those in the domain.

Initial exploration indicates that the discipline of 'simulation' includes individuals working on tasks as diverse as

- Maintaining a helicopter flight simulator
- Designing a way to gauge support for a community activity
- Managing health professionals' learning in a simulation suite
- Planning major relocation of hospital staff and patients
- Leading the rehearsal of a military deployment
- Facilitating a role play teaching communication skills
- Planning the architecture of an entirely new approach to computerizing a nation's health records, etc.
- Designing online games and 3rd World environments
- Commissioning major investment in simulator technology

Our aim is to demonstrate how people involved in these activities share a common core body of knowledge with comparable skill sets linked to this knowledge and share specific ethical sensibilities and responsibilities. However there is not yet a widespread awareness that such individuals do have a lot of things in common – let alone sharing membership of a 'simulation profession'. In effect, what is involved in being a 'simulation professional' is not yet agreed, and individuals undertaking any of the above tasks are likely to identify with established professions. The task of achieving agreement on this will be complex and extended.

4   What Are Competencies?

Competencies are defined *as a cluster of related abilities, commitments, knowledge, and skills that enable a person (or an organization) to act effectively in a job or situation* (Business Dictionary, 2013).

'Competency statements' are outcome-oriented descriptions of career-relevant capabilities. In Australia the Australian Qualifications Framework (AQF 2013) is a nationally endorsed strategy that

> ... *incorporates the qualifications from each education and training sector into a single comprehensive national qualifications framework.*

While not all learning activity is competency-based in Australia – all formally recognized qualifications have a link to competency-based documentation. For example the "Blueprint for Career Development" (Blueprint 2012) documents key career development competencies and is intended as a guide for all career-focused educators. Extensive development of industry and/or skill specific competency standards has also been completed. In short, Australia is basing much of its career education activity on competency-oriented (i.e. 'outcomes' based) education.

However, during the time that work on competencies has evolved, some career arenas remain hard to codify. For example while Project Management has codified its core practices, its proponents have had to work out how to incorporate the reality that various components of that discipline occur, and are practiced, in other areas. Like simulation, Project Management is both cross-disciplinary and highly complex, and thus is not easily reduced to industry or task specific documentation, and work completed by those experts (see for example AIPM 2012) is helpful in pointing the way ahead for disciplinary areas that are inherently multi-focused, like simulation.

5   How to Define 'simulation'?

This is both the core of the problem and a most fascinating aspect of it, since it is just as possible to ask "What is A simulation?" or even "What is a simulator?" and get answers that are superficially the same. The images in Figure 1 are 'Wordles' (www.wordle.net) built by combining the text of nine web-based dictionary definitions of 'simulation'.

Fig. 1. "Wordles" built from web-based dictionary definitions of 'simulation'

Together they highlight the large number of common words and also the complexity of choosing a definition that can address the range of issues involved. At the beginning of this project they help indicate the complexity of the task, but do not greatly assist in establishing any clarity about routes to take towards achievement of the goals. To arrive at a definition for the project we turned to consideration of the core essentials and proceeded via what has become an application of Occam's Razor to the question of 'what are these 'essentials' without which simulation would not be 'simulation'.

6   So - What Are the 'Essentials' of Simulation?

The basis for the definition being used in this project was proposed by Michael McGarity in 2011, and the simplicity of his definition belies its complexity

"Simulation is the abstraction of reality for a purpose."

To enable development of the kind of documentation envisaged by this project this has been extended, as follows –

Simulation is the facilitated abstraction of reality for a purpose. It occurs within a 'container' delineating boundaries connecting the 'real' external world, to the 'unreal' simulation, which can only occur inside the container.

The definition does not attempt to focus on techniques, tools or types preferring to name the elemental components in such a way that the intent of simulation is clearly delineated. An additional benefit is that the representation of any particular 'abstraction', is left to the needs and goals of specific designers and users. With key terms in place it becomes possible to construct a systems image of the relationships among the elements, as shown in Figure 2.

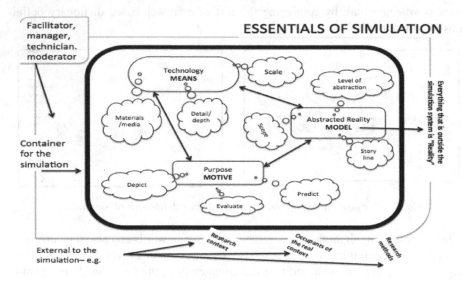

Fig. 2. A systems map of the elements of simulation

Each element in this definition requires further elaboration. And this may challenge common assumptions about aspects of each. The next section describes each element in more detail, discussing them in the order of their contribution to the definition as a whole - rather than in the order of their occurrence within the text of the definition.

Reality

Reality is generally considered to be the state of being actual or true. When something is 'real' it is actually there. There are – these days - relatively few places where 'actuality' itself is not open to contest. As education and learning have become more accessible, and human understanding has embraced the notion of 'perceptions of reality' the ability to agree on what is 'actual' declines. In regard to creating a 'simulation of reality' the term 'reality' is considered to refer to the item, situation, environment or context that is being *replicated* in some specific manner during the course of a simulation.

Real

As with 'reality' so with 'real'. It is easier to achieve agreement, for example, when what is being considered is a tangible object or location, it is less so when consideration is being given to concepts, ideas, and intangibles such as emotions and relationships. Simulation aims to achieve a condition in which participants can agree that they were experiencing things '*as if*' they were real, while being able to acknowledge that they were not actually so.

'Real' exists beyond the simulation experience as something from which participants have been withdrawn for a time – and to which they will return. It remains as a parallel entity outside – external to – the immediate experience being created by the process.

Unreal

Paradoxically, what is 'unreal' may appear to all intents and purposes as 'real' for the duration of the simulation experience. Factors such as 'fidelity' and 'validity' are vital in creating a context that replicates/represents an external reality, while being highly malleable factors subject to wide variation. What is inescapable here is that within the simulation experience everything is – to some extent unreal and participants are – and always remain – aware that 'this will end' and that they will return to the external reality, albeit with altered views about the nature of that reality.

Container

Everything has boundaries, edges or borders where one thing ends and another begins. In the normal course of events, what gets attention is the thing itself. For a simulation experience to be successful in its purpose, the container establishes the boundary conditions for immersion and is vital, even when not readily apparent. This term aligns with Jan Klabbers (2006) use of the term 'Magic Circle'. Participants inside the 'container' are freed, to a greater or lesser extent, from expectations about 'normal' behaviour. The 'unreal' becomes 'normal' and the boundary holds the entirety of the simulation experience within an enclosed time/space continuum that may last for a few minutes and occupy a few square metres, or may last for a week or more and involve people and objects spread over vast distances. In all instances everyone involved in the simulation is aware of being inside a boundary, and also that others are outside it, and therefore unengaged. Making, and sustaining, this distinction is an important part of achieving a successful 'as if' simulation experience.

Abstraction

To create this experience involves a sequence of analytical steps culminating in the creation of a stable container that is representative of – but never itself – the 'real thing'. In effect 'reality' is reduced in size and scope through a sequence of steps that are highly analytical in nature. Duke (1974) lists these essential steps in the sequence –

1. All that is known – and can be assembled – about the real context is collected for analysis
2. Aspects deemed superfluous to the purpose of the activity are removed from consideration
3. Selected items may be reintroduced to contribute to the quality of the 'as if' experience
4. Critical items are distilled to establish a small tightly defined scope for activity
5. These are arrayed and arranged in a manner that enables development of the simulation experience

This process produces a reduced set of elements that continue to represent the real conditions or context while tracing out a path that moves ever further away from the 'real' by selectively creating an abstract reduction of the original 'whole'.

Technology/Technologies

The process of abstraction may result in developing a means of representing the 'real' via a bewilderingly varied range of methods. Flight simulators are an obvious and extremely large example of such technologies. Another is the growing capacity for connecting such machines and thus producing a capacity for 'inter-operability' linking ships and aircraft with ground troops and remote Headquarters staff for large scale 'war games'. However the technology involved in creating a simulation experience may also be as simple as a game board, a deck of cards or sets of role descriptions. Because they are more 'tangible' elements in the development of the simulation experience these items may become the focus of too much attention, to the detriment of achieving effective understanding of the simulation context and experience they are helping create. In real terms over-attention on tangible items may obscure, and even distort, the nature of the experience that it is the intention to create. In some instances buying the simulator technology may even be seen to be the end of the process – whereas it is barely even the beginning of ensuring that simulation experiences become all that was intended.

Facilitated

A simulation experience is always mediated – in one way or another – by the actions of individuals (or teams) who patrol the boundary of the container. Their job is to assist participants cross the boundary in such a way that the abstraction appears sufficiently real for the designated purpose/s and then to successfully extract them from the container when it is time to re-enter the 'real world' (Leigh, 2003). Titles for this role include – but not limited to - educator, maintainer, umpire, instructor, simulation technician. They share the task of ensuring that the container is a stable and consistent representation of the external reality it replicates, for the term of the experience.

Purpose

Reasons to establish a simulation experience vary widely. Common to all of them is the prior existence of a purpose that – it has been decided – cannot be achieved efficiently/effectively by any other means. It may be a learning outcome involving acquisition of skills and knowledge, a logistics analysis prior to committing forces to action or a planning exercise intended to inform decisions about movement of large numbers of people.

When choices about simulated experiences are being made, the common factor is agreement that an interactive encounter with the process is required. 'Purpose' is more than transmission of facts and data - its presupposition is that physical, emotional and action-based engagement is essential for successful achievement of desired goals.

Summary

Simulation is complex, multi-layered and highly diverse in its manifestations. Common characteristics for all forms of simulation are the abstraction of reality for a purpose, using suitable technology within a container that is facilitated by one or more individuals who are themselves not participants in the simulated action.

These key factors are the essential ingredients, regardless of whether the simulation being examined is a miniature replication designed to assist learning about committee procedures, or a multi-million dollar technology-dominated site established to teach pilots how to fly.

This set of concepts is the basis of Simulation Australia's work. The aim is to develop a means of demonstrating to all involved in 'simulation' that 'their' particular focus has an identifiable relationship with all other forms, and that establishing the requisite level of 'abstraction' makes it possible to find a 'crossover' point where all forms touch the common points that make 'simulation' a practice, a tool and a discipline in its own right.

7   How is Simulation Built?

There are several responses to this question, all turning on what is meant, in specific contexts, by the term 'built'. One key factor to keep in mind is that a simulation is first and foremost a means of *playing with* reality. Its characteristics and features have to be conceptualised, before any physical components can be considered. 'Design thinking' is required in all/any of the modes of 'building'.

In conceptualising a simulation it is vital to realise that it occurs in three stages – 1) briefing, 2) action and 3) debriefing – and has five key components – 4) rules, 5) roles, 6) scenario, 7) recording and 8) relationships. Regardless of the technology used to materialise a simulation these eight elements must be as fully detailed as possible, prior to turning to manufacture of the physical technology. There are many possible levels of activity involved in building a simulation and different purposes dictate different choices of abstraction and of technology.

7.1   Sample Arrangement of Purposes and Form

Table 1 lists four quite different ways in which a simulated environment and related experience may be developed for a cohort of medical students. The total reality for a medical student studying to become a doctor is years of study, focused on absorption of theory and practice along with development of skills, knowledge and appropriate attitudinal stances and behaviours. To support this learning regime a medical faculty may use many types and levels of simulated experiences.

Table 1. Some simulated environments for a medical cohort in an academic setting

Purpose	Form
Establish effective communication habits	'Simulated patients' using actors
Practise giving intravenous injections	'Part task trainer' – simulated limb
Develop team work skills for surgical procedures	Simulated environment with high end manikins, and mixed team of peers and experts in an extended replication of a surgical event
Practise specific surgical procedures in real time on live subject	Conduct a procedure in a simulated theatre on a living animal [e.g. pig]

For each purpose listed in Table 1 an extensive range of research will be conducted to develop the final form for particular simulation experiences. All are developed after consideration of the specific purpose and level of abstraction. Once a concept is complete and the process and components defined, decisions are made about technology to be built or acquired to support the experience.

A communication activity may involve extensive scripting of a scenario and briefing for the actors, after which specific visible equipment is selected – bed and chairs in a hospital ward setting for example. The entire process may be unique to a particular setting and not be repeated anywhere else.

In contrast the 'part task' trainer may be developed to meet a range of potential contexts and skill needs, and made available for use in a wide variety of settings and acquired by specific institutions, whose staff then make further decisions about how it will be used.

A team skills activity may require months of scenario development, bring together many differently skilled personnel, and be intended for regular reuse and shared activity across a number of institutions.

Finally a decision to use live subjects in simulated operations will necessitate ethical considerations and intensive exploration of the validity of the stated purpose and how this solution actually supports the intended goals.

This particular case study illustrates the complexity of simulation and suggests some of the factors to be explored in the time ahead. Many similar case studies of quite different settings will be developed and analysed as we proceed.

8   Getting Underway

2013 will be a busy year of complex activity across many simulation domains. The Australian government – via its Health Workforce Authority – has contracted Simulation Australia to manage funding research on what is needed to ensure that suitably qualified personal are employed in the many simulation centres it has sponsored in hospitals and universities (HWA 2013). The HWA project is also addressing the question of accreditation of simulation centres. Balci and Ormsby (2007) explored the value of developing, using and re-using conceptual modelling as part of assisting communities of practice to expand and share their resources in this regard. The interlinking of efforts to establish the means of accrediting centres and certifying practitioners is a first, and promises to give Australia a lead – most especially because of the nation-wide focus of the project.

Private employers with major investments in building, using and maintaining simulation environments for defence and aviation are also exploring how to develop certification strategies for their staff. As members of Simulation Australia their interests are aligned, and also constrained by the need for 'commercial in confidence'. The overriding issue will be how to collaborate on the venture while sustaining separate commercial goals.

Simulation Australia's PD committee will be directing its attention to drawing these diverse interests together to achieve a united approach to certification of simulation professionals. Simulation Australia aims to use its role as a national body of simulation professionals in a way that demonstrates a professional and soundly educational approach to the work ahead. We will be establishing what documentation exists, what is needed and what clients, users, builders and learners all expect to have available for their use as the 21st Century makes ever more use of simulation. This project will alter many, many of the things we have taken for granted about simulation in the past.

References

1. AIPM (2012), http://www.aipm.com.au/AIPM/CERTIFICATION/COMPETENCY _STANDARDS/3G/P/pcspm.aspx?hkey=32ad63cc-73d1-4ba5-ae27-4a0a78ecbb86
2. AQF (2013), http://www.aqf.edu.au/AbouttheAQF/TheAQF/tabid/108/Default.aspx
3. Balci, O., Ormsby, W.F.: Conceptual Modeling for Designing Large-Scale Simulations. Journal of Simulation 1(3(Aug.), 175–186 (2007)
4. Business Dictionary (2013), http://www.businessdictionary.com/definition/competence.html#ixzz2Qmb1ZapH
5. Duke, R.D.: Gaming: the Futures Language. Halsted Press, New York (1974)
6. HWA, Simulated learning: Enabling the adoption of simulation (2103), http://www.hwa.gov.au/work-programs/clinical-training-reform/simulated-learning-environments-sles/enabling-adoption-simula
7. Klabbers, J.H.: The magic circle: Principles of gaming & simulation. Sense Publishers (2006)
8. Leigh, E.: A Practitioner Researcher perspective on facilitating an open, infinite, chaordic simulation. Learning to Engage with Theory while Putting Myself Into Practice UTS, unpublished thesis accessible (2003), http://epress.lib.uts.edu.au/research/handle/2100/308
9. Wills, S., Leigh, E., Ip, A.: The Power of Role-based e-Learning: Designing and Moderating Online Role Play. Routledge, London (2012)
10. Nygaard, C., Courtney, N., Leigh, E.: Simulations, Games and Role Play in University Education. Libri Press, UK (2012)
11. Lewis, F., Rowe, P.: The Certified Modeling & Simulation Professional (CMSP) Program, SCS M&S Magazine – (January 2010), http://www.scs.org/magazines/2010-01/index_file/Files/article_Lewis-Rowe.pdf
12. Garrett, S., SA Guide to Professional Skills Development in Australia (2011), http://www.simulationaustralia.org.au/education
13. Rutledge, A., Design Professionalism (2011), http://designprofessionalism.com/
14. Simulation Australia (2011), http://www.simulationaustralia.org.au/files/upload/pdf/AnnualReport~2011-2012.pdf
15. Wikipedia (2013), http://en.wikipedia.org/wiki/Profession

Author Index